WHAT READER

I was both challenged and comforted. [...] stories, and biblical narratives, Ted and Mark answer the most pressing questions we have about forgiveness and the challenges we face to forgive. As a resource for reconcilers, this book will be invaluable.

DWIGHT SCHETTLER, PRESIDENT, AMBASSADORS OF RECONCILIATION

Sin, forgiveness, and reconciliation! These are concepts unfolded in stories, many of which are deeply personal ones of the authors and are the center-pieces of this richly moving and in many ways provocative book. Ted Kober and Mark Rockenbach provide Bible studies, narratives, thoughtfulness, hymns, prayers, and reflective exercises. Get it! Read it! Do it, led by God's Spirit, and bathe in the forgiving love of God in Jesus!

BRUCE M. HARTUNG, PHD; PROFESSOR EMERITUS, PRACTICAL THEOLOGY,
CONCORDIA SEMINARY, ST. LOUIS

The conversation that these two brethren offer in their book and the con-solation it brings open up the depths of the powerful impact of Christ's for-giveness on Christians' interaction with others. The authors weave together personal experiences with biblical narratives to tell of the imprisoning might of unforgiveness and to shed light on how the Holy Spirit guides us through contemporary believers' practice of forgiving and that of Joseph, Jonah, David, and others. Newly written hymn verses and an outline for personal meditation and prayer lead readers to the Spirit's power to for-give, reconcile, and live together with those who have harmed us. This well-crafted proclamation and instruction will aid readers in enjoying the liber-ation Christ's death and resurrection provides in daily life.

ROBERT KOLB, PROFESSOR EMERITUS, SYSTEMATIC THEOLOGY,
CONCORDIA SEMINARY, ST. LOUIS

Ted Kober and Mark Rockenbach have provided a great tool for those who have ever struggled with unforgiveness. We see all around us how conflict causes pain in relationships in marriage and family, the workplace, church, and beyond. Filled with real-life examples, the book is an easy read and accessible for everyone. What is most helpful is how the authors consis-tently return to the faithful promises found in God's Word for the guid-ance and hope that we need in confronting sin. The discussion questions are helpful and make this a suitable resource for discussions among church leaders or those assisting with reconciliation.

REV. DR. R. LEE HAGAN, PRESIDENT, LCMS MISSOURI DISTRICT

The challenge for each Christian living in this sin-filled world is to "forgive the unforgivable just as God in Christ has forgiven us." Reminding readers of their own "unforgivable" nature before God, deserving His "temporal and eternal punishment," Kober and Rockenbach share the unbelievable Good News of God's grace and love in that "while we were yet sinners, Christ died for us." Over and over again, they focus the reader on this miraculous gift that comes from God and empowers us to move from a spirit of unforgiveness to "forgive as we have been forgiven." Each chapter speaks to different aspects of this spirit of unforgiveness, illustrating with contemporary and biblical stories, challenging the reader through a series of questions to grapple with the theme, and concluding with suggestions for prayer as the reader takes the journey from unforgiveness to forgiveness.

REV. DR. RALPH MAYAN, PRESIDENT EMERITUS, LUTHERAN CHURCH—CANADA

Repeatedly, Kober and Rockenbach root the power to forgive in the forgiveness Christians receive in Jesus Christ. The Christian Gospel pervades their work not just as an example of forgiveness but as the motivating power for Christians to forgive. The catechetical approach of the book is winsome and practical. The question chosen for each chapter is the right question, the necessary question, that is, a question of real, practical concern for Christians seeking to forgive. The simple prayer format to close out each chapter shows the value of prayer along the way of forgiveness. Though readers may select specific chapters most relevant to their situations, reading the chapters in sequence can have a valuable cumulative effect in enhancing one's understanding and practice of forgiveness. The poetry of hymn lyricist Ken Kosche adds an artistic beauty to the work and a winsome introduction to the focus of each chapter.

DEAN NADASDY, PRESIDENT EMERITUS, LCMS MINNESOTA SOUTH DISTRICT

Kober and Rockenbach have listened carefully for decades to people who struggle with forgiveness; they've heard their questions and answer them superbly in this book. "What if I've forgiven but still feel hurt or angry? What about abuse? What if I can't forgive myself?" and many others. The authors are consummate storytellers, and their book is deeply steeped in Scripture and the forgiveness of Jesus Christ. You won't just read this book once but will return to it again and again for help in sharing Christ's forgiveness with others (especially in difficult situations) and in believing that His forgiveness is for *you*!

RICK MARRS, MDIV, PHD; SENIOR PROFESSOR OF PRACTICAL THEOLOGY, CONCORDIA SEMINARY, ST. LOUIS; LICENSED PSYCHOLOGIST; AUTHOR OF *MAKING CHRISTIAN COUNSELING MORE CHRIST CENTERED*

UNFORGIVABLE?

HOW GOD'S FORGIVENESS
TRANSFORMS OUR LIVES

Ted Kober | Mark Rockenbach

Published by Concordia Publishing House

3558 S. Jefferson Avenue, St. Louis, MO 63118-3968

1-800-325-3040 • cph.org

1 2 3 4 5 6 7 8 9 10   32 31 30 29 28 27 26 25 24 23

CONTENTS

FOREWORD

A burdened heart may be why you're getting into this book. Something is so seriously wrong in a relationship that you've decided, "Hard as this may be, I've got to move on to a better place." Maybe your book club or Bible study group has decided to read *Unforgivable?* Right now, you're feeling fine about your life, but you suspect reading and discussing forgiveness and unforgiveness may open an old wound. Or maybe a friend who thinks you have an issue with forgiveness and unforgiveness encouraged you to look at this book.

Lots to mull over—yes, there will be some struggle, some wrestling with emotions—but isn't this the way life really is? Whatever thoughts and feelings you experience as you work through the following chapters, first congratulate yourself for making the effort! At the same time, immediately look forward with hope. Trust that setting out on this journey from unforgiveness to forgiveness can bring you to a much better place.

Let's start by zooming out from any interpersonal problems we might have. Growing up in the south suburbs of Chicago, I never thought about the stars. Streetlights made it impossible to see all but the brightest stars. Today we call it light pollution. The first churches I served were in rural America, and wow! Many a night or early morning I would look up at the countless stars and be filled with wonder. In the decades since, scientists have increased the wow factor. Humans landing on the moon and someday on Mars, space probes within and beyond our solar system, the Hubble Space Telescope and now the James Webb Space Telescope—we are seeing with our own human eyes the incomprehensible vastness of creation. For some people this vastness is depressing: *I don't matter. Life has no purpose.* But there's another way to think of our place in this vast universe. This is the way of wonder. Perhaps we're not the chance result of evolution; perhaps there is a great Creator of heaven and earth. The Bible puts it this way: "Lift up your eyes on high and see: who created these? . . . Have you not known? Have you not heard? The Lord is the everlasting God, the Creator of the ends of the earth" (Isaiah 40:26, 28). Wonder over the Creator's work can lead us to awe, and that is the beginning of wisdom (see Psalm 111:10).

On December 24, 1968, Apollo 8 was orbiting the moon. During one orbit, astronaut William Anders looked out his window and saw Earth rising over the moon's horizon. He took a photo that we know as "Earthrise," with our beautiful blue, green, and white planet shining against a dark and foreboding background. Here's an amazing fact: in all the millennia of human history, we are the first generations to see from space this home that the great Creator made for us. None of the people in the Bible, none of the people in world or US history, none ever saw what science has enabled us to see. You might call it a God's-eye view of Earth.

And what has the Creator seen over thousands and thousands of years? Strife, envy, hatred, crimes of every sort, wars, genocides, potential nuclear annihilation . . . and whatever unforgiveness you might be harboring or causing. Now join that sad picture of sinful humanity with the purpose of this book. By all rights, the Creator could have said, "Enough! I've had it with these sinful people. I'm going to put a few asteroids into My slingshot and kerplowee!" Our sad human record of sin has earned God's punishment, not forgiveness.

But what did the Creator do? Something awesome. "God so loved the world, that He gave His only Son, that whoever believes in Him should not perish but have eternal life. For God did not send His Son into the world to condemn the world, but in order that the world might be saved through Him" (John 3:16–17). Our wonder at the incomprehensible vastness of creation becomes awe that, in love, our Creator forgives you and me. The awesome love of the unseen God now has a face. We not only have a Creator; we also have a Savior who by His cross and resurrection has reconciled us to God. "For God, who said, 'Let light shine out of darkness,' has shone in our hearts to give the light of the knowledge of the glory of God in the face of Jesus Christ" (2 Corinthians 4:6).

And we have a Helper for this not-so-easy move from unforgiveness to forgiveness. Jesus says, "I will ask the Father, and He will give you another Helper, to be with you forever, even the Spirit of truth" (John 14:16–17). Do you ever think, "Well, Jesus was active in the first century and someday will come again, but what's He doing now?" Jesus is not absent from daily life, not waiting until His reappearance on the Last Day. Jesus is, in biblical talk, "seated at the right hand of God" (Colossians 3:1). That means He's exercising all the power of His divine being, lovingly guiding us and all His believers to the glorious heaven He has won by reconciling us to the Father. He who suffered on the cross for our sins and was raised from the dead loves you and all who believe in Him. Now He hears your prayers. He feels your sighs. He knows your heart. And to help you on your heavenward way, your ascended Lord is giving you the Holy Spirit, the Helper whom He promised.

From the vastness of creation, the Spirit of the ascended Lord zooms us in on the awesome love of God, love that motivates and enables you on the journey from unforgiveness to forgiveness. When you slip back into unforgiveness, as we all do, Jesus knows. He will continue to use His Word to bring you back to forgiveness for yourself and for others. It's a process, a journey, and not always easy, but what a can't-wait-for-it goal! "From sorrow, toil, and pain, and sin we shall be free and perfect love and friendship reign through all eternity" (*LSB* 649:5).

We're not there yet, but we are on the way. That's why Ted Kober and Mark Rockenbach wrote this Christ-centered book. They are well qualified to lead you on the not-so-easy journey from unforgiveness to forgiveness. They write clearly and to the point. The content is laid out in short paragraphs, with space that invites you to think about what you've just read and jot notes on the page. The authors' regular encouragement to write about unforgiveness and forgiveness will help you focus your struggles. Hymn stanzas by Kenneth Kosche and suggestions for prayers from the authors will help you take your reflections to the God of help and hope. Frequent quotations of Bible passages offer you immediate comfort and hope from God's Word. You need not set out to read the book cover to cover; after the introduction, you can go to chapters whose titles seem especially relevant to your situation. May this book help lead you to ever-increasing awe at the love the Creator has for you and for all in Jesus Christ.

Now to Him who is able to do far more abundantly than all that we ask or think, according to the power at work within us, to Him be glory in the church and in Christ Jesus throughout all generations, forever and ever. Amen. (Ephesians 3:20–21)

Dale A. Meyer
President Emeritus
Concordia Seminary, St. Louis

ACKNOWLEDGMENTS

We praise our forgiving God for the cleansing of our sin through the blood of our Savior, Jesus Christ (see 1 John 1:7), and we dedicate this book to the glory of God.

We cherish the supporting roles our families played in writing this book. I (Mark) acknowledge the love and support from my wife, Darlene, and our children, Joshua, Rachel, and Andrew. I (Ted) appreciate the patience and encouragement given me by my wife, Sonja, and son, David.

We also acknowledge the special contribution to this book by Dr. Kenneth T. Kosche. We commissioned him to write hymn stanzas to introduce each chapter of this book. He wrote them to be sung with a hymn tune as indicated in the "Suggested Hymn Tunes" section. For easy reference, he also identifies the tune from *Lutheran Service Book* (e.g., KINGSFOLD [*LSB* 444]).

Ken wrote these hymns to help anyone preaching or teaching from this book to reinforce the instruction in a devotional setting. Not only can they be sung but these lyrics also serve as prayers to begin or end a session. The lyrics in poetic form communicate the message in a medium that speaks to the heart. Music touches the soul and aids in learning and memory.

We thank God for Ken sharing his gifts with us and our readers. We hope your heart and soul will be touched by Ken's lyrics in your journey to overcome unforgiveness.

INTRODUCTION

Who is the unforgivable in your life? Is it someone who hurt you or someone you love? Do you consider yourself unforgivable?

What is the unforgivable sin? What was the offense that is so painful for you? What seems beyond any hope for forgiveness?

FROM TED

A teenage girl had been sexually molested by her father. When she told her mother, her mother refused to believe or support her. The betrayal and hurt by both her parents led her to rebel in her late teens, and she earned a reputation as a wayward daughter among extended family and friends. When she was an adult, her bitterness evolved into resentment and open disrespect for her parents. Of course, that served to reinforce her reputation as the black sheep of the family. As I worked for several days with both sides in mediation, it appeared that there was no hope for forgiveness or reconciliation. Irreparable harm over many years had destroyed their relationship.

As a reconciler for three decades, I have found that unforgiveness is the most difficult challenge for Christians in conflict to overcome. It can be difficult for some to admit their own contribution to a conflict or recognize their sin in a dispute. But when it comes to forgiving someone, even oneself, many find it impossible.

What are some of the declarations I've heard?

> I can't forgive him!
>
> I will never forget what she did!
>
> I can't forgive myself!
>
> When I pray the Lord's Prayer, I skip "forgive us our trespasses as we forgive those who trespass against us."
>
> He doesn't deserve forgiveness!
>
> There can be no peace without justice.
>
> I will not forgive her until I am satisfied with her repentance.
>
> He has to prove himself to me before I'll forgive.
>
> God damn him for what he has done!
>
> Why can't I just forgive and forget?

Perhaps you have said similar things.

Unforgiveness sentences you to a prison that leads to all kinds of suffering—emotional, mental, spiritual, and physical. Throughout my ministry, I have reflected on what helped people escape from the prison of unforgiveness. I have witnessed miracles of forgiveness that defy human understanding. I have met people who suffered the consequences of unforgiveness but were freed from its torments. I have personally learned to overcome unforgiveness in my own life as well.

One of the miracles I witnessed was the woman who was molested by her father. Though it appeared to be impossible, God enabled her at the end of our scheduled time to forgive as the Lord had forgiven her. It was easy to understand her unforgiveness. It was astounding to see her forgiveness and reconciliation with her parents. I continue to be awed when I see miracles of forgiveness.

I have come to appreciate the role that the Bible and faith in Christ plays in healing people and moving them to receive forgiveness and to forgive. Thus, I have desired for years to write a book for readers like you—most of whom I'll never meet this side of heaven—to find hope and comfort in your suffering.

I invited Mark to coauthor this book. Mark is a friend and colleague who shares similar observations from his own experience and background on the hope for overcoming unforgiveness.

FROM MARK

I have served as a pastor, a mental health counselor, and a seminary professor. I have had the opportunity to counsel, teach, and do research about forgiveness. While earning my PhD in psychology, I studied the lived experience of nonclergy Christians who forgave an interpersonal transgression. I limited my sample population to Lutherans because the research methodology required a small sample size, and it was convenient to access people from my own denomination. What I learned from this research project and from my professional experience with helping people to forgive shaped and formed my contribution to this book. Throughout the book, I will be sharing experiences from my research participants, though I have changed names and other identifying information to protect confidences. My phenomenological approach to research influences how I understand the experience of forgiving. Yet, my faith and God's Word are the foundation for what I believe and how I live out forgiveness. My psychological background informs me, but my theological background drives me.

People often seek mental health counseling for help in forgiving a broken relationship. For years, the mental health community was not prepared to provide such assistance. But various researchers began to study forgiveness and provide resources that would assist mental health professionals to counsel people through a forgiveness process. The various forgiveness processes tend to have one thing in common: they offer coping mechanisms that help clients create strategies that will help them cope.

Coping mechanisms are not new to the psychological world; rebranding them as forgiveness, however, is a new approach. The rebranding of coping mechanisms as forgiveness satisfies the client's desire to forgive, but it does not faithfully represent what God means by *forgiveness*.

Psychologist Michael McCullough and his colleagues focused on a process of motivational prosocial changes that encourage people to be less avoidant and revengeful toward their offender.[1] Robert Enright provided a complex model that walks people through a process that will help them end avoidance and revenge, which leads to forgiveness.[2] Both approaches help people to cope with transgressions against them. However, learning to personally manage a transgression ignores the life, death, and resurrection of Jesus Christ. The ability to forgive, according to most psychological models, comes from within the person. The burden to forgive is on the person. This is an interesting approach that may have some limited benefits. But it misses the richness of the Gospel. Forgiveness is not from within us. Forgiveness is not something we can do by means of managing a situation. Forgiveness is something that takes place outside of us and is given to us as a gift from God.

God says, "I, I am He who blots out your transgressions for My own sake, and I will not remember your sins" (Isaiah 43:25).

God declares, "And no longer shall each one teach his neighbor and each his brother, saying, 'Know the LORD,' for they shall all know Me, from the least of them to the greatest, declares the LORD. For I will forgive their iniquity, and I will remember their sin no more" (Jeremiah 31:34).

"To Him all the prophets bear witness that everyone who believes in Him receives forgiveness of sins though His name" (Acts 10:43).

---

1   See Michael E. McCullough, Kenneth Ira Pargament, and Carl E. Thoresen, eds., *Forgiveness: Theory, Research, and Practice* (New York: Guliford Press, 2000).
2   See Robert D. Enright, *Forgiveness Is a Choice: A Step-by-Step Process for Resolving Anger and Restoring Hope* (Washington, DC: American Psychological Association, 2001).

God accomplished this gift of forgiveness through His Son, Jesus Christ. John the Baptist proclaimed, "Behold, the Lamb of God, who takes away the sin of the world!" (John 1:29). Jesus forgives sins.

The apostle Paul says,

Therefore, if anyone is in Christ, he is a new creation. The old has passed away; behold, the new has come. All this is from God, who through Christ reconciled us to Himself and gave us the ministry of reconciliation; that is, in Christ God was reconciling the world to Himself, not counting their trespasses against them, and entrusting to us the message of reconciliation. (2 Corinthians 5:17–19)

God worked through His Son, Jesus Christ, to forgive the sins of the world.

What would it have looked like if God attended mental health counseling to learn how to deal with the sinful brokenness of His creation? A mental health counselor might suggest that God practice deep breathing exercises to calm Himself. The counselor might suggest that God distance Himself from the stressor—His creation. The counselor might suggest that God lower His expectations or seek emotional support from His fellow gods.

God does not cope with our sins. He forgives them. That required the shedding of His Son's blood. Jesus was not coping with the sins of the world while hanging on the cross. Jesus suffered the punishment for our sins and died for us. This is a radically different approach from any that a psychological method has to offer. God did not cope with our sin; He forgave it through the suffering, death, and resurrection of His Son, Jesus Christ. This is good news for you! To forgive as God forgives, you need not merely cope with sin. Rather, believe and trust that it has been forgiven through the suffering, death, and resurrection of Jesus Christ. Forgiveness is something that Christ has done, and we benefit from His work.

Yet, it can be easy to get caught up in foreign definitions and techniques to forgive. When we treat forgiveness as simply a way to cope with a transgression, we often end up in a never-ending loop of unforgiveness. A common coping strategy that produces negative results is rumination, also known as cognitive looping. Rumination occurs when a person has excessive negative thoughts or feelings about a particular situation. People will replay the transgression over and over in their mind or in conversation with others. The looping is based on assumptions that are not true, but it impacts how we think or feel about the transgression.

For example, a person will assume that forgiveness is not possible. Every time he replays the situation and ruminates on it, he engraves the lie into his life that the transgression is unforgivable. Over time, as he continues to ruminate on the situation, he becomes comfortable with the lie. He has relived it in his mind or with others so many times that he reflects on the situation with little effort. In addition, he may have people around him who encourage him to keep reliving the transgression in this way.

This coping method encouraged by mental health professionals only keeps you in the endless loop of rumination. You may be able to reduce your anger and desire for justice. Or you may be able to avoid people involved in the transgression. But you are still in the loop. And labeling this coping method "forgiveness" is not appropriate. This is not true forgiveness. The more you ruminate on the transgression in this way, the further down a dark hole of unforgiveness you will find yourself.

How can the cycle of rumination and unforgiveness be broken? The cycle is interrupted by godly forgiveness.

FROM BOTH AUTHORS

At different times in our lives as Christians, each of us is confronted with opportunities to receive forgiveness and to forgive. And God commands that we forgive as He has forgiven us. Why, then, does such a common occurrence seem so unattainable?

Actually, to forgive as God forgives us is impossible—on our own strength. It takes divine power to forgive as He does. So how can we, weak and feeble sinners, do the divine work that God expects of us?

Paul clues us in when he writes, "I can do all things through Him who strengthens me" (Philippians 4:13).

But what does that look like in today's world? How can that work for me? for you? for others?

This book is written for all those who struggle with unforgiveness in the hope that God's Word will strengthen you for this divine work. We share true stories to illustrate what a difference God's promises in the Bible have made for others to encourage you that it does work.[3]

In our sixty years of combined experience, we have helped people deal with unforgiveness by addressing key questions. We have devoted a chapter to each

---

3   Except when we share stories of our own families, names and other details are changed to protect confidences unless otherwise noted.

of eighteen such questions, as listed in the table of contents. You can choose to read first the chapters that most relate to your situation. Then we encourage you to read the rest, as each one gives additional insight into questions you have not yet asked.

The journey to receive forgiveness and forgive as you have been forgiven is not easy. Yet, God never intended for us to be on such a journey on our own. He doesn't promise that life will be easy or fair or without suffering. But He does promise to be with us every step of the way:

I will not leave you or forsake you. (Joshua 1:5)

And behold, I am with you always, to the end of the age. (Matthew 28:20)

God provides fellow believers to encourage us and share in our burdens and joys. He has given us one another to listen, pray, and share God's Word together. We recommend that as you embark on this journey, do so with your pastor, counselor, close friend, or another loved one to discuss what you are learning and to receive support. Choose someone who is spiritually mature and will hold your discussions in confidence. Find a person who will pray for you, encourage you, and lovingly challenge you. Intentionally select someone who will proclaim God's forgiveness to you throughout your journey.

Each chapter includes application questions. Take time to answer them relative to your present struggle. Write down your answers because that helps you take time to think more thoroughly. Written answers provide you opportunity to review your thoughts later. It also gives you something to discuss with the person on the journey with you.

We pray for you, our readers, with the words of Paul: "May the God of hope fill you with all joy and peace in believing, so that by the power of the Holy Spirit you may abound in hope" (Romans 15:13).

In Christ's service,
Ted Kober and Mark Rockenbach

CHAPTER 1

WHAT IS UNFORGIVENESS?

Our unforgiveness is a curse;
It drives a wedge, walls us apart
Creating enemies and—worse—
Imprisons both our minds and hearts.

O Christ, who burst the bonds of hell,
Break down the prison walls as well
That we erect and wall about
To fence us *in* but others *out*.

Lord, tear them down in Your dear name,
Nor let a barrier remain
For You have bought our liberty;
Your resurrection sets us free.

TED

"I hope she burns in hell!"

That's how I felt when my stepmother kicked the pastor out of my father's hospital room.

The relationship between my stepmother and me had been bad for years. At first, I was grateful that my father remarried after my mother passed away. He suffered for years as his first wife was dying.

My relationship with her soured when she began to cause separation between my father and many friends and family, including us children. Her verbal assaults on all of us were mean-spirited. Following two public family celebrations where she physically assaulted family members, my siblings and I invited our father and stepmother to join us in counseling. Her behavior was unacceptable and unpredictable. We feared more people would be assaulted, including our young children. When our parents refused to join us, our counselor advised we set up boundaries. She was no longer allowed in our homes for the safety of our children until we could meet together with a counselor. When we told our father, he said if his wife was not welcome in our homes, he was not welcome either.

For two years, we did not talk to her. We visited our father at his office, but the relationship was strained. He rarely saw his grandchildren after that.

Then one day, my stepmother called me. "Your dad needs you. He has cancer." The news was awful—doctors gave him ninety days.

My father had not been in church for the thirteen years since his second marriage began. I was concerned about his eternal welfare. He didn't know our pastor, although he was officially still a member. Our pastor, who was a kind and gentle man, visited him in the hospital to pray with him when my stepmother was out for a break.

When she returned and saw the pastor there, she screamed at him to get out and never come back. She called him various swear words and followed him down the hall, yelling. She threatened hospital staff to never allow this ****
back in her husband's room again. My pastor had never experienced such hostility while ministering to someone, and he was quite shaken.

I was beside myself with anger. My father was dying, and I was concerned about his eternity. My stepmother had chased away spiritual care just when he needed it the most.

Unforgiveness can range from simply ignoring someone to a progression of anger, bitterness, rage, hatred—even murder.

Unforgiveness occurs in two ways. Some people *refuse* to forgive. Others *struggle* to forgive. In both cases, the effect on the unforgiving person is similar. And when someone withholds forgiveness, the person yearning to be forgiven may suffer with guilt or shame.

The one who does not forgive slowly dies in a prison of anguish. Unforgiveness is a poison that wracks the mind, spirit, and body of the unforgiver. Left unchecked, it can kill a person emotionally, spiritually, and even physically.

Simply put, unforgiveness is what happens when we do not want to or cannot forgive.

Doctors of both psychiatry and medicine have observed the toll that unforgiveness takes on the one who doesn't forgive. Mental health professionals have long counseled their patients to forgive for their own personal well-being.

Accordingly, scores of books have been written on forgiveness. In this book, we will explore what it means to forgive as God has forgiven us and why that is a key to overcoming unforgiveness.

To understand what unforgiveness entails, let's begin by considering its opposite—forgiveness.

A MIRACLE OF GOD

A few weeks after the hospital incident, I met with my stepmother and father. He asked me to serve as his co-personal representative for his estate. He had major ownership in more than thirty active companies. He had thousands of employees, and he had several key friends and experienced businessmen whom he could have asked to serve. As a young man in my early thirties, I was humbled and privileged to serve his estate this way.

But there was a condition: I would serve as a co-personal representative with my stepmother.

I had begun to see how much she loved my father. She sacrificed her own well-being to be his twenty-four-hour caregiver. But I still despised and feared her. Yet, I agreed to serve my father in this way.

Then he asked if I would look after her when he died. In my grief and love for him, I promised to do so. The next day, they left town to seek treatment for his cancer in another state. He died several weeks later. I never saw him again.

Those first several months when my stepmother came home were challenging. She had created many enemies during her marriage to my father. She hated all but a few of his friends, family, and business associates, and she feared many. She didn't trust me, and I didn't trust her. But we were bound together by this strange circumstance to work together on Dad's estate.

One day she told me she bought a weapon and was going to kill some of Dad's business partners. I sought legal counsel to see if I could have her committed to a mental health institution but learned that was highly unlikely. I did not want to have anything to do with her plans for murder, so I planned to resign as co-personal representative. Her financial adviser talked her into resigning as co-personal representative and leaving the estate management to me.

And so our new relationship began. She was the major beneficiary for whom I worked as a fiduciary. I also needed to pay off the sixty creditors who filed claims against the estate. Early on, some minority partners tried to pit my stepmother and me against each other by telling us lies about the other so that they could take control of a company. She and I met to confront each other about the lies. We learned we had been set up, and we agreed not to let anyone come between us. That was our financial arrangement as beneficiary and personal representative.

I was committed to paying off all my father's creditors to honor his reputation with them. I also wanted to treat his partners and dedicated employees fairly. And if there was to be any benefit from the estate, I needed to devote full-time attention to overseeing the business for all the creditors and beneficiaries. I resigned from my career to work full-time for the estate.

I had made a commitment to my father to look after my stepmother. But personally, I had to decide how I would think about her. My unforgiveness and bitterness toward her conflicted with my faith in Christ. I chose to forgive her for the many hurts to me and those I cared about. Then, I decided to love her as God loves me—unconditionally.

Had she repented of any of the hurtful things she did? No. Did she change any of her attitudes or behaviors toward others I cared about? Rarely. Was there anything she could do to earn or deserve my forgiveness? Not a thing.

Then why did I make the decision to forgive and love her?

My faith took me to the cross of Jesus. In God's eyes, I am a sinful creature from conception who continues to sin against Him daily. There is nothing I can do to earn any merit from God. By nature, I am a worthless beggar who can only ask for mercy. God loves me so much that He sent Jesus to take on my sin, to suffer my punishment, and to die for me. In return, God gave me the righteousness of Jesus. God made me His child, an heir of His heavenly promises. My forgiveness in Christ is a miracle.

If God can love me that much, then how can I not do the same for people around me? Yes, even the woman I wanted to burn in hell. After all, Jesus died for her sins as well, whether she believed it or not.

The decision to forgive and love was a miracle in my life. However, living out that decision was another miracle that was tested for many years. Although she didn't attack me after Dad died (except for my faith), my stepmother often said hurtful things about people I cared about. Disputing her claims only resulted in tirades. I needed God's Word regularly to forgive repeatedly. I prayed for His help on those days it was most difficult. My loving wife, caring pastors, and mature Christian friends helped me in this difficult journey.

With God's help, I came to truly love and care for my stepmother, and she loved me. I defended her vigorously when others tried to steal from her. I protected her from people who wanted to take advantage of her. In later years, she entrusted me to make her health decisions. She empowered me to manage her estate. She learned to trust me more than anyone else.

Did she change her attitudes or behaviors toward others? No. But long after my decision to forgive, I learned how she had been cruelly abused by many from childhood into adulthood. She told me of one incident when a former husband nearly killed her. In her pain, she learned to hurt others before they hurt her. She trusted no one except for her grandmother, my father, and eventually me.

Did her pain justify all the hurt she caused others? Of course not. But learning about her past helped me understand her better. Did she earn my forgiveness and love? No. But in later years, she treated me as her own son. Did I condone the ways she hurt people? Certainly not.

I began to see her in a new light. I learned to have compassion for her. After I forgave her, I was able to see some of what led to her fears, anger, bitterness, and mistrust. I saw a person who had been deeply wounded over and over again. I have never experienced that kind of repeated abuse, and it's difficult to judge someone when you haven't experienced what she has suffered. I also learned she could be fun and loving in surprising ways.

When her mother died, a church elder told this seven-year-old girl that God needed her mother more than she did. That day, she determined to hate God and reject anything connected to Him. (Learning this helped me understand her reaction to the pastor in the hospital.) She rarely allowed me to talk about Jesus without her becoming angry. But she did allow me to show her the love, compassion, and forgiveness of my Savior. She received decades of my living witness, even when she refuted my verbal witness. However, I confess it was rarely easy, and my forgiveness for her was tested regularly.

In God's eyes, I am no more deserving of His love and forgiveness than she was. I am ashamed for wanting her to go to hell. I prayed that God would forgive me for my hateful attitude toward her. For many years, I prayed God would change her heart toward Him so that she could spend eternity with Him in heaven. Because I lived in another state, I was not with her the last days of her life, and I don't know whether she received God's gift.

Christians and non-Christians recognize that forgiveness in such situations is not normal. It's a miracle.

In this book, we define *forgiveness* in a narrower sense than the typical approach. That's because we believe the key to forgiving others lies in knowing how forgiven we are in Christ. As a result, we expect that some will take issue with our definition and our approach.

As authors, we confess a faith in the triune God as revealed in the Bible. We believe that this Word of God makes life-changing differences, not only for eternity but also for this life. We have personally witnessed miracles of forgiveness that defy human reasoning. We apply this approach because we firmly believe that addressing unforgiveness in the most healing way possible happens when we focus on the forgiveness we have in Jesus. We'll explore what the Bible says about forgiveness and unforgiveness, and then we'll share true stories of how applying biblical forgiveness has healed people from ancient times to this day.

OUR FORGIVENESS FLOWS FROM GOD'S FORGIVENESS

Our definition of forgiveness is built on a biblical understanding. Specifically, we define forgiveness based on the way God forgives, since Christians are called to forgive as the Lord has forgiven them.

Be kind to one another, tenderhearted, forgiving one another, as God in Christ forgave you. (Ephesians 4:32)

As the Lord has forgiven you, so you also must forgive. (Colossians 3:13)

We are called to forgive, not as the unbelieving world does but rather as God has forgiven us.

Consider what Scripture says about God's forgiveness. Forgiveness means that our entire debt to God for our sins has been paid in full (see John 19:30). Forgiveness releases us from the judgment of condemnation from God (see Romans 8:1). Forgiveness means that our iniquities have been removed from us as far as the east is from the west (see Psalm 103:12). Forgiveness means that through Christ we have been made righteous before God (see 2 Corinthians 5:21).

FORGIVENESS—NOT WHAT WE DESERVE

In God's view, we are all guilty. We are born sinful, unable to please God in any way on our own. "Behold, I was brought forth in iniquity, and in sin did my mother conceive me" (Psalm 51:5).

Not only are we sinners from conception, but we are sinners in action. Yes, *all* of us. "As it is written, 'None is righteous, no, not one; no one understands; no one seeks for God. All have turned aside; together they have become worthless; no one does good, not even one.' . . . For all have sinned and fall short of the glory of God" (Romans 3:10–12, 23).

Perhaps some feel that they have been good in almost every way—or at least they haven't done anything *really* bad. However, God judges by a different standard: "Whoever keeps the whole law but fails in one point has become guilty of all of it" (James 2:10).

Yikes! Even if I think I have slipped only a little bit, God declares me guilty of breaking the entire law. Of course, we are good at justifying ourselves and minimizing our sin. Nevertheless, God turns His face away from those who break His commandments. He declares that before we were reconciled through Christ, we were considered enemies of God.

> But your iniquities have made a separation between you and your God, and your sins have hidden His face from you so that He does not hear. (Isaiah 59:2)

> For if while we were enemies we were reconciled to God by the death of His Son, much more, now that we are reconciled, shall we be saved by His life. (Romans 5:10)

Although we may think more highly of ourselves, we are unclean and worthless according to God's standards. We have nothing to bring God to pay for our transgressions. Even our best deeds fall short. We can only approach Him as beggars, seeking mercy.

> We have all become like one who is unclean, and all our righteous deeds are like a polluted garment. (Isaiah 64:6)

> For we brought nothing into the world, and we cannot take anything out of the world. (1 Timothy 6:7)

Although Christians are made righteous in Jesus, and we know better, we still struggle with our sinful nature. Although we are His forgiven people and strive to live according to His precepts, we are in continual need of God's mercy and grace.

> Who can bring a clean thing out of an unclean? There is not one. . . . What is man, that he can be pure? Of he who is born of a woman, that he can be righteous? (Job 14:4; 15:14)

Paul anguished over his inability to keep God's commands, even as an apostle:

> For I know that nothing good dwells in me, that is, in my flesh. For I have the desire to do what is right, but not the ability to carry it out. For I do not do the good I want, but the evil I do not want is what I keep on doing. . . . Wretched man that I am! (Romans 7:18–19, 24)

> For the desires of the flesh are against the Spirit, and the desires of the Spirit are against the flesh, for these are opposed to each other, to keep you from doing the things you want to do. (Galatians 5:17)

Our holy, almighty, all-knowing, present-everywhere Creator calls us to live righteous lives. But as those conceived and born in sin, we must acknowledge that is impossible. No matter how hard we try, we miss the mark. God's righteous judgment declares us guilty, unworthy of His love, mercy, and grace. Yes, according to God's perspective, we are unforgivable.

The result? We deserve eternal separation from our Maker. "For the wages of sin is death" (Romans 6:23a). We don't deserve forgiveness from our holy God. We deserve hell. Yes, *all* of us.

That's what makes God's forgiveness so unfathomable, so incredible, so over the top. Despite who we are by nature, regardless of our inability to keep His commandments even as believers, God loves us. He loves you so much that

He put all your sins—past, present, and future—on His Son and condemned Him to die in your place. In return, He gave Jesus' righteousness to you. You deserve to go to hell, but Jesus suffered hell for you. You deserve to be separated from God eternally, but God chose you to be His child, to live with Him in heaven forever. You deserve the wages of sin, but God paid the full price for your redemption. You are precious to Him.

Forgiveness is mercy and grace. Mercy is not receiving what you deserve. It's a release from the consequence of eternal death. Forgiveness is the mercy of undeserved justification. Grace is receiving what you do not deserve. It's a gift without strings. Grace is God's undeserved love revealed in forgiveness.

FORGIVENESS—A FREE GIFT

Forgiveness is God's gift to you. You do not deserve the gift. You cannot buy it anywhere. And there is nothing you can do to earn any part of it. It is a free gift.

But the free gift of God is eternal life in Christ Jesus our Lord. (Romans 6:23b)

For by grace you have been saved through faith. And this is not your own doing; it is the gift of God, not a result of works, so that no one may boast. (Ephesians 2:8–9)

It's like the gift I gave my stepmother. She didn't deserve it. There was nothing she could do to earn my forgiveness. No matter how well she may have treated me in later years, her goodness to me could never earn any part of my forgiveness and love. It was a free, undeserved, miraculous gift.

But my gift to her was not initiated by me. I was simply giving her the gift I received through Jesus Christ.

FORGIVENESS MAKES US NEW

Through this free gift, we are at peace with God. We are freed from the consequences of our sin, both our inherited sin (see Psalm 51:5) and our own sinful actions. We are healed from the brokenness of our condition. We are no longer in danger of perishing forever in hell but rather have been given eternal life. God's gift makes us new creations.

But He was pierced for our transgressions; He was crushed for our iniquities; upon Him was the chastisement that brought us peace, and with His wounds we are healed. (Isaiah 53:5)

For God so loved the world, that He gave His only Son, that whoever believes in Him should not perish but have eternal life. (John 3:16)

For when I kept silent, my bones wasted away through my groaning all day long. For day and night Your hand was heavy upon me; my strength was dried up as by the heat of summer. I acknowledged my sin to You, and I did not cover my iniquity; I said, "I will confess my transgressions to the LORD," and You forgave the iniquity of my sin. (Psalm 32:3–5)

From now on, therefore, we regard no one according to the flesh. Even though we once regarded Christ according to the flesh, we regard Him thus no longer. Therefore, if anyone is in Christ, he is a new creation. The old has passed away; behold the new has come. (2 Corinthians 5:16–17)

FORGIVENESS CHANGES US FROM ENEMIES TO HEIRS

Because of His forgiveness, God no longer considers us enemies, separated from Him and deserving of judgment. Instead, He redeemed us from the slavery of sin, made us heirs of His heavenly promises, adopted us as His precious children, and lavished us with His steadfast love.

But when the fullness of time had come, God sent forth His Son, born of woman, born under the law, to redeem those who were under the law, so that we might receive adoption as sons. And because you are sons, God has sent the Spirit of His Son into our hearts, crying, "Abba! Father!" So you are no longer a slave, but a son, and if a son, then an heir through God. (Galatians 4:4–7)

But now in Christ Jesus you who once were far off have been brought near by the blood of Christ. (Ephesians 2:13)

See what kind of love the Father has given to us, that we should be called children of God; and so we are. (1 John 3:1)

But to all who did receive Him, who believed in His name, He gave the right to become children of God, who were born, not of blood nor of the will of the flesh nor of the will of man, but of God. (John 1:12–13)

Because you are precious in My eyes, and honored, and I love you, I give men in return for you, peoples in exchange for your life. (Isaiah 43:4)

JESUS' BLOOD REDEEMS US

By nature we are slaves to sin and under God's judgment. But through Christ's blood, we have been cleansed and purchased from our condemned state. Redemption occurs when someone frees a slave by purchasing him and setting him free. Because we are redeemed by Him, we belong to Jesus.

The blood of Jesus His Son cleanses us from all sin. (1 John 1:7)

Knowing that you were ransomed from the futile ways inherited from your forefathers, not with perishable things such as silver or gold, but with the precious blood of Christ, like that of a lamb without blemish or spot. (1 Peter 1:18–19)

Christ redeemed us from the consequences of our sin. He paid the ultimate price so that we would be forgiven. We belong to the One who purchased us by His blood.

FORGIVING OTHERS MEANS...

To forgive as the Lord has forgiven us means to share the gift He has given us—undeserved mercy and grace. We no longer judge the offender as our enemy but as another sinner for whom Christ died and was raised again. Jesus died for all people—not only believers but also those who do not yet believe in Jesus (see John 3:16). Instead of judging and condemning others, we freely give up the right to be angry, bitter, full of rage, hateful, and murderous. We offer the same love God has given us. We forgive.

This kind of forgiveness is not of this world. To forgive as God forgives is a divine act. It is not our human nature. Instead, it is sharing a miracle that only God, and those who receive God's gift, can offer.

Forgiveness is not a coping mechanism. The mental health community defines coping mechanisms as healthy or unhealthy strategies to address stressful situations. A person may choose to drink an excessive amount of alcohol to cope with a conflicted marriage. This would be an example of an unhealthy coping mechanism. A person may learn relaxation techniques from a mental health counselor to help them cope with the extreme pressures of work. This would be an example of a healthy coping mechanism. Forgiveness does provide relief similar to healthy coping mechanisms. But forgiveness is more than a strategy to reduce tension in a stressful situation. A coping mechanism looks within a person for strength and hope. Forgiveness looks outside of a person to Christ for strength and hope.

Forgiveness is not excusing sin. The very fact that forgiveness is needed means that someone has sinned. It also means that someone needed to be punished for it. God's punishment for sin is death, and Jesus paid that price for all. Justice required blood; Christ's blood atoned for our sins. "Indeed, under the law almost everything is purified with blood, and without the shedding of blood there is no forgiveness of sins" (Hebrews 9:22).

Forgiveness means setting aside the right to recall another's sin and use it against him. God promises, "I will forgive their iniquity, and I will remember their sin no more" (Jeremiah 31:34).

Notice that forgiving is not the same as forgetting. When God says, "I will remember their sin no more," it's not because He's getting old and forgetful. He chooses not to remember. God does not dwell on our sin, stirring up more anger and wrath. He doesn't get stuck in the loop of replaying our offenses over and over. You see, forgiveness is a decision, an act of the will. It is not passive, waiting for time to pass so that we forget. Remembering no more is a commitment not to dwell on the offense.

Forgiveness is not dependent on the sinner's actions. There is nothing you can do to earn God's forgiveness. Imagine if God were to say to you, "I'll forgive you, but only when you jump through all these hoops and prove that you're worthy." Impossible! We can never do enough good to pay for our sin. Accordingly, when we forgive others as God forgives, we forgive without conditions, without requirements, without demands. Remember, it is an undeserved, unearnable, free gift. (See chapter 8, "What If They Don't Repent?" to understand how those who do not believe in God's gift do not benefit from it.)

God also does not punish us by withholding forgiveness. He doesn't say, "Well, you dirty rotten scoundrel, I'm going to withhold forgiveness from you for a thousand years just to punish you." His forgiveness is instantaneous, constant, eternal—an expression of His steadfast love.

> The LORD is merciful and gracious, slow to anger and abounding in steadfast love. He will not always chide, nor will He keep His anger forever. He does not deal with us according to our sins, or repay us according to our iniquities. For as high as the heavens are above the earth, so great is His steadfast love toward those who fear Him; as far as the east is from the west, so far does He remove our transgressions from us. . . . But the steadfast love of the LORD is from everlasting to everlasting on those who fear Him. (Psalm 103:8–12, 17)

HEALING AND FORGIVENESS

Forgiveness blesses both the forgiver and offender in many ways, including healing. Listen to the words of David and note the benefits that flow from forgiveness:

> Bless the LORD, O my soul, and forget not all His benefits, who forgives all your iniquity, and heals all your diseases, who redeems your life from the pit, who crowns you with steadfast love and mercy, who satisfies you with good so that your youth is renewed like the eagle's. (Psalm 103:2–5)

From forgiveness flows healing of diseases, redemption from the pit, crowning with steadfast love and mercy, satisfaction with good, and the renewing of youth. Forgiving someone frees one from the prison of anger, bitterness, rage, and even the desire to murder. As psychiatrists and medical doctors have observed, it brings healing to the mind and body.

But knowing how forgiveness benefits the forgiver is not what enables us to forgive. God's forgiveness empowers us to forgive as He has forgiven. The benefits of our forgiveness flow out of God's forgiveness. Notice what compels us to live as God's people, including forgiving others:

> For the love of Christ controls us, because we have concluded this: that one has died for all, therefore all have died; and He died for all, that those who live might no longer live for themselves but for Him who for their sake died and was raised. (2 Corinthians 5:14–15)

The power of the cross empowers us to live the sanctified life—that is, to die to sin and live to righteousness.

He Himself bore our sins in His body on the tree, that we might die to sin and live to righteousness. By His wounds you have been healed. (1 Peter 2:24)

Remembering our forgiveness in Christ, earned for us by His death and resurrection, enables us to die to sin and live to righteousness. Focusing on Jesus, we have hope to forgive as God forgives. As we struggle to put aside our sinful ways, we are directed to the foot of the cross for Jesus' strength. With Paul, we confess, "I can do all things through Him who strengthens me" (Philippians 4:13).

WHAT IS UNFORGIVENESS?

Forgiveness is sharing God's gift. Unforgiveness is withholding God's gift.

When someone withholds forgiveness, the unforgiving person suffers all kinds of consequences. Unquenched anger leads to long-term bitterness and rage. A desire to hurt—even to murder—the offender may arise. Maybe the unforgiver wouldn't physically kill their offender, but in their mind, they murder him again and again in the loop of recall. (Remember that Jesus compared anger to murder in Matthew 5:21–22. See also 1 John 3:16.)

A demand for justice on the terms of the offended evolves into an expectation that cannot be met. Some may seek personal retribution, which carries consequences for the unforgiver. Whatever consequences the offender may experience, it's not enough to satisfy the rage of the offended. We often hear that a victim's family can "have peace" when the offending criminal has been convicted and sentenced, and justice served may give some satisfaction. But on its own, it does not give peace. Only God's forgiveness for both perpetrator and offended can bring peace that transcends all understanding.

Withholding forgiveness results in suffering for the offended.

It's nearly impossible to work through the grief over the loss of a loved one when you dwell on bitterness and rage against the perpetrator. If you are personally hurt or disabled, your own healing is impaired while you rehearse your anger.

Anger consumes one's entire being and gives birth to all kinds of evil. "Be angry and do not sin; do not let the sun go down on your anger, and give no opportunity to the devil" (Ephesians 4:26–27).

Anger that feeds unforgiveness gives opportunity for the devil to gain a foothold in your life. Unquenched anger matures into bitterness, a long-term anger that poisons the entire body. Eventually, bitterness can separate you from God.

Unforgiveness can create a perception of leverage over another person. You may make demands of the offender, internally or openly, because you want retribution for the offense. Leverage may evidence itself as you talk about the offender, continually tearing down his reputation, hoping to gain agreement and acceptance from others.

When we dwell on an offense, we play it over and over again in our minds. It's like a vinyl record where we keep the needle in one spot so we can hear it play again and again. As it does, it keeps us stuck in anger and hurt. We relive the suffering repeatedly, making the pain worse. As the event repeats in our mind, some of the details become rewritten. Often, our remembrance of certain aspects becomes worse to justify and inflame our bitterness. It becomes a downward spiral that causes even more pain and suffering. The loop leads to a kind of unforgiving hell.

Being filled with rage harms our other relationships too, not just with the offender. Although unintentional, the effects of wrath and malice impact relationships with those we cherish. Bitter, angry people sour good relationships. And when those loved ones don't join in our bitterness, we cut them off. We reason that they don't love us or support us. They don't understand or appreciate our suffering and pain. Consciously or not, we judge them unworthy of our affection. In any case, we lose the support and affection of loved ones.

Unforgiving people suffer loneliness caused by their own destructive patterns.

Unforgiveness is a poison we ingest, hoping the other person will die.

Thankfully, God has mercy on us sinners who struggle to forgive. Even unforgiveness is forgivable through Jesus. We find hope, healing, and spiritual health when we focus on the cross of Christ.

CAN NONBELIEVERS FORGIVE?

Anyone can forgive from a worldly perspective. That is, all people can try to let go of bitterness and anger, decide not to dwell on the hurt, avoid bringing up the offense, and not talk to others about the offense. They can employ coping mechanisms to ease their suffering. Because it is so difficult to do this, they may end up denying their pain, internalizing it. Mental health professionals may be helpful in guiding them through a process of forgiveness for their personal health, but those offended may end up stuck in a loop they cannot escape.

Others may try to medicate with drugs or alcohol or other self-destructive behaviors as a substitute for forgiveness.

But nonbelievers cannot forgive as the Lord forgives because they themselves do not believe they are forgiven by God. You can't give what you don't have. Only a person who has received the gift of Jesus' forgiveness can give that forgiveness to others.

So, here's the main point of this book.

To overcome unforgiveness, you must first receive and remember God's gift of forgiveness for you—and for the other person. Then, and only then, you can share the gift you have received. You can forgive as the Lord forgave you.

HOW DOES THIS APPLY TO ME?

1. Who is the most unforgivable person in your life?

2. What was the offense that seems unforgivable?

3. How have you been responding to the unforgivable event?

4. If you are unforgiving of someone, is that more a refusal to forgive or a struggle to forgive? Why do you think that is?

5. If you are in need of forgiveness from someone, read some of the Bible passages referenced in this chapter, such as Psalm 103:1–13; 2 Corinthians 5:21; and 1 Peter 2:24. What comfort do you find in these words?

6. How might defining forgiveness as sharing God's gift help you in your journey to forgive or your desire to be forgiven?

7. Write a prayer asking for God's help and hope in your journey to overcome unforgiveness. Then ask someone to pray this prayer out loud with you, inserting your name in the prayer.

PRAYER TEMPLATE

(See chapter 3, "How Should I Pray?")

INTRODUCTION

REFERENCE TO GOD'S WORK

PETITION

RESULT

CONCLUSION

CHAPTER 2

WHO ARE YOU?

Saint or sinner, who am I
  That for me in my condition
Jesus would consent to die,
  Granting free and full remission
Of my sins that I might be
  Called a saint eternally?

My sense of identity
  Ought not differ from my neighbors.
Let them all the Gospel see
  Lived out through my words and labors,
As forgiveness I proclaim
  To them all in Jesus' name.

TED

In 2019, my colleague Dwight Schettler and I traveled to Rwanda, twenty-five years after the infamous genocide. We were asked to train pastors, their wives, and other church workers to minister to people still traumatized from the genocide.

Although I had met with people who had suffered personal traumatic events including murder and sexual abuse, I had never encountered trauma of this scale: an entire society where everyone who was alive in 1994 was either a victim, a perpetrator, or both. In only one hundred days, at least 800,000 people were brutally slaughtered.[4] Others were raped or maimed. The carnage was not carried out by an enemy country but rather by neighbors, friends, and even relatives. Inconceivably, at the time of the genocide, about 90 percent of the country professed to be Christian.[5]

Two ethnic groups that shared a common language and customs were pitted against each other. Hutus were attacking Tutsis—men, women, and children. They also slew moderate Hutus who refused to participate in the bloodbath. Genocide leaders intentionally targeted children as part of their plan to exterminate all Tutsis. (They labeled the Tutsis "cockroaches").

The butchering and bloodshed defy description. Although Dwight and I tried to learn as much as we could about what happened, it is impossible for us to truly understand the depth of the trauma that these people experienced. I can tell you that it was personally painful and sickening just to learn about it. I shed many tears on that assignment. It took little time for us to realize that those who wanted to minister to others were themselves traumatized.

Since 1994, many had come to offer help in forgiveness and reconciliation. We studied as much as possible the efforts that preceded our work. Amazingly, there were countless stories of people who had lost loved ones or were deeply wounded yet who had forgiven the very people who had attacked them. Incredibly, many of the perpetrators who had fled for fear of retribution or who were being released from prison were returning to their villages and living next door to their victims.

So much had been done to teach and comfort these people in their trauma. As trainers of reconcilers, what more could we offer?

---

4   See *Encyclopedia Britannica*, s.v. "Rwanda Genocide of 1994," August 8, 2023, https://www.britannica.com/event/Rwanda-genocide-of-1994. Some sources put the death toll at over a million.

5   See Timothy Longman, *Christianity and Genocide in Rwanda*, African Studies (Cambridge: Cambridge University Press, 2009), 4, https://doi.org/10.1017/CBO9780511642043.

Before arriving, we studied what had been done and asked many questions. We identified two specific approaches that we perceived had not been widely applied before. One was to proclaim God's forgiveness to everyone based on the teaching of the Bible. The other was to remind people of their identity in Christ.

Seminars had been presented for years directing people to forgive others as they had been forgiven in Christ. Many faithfully did as they were instructed. Yet, those who lost loved ones (including entire families) or endured rape or disabling mutilations felt guilt, still wrestling with anger, fear, and a desire for retribution. Those who participated in the crimes, sometimes at the threat of being killed if they refused to kill, experienced depression and self-isolation because of guilt. Quoting Scripture, we intentionally proclaimed forgiveness to the church leaders over and over again. Only God's Word of forgiveness can bring healing, comfort, and hope to people who struggle with guilt. It proved to be healing for many.

The other approach was to remind them whose they were. In other words, we spoke extensively about their identity in Christ.

Identity had become a key issue in Rwanda. To avoid another war between ethnic groups, the government forbade anyone to talk about their identity as Tutsi or Hutu. In other words, they were to forget their own heritage. They were told to talk only about their identity as Rwandans.

How we identify ourselves shapes our perspective. To lose one's identity equates to losing one's very being or worth. The identities we cherish most affect how we view others and respond to conflict.

When we reminded our Rwandan friends that their identity is found in Christ, it created new perspectives for them in terms of trauma, forgiveness, and reconciliation. It reduced the focus on viewing one another based on family history because they realized that in Christ they are all part of His Body. They belong to the same family as brothers and sisters in Christ. When we die and enter into heaven, the only identity that matters is our status as forgiven children of God. Our worldly heritage, our achievements, our failures, our vocations—none of those matter in the eternal perspective. As people who will spend eternity together, what matters is that we are all related by the blood of Christ. We are His people, knit together by His blood.

They so appreciated the focus on their identity in Christ. As they fixed their eyes on Jesus, who gives them value and identity, their pain decreased and they viewed one another as members of the same Body. Yes, they are all Rwandans.

They all came from Hutu or Tutsi families. More important, they are children of God through Jesus Christ.

IDENTITY AND PERSONAL WORTH

How do you identify yourself?

We typically identify ourselves in multiple ways:

- Profession
- Position in family (wife, husband, parent, child, sibling, grand-parent, etc.)
- Accomplishments (athletic, educational, work awards, salary, number of grandchildren, etc.)

Some identify themselves according to their challenges or failures:

- Unemployed
- Divorced
- Angry person
- Disabled
- Alcoholic
- Depressed

Others identify themselves by their socioeconomic status, ethnic heritage or native language, marital status, sexual orientation, political affiliation, and more.

PAUSE FOR A MOMENT. LIST SOME OF THE WAYS YOU IDENTIFY YOURSELF:

How we identify ourselves, or how others identify us, influences our sense of self-worth or personal value. And self-worth affects how we respond to conflict in our relationships with others.

As mentioned above with our Rwandan friends, many forgot their identity in Christ. And yet, we authors would suggest that this is our most important identity. In terms of salvation, when you die and face your Maker, what you have done or accomplished or failed to do in life makes no difference. What God has done for you in Christ makes all the difference.

But identity in Christ makes more difference than just when you enter heaven. It also makes all the difference in life this side of heaven.

GOD'S PERFECT CREATION AND OUR BROKEN IDENTITY

God created all things, including you. You are not a mistake nor are you unexpected. You are part of God's creation. You were intentionally put together by God, and you are precious to Him.

> For You formed my inward parts; You knitted me together in my mother's womb. I praise You, for I am fearfully and wonderfully made. Wonderful are Your works; my soul knows it very well. (Psalm 139:13–14)

Nevertheless, God's perfect creation fell victim to sin when Adam and Eve disobeyed God and ate of the forbidden fruit (Genesis 3). God created you, and you are wonderfully made. But your identity as His creation is broken because of sin. The psalmist says, "Behold, I was brought forth in iniquity, and in sin did my mother conceive me" (51:5).

Our identity from birth is sinner. Paul declares, "Therefore, just as sin came into the world through one man, and death through sin, and so death spread to all men because all sinned" (Romans 5:12).

Our identity in action is sinner. Isaiah proclaims, "All we like sheep have gone astray; we have turned—every one—to his own way; and the LORD has laid on Him the iniquity of us all" (53:6).

Jesus defines what it takes to be righteous before God. "You therefore must be perfect, as your heavenly Father is perfect" (Matthew 5:48). It's an impossible standard for any sinner to achieve on his own merits.

James further clarifies our unforgivable status when he says that "whoever keeps the whole law but fails in one point has become guilty of all of it" (2:10). What a hopeless condition!

God declares us all sinners. We are unable to keep His commandments or live perfectly according to God's will. Even as Christians, we end up sinning against God and our neighbors. Talk about unforgivable!

Nonetheless, God loves His creatures, even though we are sinful. God loves the unforgivable. God loves you. Like all enemies of God, you don't deserve His love because according to His law, you are unforgivable.

Have you gossiped and slandered your neighbor? That's unforgivable in light of God's commands! Have you spoken hateful words or even just had evil thoughts about your neighbor? Unforgivable! Have you coveted what others have or wished you could have more? Unforgivable! Have you gained anything desirable by means contrary to God's design? Unforgivable! Has your anger led to you to murder your neighbor in your heart? Unforgivable! Have you sinned against God and others in any way, even in your private thoughts? Sorry . . . according to God's law, you are unforgivable!

Your transgressions make you an enemy of God—unforgivable based on your sinful identity from birth and your sinful thoughts, words, and deeds.

When my relationship to God is an enemy, I am condemned to eternal punishment. On my own, I can do nothing to escape from hell.

A BROKEN CREATION MADE NEW

Nonetheless, Isaiah proclaims hope to us unforgivables: "The LORD has laid on Him the iniquity of us all" (53:6).

God promised a Savior that would make us new again. Isaiah describes the Savior: "He was oppressed, and He was afflicted, yet He opened not His mouth; like a lamb that is led to the slaughter, and like a sheep that before its shearers is silent, so He opened not His mouth. . . . He bore the sin of many, and makes intercession for the transgressors" (53:7, 12).

God promised that His Son would bear the full punishment for our sin so that we would be forgiven. We would be viewed by God as holy, sanctified, and washed clean. And that is what Jesus did.

> For even the Son of Man came not to be served but to serve, and to give His life as a ransom for many. (Mark 10:45)

> Christ redeemed us from the curse of the law by becoming a curse for us—for it is written, "Cursed is everyone who is hanged on a tree." (Galatians 3:13)

Jesus Christ died so that every created person can be forgiven by His death and resurrection—and that includes you! Jesus says, "For God so loved the world, that He gave His only Son, that whoever believes in Him should not perish but have eternal life. For God did not send His Son into the world to condemn the world, but in order that the world might be saved though Him" (John 3:16–17).

God no longer identifies us as His enemies—unforgivable, broken sinful beings. Although there is nothing we can do on our own to gain favor with God, in Christ we are made new again.

> But God shows His love for us in that while we were still sinners, Christ died for us. (Romans 5:8)

> From now on, therefore, we regard no one according to the flesh. Even though we once regarded Christ according to the flesh, we regard Him thus no longer. Therefore, if anyone is in Christ, he is a new creation. The old has passed away; behold, the new has come. (2 Corinthians 5:16–17)

Our hope is found in Jesus Christ who took the sin of the world upon Himself. And He did this for all created people. What great news!

Jesus' blood gives us a new identity.

We have been changed from unforgivable enemies of God to forgiven children of God. No longer in danger of God's wrath and condemnation, we have been made heirs of His heavenly promises. We are the precious children of God. "See what kind of love the Father has given to us, that we should be called children of God; and so we are" (1 John 3:1).

Sometimes we might wonder why God does not judge the unforgivable. Why does He not destroy them? But God has decided to act according to His promise. God is not arbitrary or haphazard in His relationship with His creation. He is not a God of uncertainty. If He were, it would keep us on the edge of our seats, not knowing, always in a state of uncertainty.

This is the case when we think forgiveness is based on us. There surely must be something we can do, must do, to be forgiven. But how would you know when you have done enough? How would you know if you have prayed enough, given enough, performed enough good works, made sufficient satisfaction for your sin? None of that would do any good.

Thank God, none of that is necessary according to His promises. The good news is that God promised to forgive though His Son, and He did it. There is no uncertainty. There is only certainty in the promise. God forgives the unforgivable. And that gives us a new identity.

WHO BENEFITS FROM THE NEW IDENTITY?

Not everyone benefits from Christ's forgiveness.

Whoever believes in Him is not condemned, but whoever does not believe is condemned already, because he has not believed in the name of the only Son of God. (John 3:18)

For with the heart one believes and is justified, and with the mouth one confesses and is saved. . . . For "everyone who calls on the name of the Lord will be saved." (Romans 10:10, 13)

Although forgiveness is available to everyone in the world (John 3:16), not everyone benefits. Those who reject God's gift in unbelief reject the forgiveness that could be theirs. In other words, the judgment for their own sinful condition and sinful acts remains in place.

God does not force the sinner to believe. He gives us His Word (the Bible) and the Sacraments (Baptism and the Lord's Supper) to create, nurture, and strengthen our faith in Jesus.

The Bible tells us what is needed to benefit from God's gift: "Whoever believes and is baptized will be saved, but whoever does not believe will be condemned" (Mark 16:16).

Those who do not believe in the promise and forgiveness of God do not acknowledge that He created them and forgives them. Only those who believe and trust in forgiveness through Christ receive the benefits of the gift.

IDENTITY REFLECTS OUR WORSHIP

Our core identity reveals what we worship. What or whom we worship shapes how we speak, act, think, and feel. What we fear, love, and trust most of all is exposed in how we respond to others, especially in conflict.

For example, if I fear what others think of me (called "fear of man" in Proverbs 29:25), I may respond with defensiveness, self-justification, or cutting others off who criticize me. I might resort to retribution.

If I cherish my worldly possessions or financial well-being, I may judge those who threaten my goods in any way. I may choose to return evil for evil and take something precious from them. Or I may do something desperate to protect my possessions, even if I have to use sinful means.

If I trust my own desires, I may do whatever it takes to get what I want. This may include judging anyone who gets in my way or disagrees with me. It might mean doing something dishonest. I may think that the end justifies the means.

Human nature drives us to assert ourselves as god. We may not say that in so many words, but our thoughts and actions expose our heart's intent. Phrases in our culture reveal our inclination:

- I'm the god of my own destiny.
- I did it my way.
- I'm king of my castle.
- I'm a self-made man.
- No one will tell me what to do.

If I see myself as a self-made person, the god of my own destiny, the king of my domain, I have made myself god. I replaced the true Creator with a false representation. The result? My thoughts, words, and actions are all about serving me and my desires.

On the other hand, if I focus on my identity as a child of God, my fear, love, and trust in Jesus will be revealed in the way I treat others. Just as Jesus did, I will treat others with love, kindness, and forgiveness, even if they have wronged me.

My fear of God is shown when I don't fear people or things more than Him.

My love of God becomes clear when I set aside my personal agenda and worldly ways to live according to His ways.

My trust in God is revealed when I trust His Word and respond to others, even my enemies, with love and forgiveness.

HOW DOES MY IDENTITY AFFECT MY RELATIONSHIP TO MY NEIGHBOR?

God created us to be in relationship with Him and others. Our relationship to God was initiated by Him. He created us, and He loved us even when we sinned against Him. He gives us the gifts of life and salvation. We receive from God that which we do not deserve. It is a gift. We respond to His gift by worshiping Him, acknowledging that He is our God and Lord. We worship Him when we live according to His precepts.

The relationship we have with our neighbor is active. We either enhance that relationship or harm it by how we treat one another. And our actions toward our neighbor reveal who is truly our God and Lord. If we love our neighbor as ourselves, we worship the one true God. If we despise our neighbor, we make ourselves to be gods. We declare ourselves judges who determine whether someone shall receive forgiveness.

Our relationship with God shapes our relationship with our neighbor. If we turn away from God and reject His gift of forgiveness, we will not forgive our neighbor. We trust our own ways over God's. We will be bitter, angry, resentful, and judgmental. A relationship that rejects or ignores God is a relationship that will also reject our neighbor.

CAN OTHERS' VIEWS OF US CHANGE OUR IDENTITY?

Nope. We may be tempted to think so, but that would only lead us away from God's truth.

Our identity as children of God contradicts what others may say about us. Some may see us as merely evolved beings—but we are still God's creation. We remain God's forgiven children, regardless of what others think.

God's forgiveness frees us from what others may say about us. They may call us a failure. They may slander our reputation. They may even gossip about our worst moments, concluding that we are evil or worthless. Some may see us as defenseless victims. Through social media, people may say all sorts of unkind things about us, labeling us. They may convince others to agree with their judgment of what or who we are.

Regardless of what others think, we are still God's precious children. His view of us does not change.

> But now thus says the LORD, He who created you, O Jacob, He who formed you, O Israel: "Fear not, for I have redeemed you; I have called you by name, you are Mine. . . . Because you are precious in My eyes, and honored, and I love you, I give men in return for you, peoples in exchange for your life." (Isaiah 43:1, 4)

> But you are a chosen race, a royal priesthood, a holy nation, a people for His own possession, that you may proclaim the excellencies

of Him who called you out of darkness into His marvelous light. Once you were not a people, but now you are God's people; once you had not received mercy, but now you have received mercy. (1 Peter 2:9–10)

When our identity is shaped and formed by others, we may be persuaded to think that we are failures and enemies of God. But when we remember that God determines our most important identity, our confidence and hope is in our Father. Those who believe and cling to His promises stand strong in the face of persecution.

Regardless of what happens, the child of God clings to His promises. When others sin against us, and when we sin against them, we hold to our identity in Christ.

God keeps His promise. His promise is not conditioned on our abilities, our words, or our good deeds. God's promise is based on His Word. His promise is outside of us.

God does not promise that we won't suffer in this world. In fact, He tells us that we will suffer injustice because of our identity in Christ.

Remember the word that I said to you: "A servant is not greater than his master." If they persecuted Me, they will also persecute you. . . . But all these things they will do to you on account of My name. (John 15:20–21)

Although we will suffer in this world, God's children are never alone. The One who suffered, died, and rose again promises to be with us.

And behold, I am with you always, to the end of the age. (Matthew 28:20)

Keep your life free from love of money, and be content with what you have, for He has said, "I will never leave you nor forsake you." So we can confidently say, "The Lord is my helper; I will not fear; what can man do to me?" . . . Jesus Christ is the same yesterday and today and forever. (Hebrews 13:5–6, 8)

Because we are children of God, we can bring all our sorrows and struggles to Him. "Come to Me, all who labor and are heavy laden, and I will give you rest" (Matthew 11:28).

Our identity in Christ supersedes all other identities of this world.

Who are you? You are the forgiven child of God!

HOW DOES THIS APPLY TO ME?

1. How can remembering your identity in Christ affect how you value yourself?

2. How does remembering whose you are as a child of God affect how you view and value others?

3. Read 2 Corinthians 5:14–15. How can focusing on your identity as a child of God help you live for Christ and not yourself?

4. In what ways do you find it most difficult to live as a child of God? Why do you think that is?

5. Write a prayer thanking God for your identity in Jesus. Include a petition to strengthen your faith to live not for yourself but for Him who died and rose again for you.

PRAYER TEMPLATE

(See chapter 3, "How Should I Pray?")

INTRODUCTION

REFERENCE TO GOD'S WORK

PETITION

RESULT

CONCLUSION

HOW SHOULD I PRAY?

Uncertain as I am, dear Lord, now hear
  My inmost cry for grace and mercy new.
Though halting are my words, yet still draw near,
  Answer my prayers, my love and faith renew.

Lord, change the language of my inmost heart
  In which forgiveness seems a foreign word.
Your grace and wisdom faithfully impart
  That love sincerely spoken may be heard.

Sara was a conversationalist and enjoyed talking with all kinds of people. She was an encouragement to others, a helping hand when someone needed assistance, and a shoulder to cry on. But when she realized that her husband was having an affair, the world seemed to stop without notice.

She called her mother to report what happened. She talked with the people at her work about how ashamed she was. She told her craft club how stupid she felt. She spoke with her siblings about her deep hurt. She described to her hairdresser how painful this was.

Sara talked to everyone about the sin of her husband. Almost. She failed to talk to God about it. We tend to forget about God.

> And the people of Israel did not remember the LORD their God, who had delivered them from the hand of all their enemies on every side. (Judges 8:34)

God delivered the Israelites from the hand of Pharaoh. He parted the Red Sea for safe passage. He provided food for them. He gave them leaders. He promised them a land flowing with milk and honey. Yet, they did not remember Him, and they did not talk with Him.

One day Sara was telling her longtime friend about the affair over lunch. Her friend patiently listened. Sara was expecting her friend to give advice or sympathize with her. Instead, her friend surprised her.

"How may I pray for you?"

Sara sat there a bit stunned. Normally, finding something to say was not a problem for Sara. But her friend had introduced something new to the affair narrative—prayer. "How may I pray for you?" was not part of the script that everyone else had followed when she told the story. Sara was not prepared to answer this question.

"Uh, well, I don't know," said Sara. Her friend sat there patiently with such empathy and sincerity. "No one has ever asked to pray with me. I am not sure what I should pray for."

Introducing prayer is a way to interrupt the loop of unforgiveness. Often when people tell their story of the transgression, they get really good at recounting what took place and answering any questions. They have rehearsed it so many times that they could recite it in their sleep.

MARK

Many of my research participants discussed the importance of prayer. After they realized their inability to forgive on their own, they prayed to God.

Joyce said, "I spent a lot of time in prayer—I think coming to the realization of knowing that I couldn't forgive them on my own."

In prayer we put ourselves in a position to receive the gift of God. Like Peter, we cry out, "Lord, save me" (Matthew 14:30). And He does. God does not hesitate to grant us forgiveness. Our challenge is we get distracted by the storm around us, and we simply do not ask. But when we pray, God hears and He forgives.

WHAT IS PRAYER?

Prayer is talking to God. The psalmist reminds us of God's promise: "When he calls to Me, I will answer him; I will be with him in trouble; I will rescue him and honor him. With long life I will satisfy him and show him My salvation" (91:15–16).

The day before he died, the reformer Martin Luther wrote, "We are beggars. That is true."[6] As beggars, there is nothing within us that can forgive. After the research participants tried all sorts of internal approaches to address the transgression, they all eventually ended up as beggars, praying that God would help them.

Joyce continued to describe prayer this way: "It was like the Holy Spirit was there underneath my wings and I could actually do it, because I couldn't do it myself." Joyce came to God as a beggar, with open hands crying out to the Lord for help. And God answered her prayers. We are powerless without God, but with Him we can forgive the unforgivable.

Have faith in God. Truly, I say to you, whoever says to this mountain, "Be taken up and thrown into the sea," and does not doubt in his heart, but believes that what he says will come to pass, it will be done for him. Therefore I tell you, whatever you ask in prayer, believe that you have received it, and it will be yours. And whenever you stand praying, forgive, if you have anything against anyone, so that your Father also who is in heaven may forgive you your trespasses. (Mark 11:22–25)

---

6 Luther's Works, vol. 54, p. 476.

The power of prayer is not dependent on our ability to forgive. The power of prayer is dependent on God's ability to forgive. When we pray to God, we come with open hands ready to receive the gift of forgiveness that Jesus Christ paid for on the cross. God indeed has moved a mountain of transgressions and thrown them into the sea; they are no more. When we approach our heavenly Father in prayer, we come with the confidence of faith and believe that what God has promised and fulfilled in Jesus Christ is ours. We do not approach God in prayer with uncertainty or hesitancy. To do so reveals a weak faith. Children of God come to the throne of grace and boldly ask for that which He promised and fulfilled. Jesus bestows on us His forgiveness and says, "Peace I leave with you; My peace I give to you. Not as the world gives do I give to you. Let not your hearts be troubled, neither let them be afraid" (John 14:27).

The world says you need to fight, take control, demand your way, get your revenge. Yet, when the Israelites were trapped between the Red Sea and Pharaoh's army, the people cried out to the Lord. And Moses responded, "Do not be afraid. Stand firm and you will see the deliverance the LORD will bring you today. The Egyptians you see today you will never see again. The LORD will fight for you; you need only to be still" (Exodus 14:13–14 NIV).

Prayer is calling out to God with the full confidence of faith, receiving the gift of forgiveness promised in Jesus Christ. That mountain of sin is forgiven. "For as high as the heavens are above the earth, so great is His steadfast love toward those who fear Him; as far as the east is from the west, so far does He remove our transgressions from us" (Psalm 103:11–12).

Tears began to stream down Sara's face. Her friend did not give her assurances in the form of advice or adages. Her friend brought her to the feet of Jesus. Sara looked up at her friend and said, "Pray that we can get through this."

Asking "How may I pray for you?" turned Sara's focus off the transgression toward Christ, and it began to change how she responded to the affair.

What's the role of prayer? Prayer interrupts the circular conversations we have with ourselves and others. Prayer humbles us with the realization that we are beggars who have nothing to bring but our unforgiving hearts. Yet, we know that if we ask for forgiveness and a forgiving heart, God will grant it. "Ask, and it will be given to you; seek, and you will find; knock, and it will be opened to you" (Matthew 7:7).

HOW SHOULD WE PRAY?

The prayer of Sara's friend was simple:

Dear God,

Just as You showed mercy and grace to King David and Bathsheba, we ask that You help Sara and her husband during this most difficult time—so that Your forgiveness may reconcile their marriage and they may live together in the peace and joy of Your saving work. If it be Your will, strengthen their marriage through godly people who will support and encourage them. In Jesus' name. Amen.

Throughout this book you will have the opportunity to write prayers for particular aspects of unforgiveness. It may be difficult to know how to pray. Even the disciples of Jesus asked, "Lord, teach us to pray, as John taught his disciples" (Luke 11:1).

To help strengthen your prayer life, we offer a template you can use when crafting your prayers.

Introduction—"Dear God" or "Dear Jesus" or "Heavenly Father"

Reference to God's Work—"Just as . . ." or "When You . . ."

Petition—"I ask You to help me to . . ." or "Give me the strength to . . ." or "Enable me to . . ."

Result—"So that . . ." or "In order that . . ."

Conclusion—"In Jesus' name. Amen."

INTRODUCTION

We begin each prayer by calling on God who hears our prayers. Our God hears our prayers as a father hears the cries of his precious children, "Abba! Father!" (Romans 8:15). For example: Heavenly Father, Lord God, Almighty God, Eternal Father, Blessed Savior, and Merciful Lord.

REFERENCE TO GOD'S WORK

Our request for help should always be rooted in what God has done or has promised to do for us. Referring to His promises demonstrates our trust in His Word (see Proverbs 3:5). Consider beginning with "just as." For example, "Just as You answered the cries of Your people in Israel, I ask You to hear my pleas." You might also simply restate His promises: "You promise to give us the power to live as Your children" or "On my own, I cannot do what I ought to do. But with Your servant Paul, I know that I can do all things through Jesus, who strengthens me."

PETITION

State what you are asking for. Scripture tells us, "Do not be anxious about anything, but in everything by prayer and supplication with thanksgiving let your requests be made known to God" (Philippians 4:6). Normally, there is a close relationship between the work of God that you referenced and the petition.

Begin your petition by using the phrase "I ask . . ." or "Please grant me the ability to . . . ."

RESULT

Describe the result you want to happen. We know that when we ask to be forgiven, God will grant that request. But there may be other requests that are not promised but could be answered by God. We may ask God to heal someone who is sick, help a friend to repent of sin, or give us wisdom in making a difficult decision. Pray such petitions of desired results with the words "according to Your will." We approach God as beggars, asking Him to hear and answer us, but knowing that He may provide an answer that is different from what we ask (see Luke 22:42).

CONCLUSION

We address God when we begin our prayer, and we call on His name as we end our prayer. God encourages us, "Call upon Me in the day of trouble; I will deliver you, and you shall glorify Me" (Psalm 50:15), and Jesus says, "If you ask Me anything in My name, I will do it" (John 14:14).

Like a set of bookends, we encase our prayers in God's name: "I pray in Jesus' name."

WHAT IF MY PRAYER ISN'T PERFECT?

God promises not only to hear the prayers of His children but also to help them bring their requests to Him.

If you are a believer, the Holy Spirit dwells within you, and He helps you in your suffering. Paul assures us,

Likewise the Spirit helps us in our weakness. For we do not know what to pray for as we ought, but the Spirit Himself intercedes for us with groanings too deep for words. And He who searches hearts knows what is the mind of the Spirit, because the Spirit intercedes for the saints according to the will of God. (Romans 8:26–27)

When words fail, pray from your heart. "Lord, help me!" The One who died and rose again for you hears you. The Holy Spirit groans on our behalf. The Father hears the cries of His children.

Don't refrain from praying because you fear your prayer will be imperfect. Your prayer need not be perfect to be heard by God.

We encourage you to come before the Lord God and pray.

HOW DOES THIS APPLY TO ME?

At the end of each chapter, you will write a prayer. Use these prayers as part of your regular devotional life. Challenge yourself to write new prayers using the template explained in this chapter. At first it may seem unnatural to use the template. But the more you practice praying in this way, the easier it will become. Practice begins now.

1. Using the template, write a prayer asking God to give you a forgiving heart.

    ▶ Introduction—"Dear God" or "Dear Jesus" or "Heavenly Father"

    ▶ Reference to God's Work—"Just as . . ." or "When You . . ."

    ▶ Petition—"I ask You to help me to . . ." or "Give me the strength to . . ." or "Enable me to . . ."

    ▶ Result—"So that . . ." or "In order that . . ."

    ▶ Conclusion—"In Jesus' name. Amen."

2. Using the template, write a prayer asking God to give someone else a forgiving heart.

3. Using the template, write a prayer thanking God for the gift of salvation given by Jesus Christ.

PRAYER TEMPLATE

INTRODUCTION

REFERENCE TO GOD'S WORK

PETITION

RESULT

CONCLUSION

CHAPTER 4

AM I IN THE PLACE OF GOD?

Should I with brash temerity
 Usurp my Savior's place,
Pass judgment with severity
 Instead of showing grace,
My arrogance and pride remove;
 Lord, lead me to forgive,
That, saved by Your redeeming love,
 I may not die but live.

As a teenager in Australia, Gladys[7] determined to serve her Lord in the mission field. She trained as a nurse and took a position in India. She worked in a Christian hospital serving lepers—not just any lepers, but those who were Dalits, the untouchables, the outcasts. Dalits are the lowest level of people in a Hindu society and are considered removed from caste. Hindus believe that Dalits sinned so many times in previous lives that they were reborn as people who are worth less than animals. Lepers among Dalits were the outcasts among outcasts.

Graham Staines served as the hospital administrator. Also from Australia, he grew up in Queensland just thirty kilometers from Gladys. But they never met until they worked together in India. Graham and Gladys were married, and they had three children: Esther, Philip, and Timothy.

Graham loved the Indian people and wanted all of India to convert to Christianity. At the time, only about 4 percent of India was Christian. The Staineses worked together in the hospital and shared Jesus with their patients. Their children sang songs about Jesus as they wrapped wounds of the lepers.

Graham spoke about his faith in Christ at a conference in the jungle. Philip (age 10) and Timothy (age 7) accompanied their father. At the end of the day, they slept in their car.

Just after midnight, several Hindu activists surrounded the Staineses' vehicle. They hated Graham's message about Jesus. The leader slashed all four tires of their car to prevent them from driving away. Then they broke out the windows of the car, stabbing Graham and his boys with tridents. They kept them from escaping with the tridents as they set the car on fire, burning them to death.

How would you have felt about those killers if you were Gladys? Talk about unforgivable! Would you have wanted to condemn them to hell? Would your judgment put you in the place of God?

JOSEPH BETRAYED

Consider the life of Joseph (Genesis 37–50), a man from the Bible who had opportunity to exercise righteous judgment and unforgiveness. Although the story is familiar, let's recount the horrendous deeds of Joseph's brothers to emphasize the immensity of their crime and the miracle of Joseph's response.

---

7   I (Ted) learned the story of Gladys Staines (actual name) through a book and my meeting her. See Vishal Mangalwadi, Vijay Martis, M. B. Desai, Babu K. Verhese, and Radha Samuel, *Burnt Alive: The Staines and the God They Loved; Missionaries Murdered in Manoharpur* (Mumbai, India: GLS Publishing, 1999). Interview of Gladys Staines by Ted Kober in Townsville, Queensland, Australia, August 30, 2010.

Jacob loved his son Joseph, who was the firstborn of his favorite wife, Rachel, but the second youngest of Jacob's twelve sons.

Jacob gave seventeen-year-old Joseph a treasured coat of many colors because he loved Joseph most among his sons. This caused Joseph's brothers to despise Joseph.

Their hatred grew against Joseph when he told them about his dreams: "Behold, we were binding sheaves in the field, and behold, my sheaf arose and stood upright. And behold, your sheaves gathered around it and bowed down to my sheaf" (Genesis 37:7).

The brothers responded, "Are you indeed to reign over us? Or are you indeed to rule over us?" (v. 8). Their resentment toward him inflamed even more.

As if that weren't enough, Joseph told them more: "Behold, I have dreamed another dream. Behold, the sun, the moon, and eleven stars were bowing down to me" (v. 9). Jacob rebuked his son for implying that Joseph's father, mother, and all his brothers would bow before him. The brothers' jealousy intensified, but Jacob "kept the saying in mind" (v. 11). Later, Jacob didn't help the situation when he sent Joseph looking for his brothers to report on them.

Just as Scripture warns us today, unquenched anger gave opportunity to the devil. The brothers conspired to murder the favorite son of their father. However, the eldest brother, Reuben, interrupted their plans and told them to place Joseph into a dry pit. Reuben planned to rescue the boy later. When Joseph came looking for his brothers, they stripped him of his prized robe and threw him into the pit.

But before Reuben could save him, brother Judah devised a new evil plan, which the rest of the brothers embraced. When a caravan of Ishmaelite traders came through their area, the brothers pulled Joseph out of the pit and sold him as a slave for twenty shekels of silver. Then they took his coat of many colors and dipped it in goat's blood. They presented the robe to their father to cover up their wicked act. Jacob concluded that his precious son had been devoured by wild animals.

Not only did they sin greatly against their brother, but their deception caused years of grief for their father. Certainly, what they did was unforgivable, right?

MORE INJUSTICE AND SUFFERING

It got worse for Joseph.

The Ishmaelites sold Joseph to the Egyptian Potiphar, the captain of the guard under Pharaoh. Joseph proved himself trustworthy, and he found favor with his master. Potiphar appointed Joseph an overseer of his house and all he owned.

Joseph was a handsome young man, and Potiphar's wife made a pass at him. He rebuffed her continued advances until one day she grabbed his garment and demanded that he lie with her. He fled the house, leaving her with his garment in her hand. She cried out to the men of the household, accusing Joseph of attempting sexual assault. She repeated the accusation to her husband. As soon as Potiphar heard his wife's report, he had Joseph thrown into prison.

Because Joseph revered God and His precepts and refused her advances, he fell victim to false accusations and landed in prison.

Not only was he carried off as a slave to a foreign land where his native tongue and customs were unknown, but he also was separated from his father who doted on him and from the familiar comforts of home. Now he found himself imprisoned on trumped-up charges—all because his jealous brothers plotted to get rid of him. Although the Bible doesn't specifically indicate that Joseph resented his brothers, it's hard to imagine that he didn't blame and hate them for what they did.

After some time, two fellow prisoners had dreams that worried them. Joseph had been appointed to tend to them, and he saw that they were troubled because there was no one to interpret their dreams. Joseph invited them: "Do not interpretations belong to God? Please tell them to me" (Genesis 40:8).

The first, the former chief cupbearer of Pharaoh, told Joseph his dream. His interpretation gave hope for the cupbearer. Joseph said that the cupbearer would be released from prison in three days and restored as Pharaoh's cupbearer. Joseph asked the cupbearer to remember Joseph to Pharaoh when the cupbearer was restored to his position.

But for the second, Pharaoh's former chief baker, Joseph bore bad news. The baker would be taken out in three days and hanged.

Both interpretations proved true. But the chief cupbearer forgot to tell Pharaoh about Joseph. Once again, Joseph's suffering continued unjustly.

Imagine how Joseph felt. Because of his human nature, we would understand if Joseph got caught in the loop of rehearsing his unforgiveness against his brothers. Although the Bible does not say so, it is possible, even likely, that there were times when his bitterness grew against his brothers. Sitting in a dreadful prison would provide lots of opportunity to ruminate on what ultimately put you there.

GOD'S INTERVENTION

Two years later, Pharaoh had dreams that evaded interpretation by any of his advisers. Finally the chief cupbearer remembered what Joseph had done for him, and he told Pharaoh. Pharaoh summoned Joseph. When he had been properly cleaned up, Joseph was brought before Pharaoh, who told Joseph his dreams.

Amazingly, Joseph credited God for Pharaoh's dreams, warning him of impending disaster. Because Pharaoh was considered a god, Joseph's witness could have resulted in his death. But God protected Joseph and caused Pharaoh to believe Joseph's interpretation. There would be seven years of plenty followed by seven years of famine. Pharaoh could use the seven abundant years to prepare for the seven years of scarcity. Joseph advised Pharaoh to appoint overseers throughout Egypt and to select a wise and discerning man to direct the storing of food during the years of plenty.

Pharaoh replied,

Can we find a man like this, in whom is the Spirit of God? . . . Since God has shown you all this, there is none so discerning and wise as you are. You shall be over my house, and all my people shall order themselves as you command. Only as regards the throne will I be greater than you. (Genesis 41:38-40)

Pharaoh gave Joseph the authority and position to execute a plan to prepare for the famine. At that time Joseph was thirty years old. Pharaoh gave him an Egyptian name and wife. Before the famine began, they had two sons. The firstborn he named Manasseh, "'For,' he said, 'God has made me forget all my hardship and all my father's house'" (v. 51). The second son he named Ephraim.

Joseph succeeded in storing enough grain for Egypt. In fact, he had gathered enough even to sell to foreigners.

And that's what brought his estranged brothers to him.

JUSTICE OR RECONCILIATION?

The famine hit Canaan as well. So Jacob sent ten of his sons to Egypt to buy grain. He held back Joseph's brother Benjamin because he feared harm might come to his only remaining son from his deceased wife Rachel. The ten brothers approached the governor of Egypt to purchase grain. They did not recognize their brother Joseph, but he recognized his brothers.

Think for a moment. Who of us today would have judged Joseph harshly for making his brothers pay for their crimes? He had both the just right and the authority to execute judgment on them. He restrained himself from doing so. At the same time, he took time to test his brothers and consider his options.

Speaking through an interpreter, Joseph accused his brothers of being spies, which they denied. The brothers told Joseph about their family, saying that they were twelve brothers from one father. They answered Joseph's questions about their father and brother at home. But Joseph insisted they were spies. The brothers began to reflect on what they had done to Joseph. Reuben shamed them regarding their past deeds, declaring that there now came a reckoning for their sins against their brother. They expressed regret among themselves, not realizing that Joseph understood what they were saying. Joseph turned away in tears when he saw their contrition.

He continued to accuse them of spying. To test their honesty, he held back Simeon and sent the others back to Canaan, instructing them to bring back their youngest brother. He sold them grain, but he directed his servants to hide their money in the grain sacks. When they later discovered the money, they feared what would happen to them.

Once the food they purchased was gone, the brothers planned to return to Egypt. Jacob resisted sending Benjamin back with them, blaming his boys for disclosing they had a younger brother at home. Judah vowed to protect Benjamin and bring him back alive. With few options left, Jacob relented, allowing Benjamin to go with his brothers. He instructed them to take gifts and double the money needed so they could repay what they had initially purchased.

Joseph welcomed his brothers back with a dinner, but the brothers were afraid. Before entering the house, the brothers explained that they found their initial payments with their grain. Joseph comforted them, telling them not to be afraid and saying that God put treasure in their sacks. He released Simeon to them. As they entered Joseph's house, he saw his younger brother, Benjamin. Emotions overcame Joseph and he left to weep. After washing his face, he again approached them.

After they ate, Joseph commanded the steward to fill their sacks with grain and put their money back in their sacks as well as a silver cup. The next morning, Jacob's sons left with their purchases. Shortly after, Joseph sent his steward to chase after them and accuse them of stealing. The brothers denied any wrongdoing, and they vowed that if the cup was found in any brother's sack, that brother should die and the rest would remain as servants. To their horror, the cup was found in Benjamin's sack, and their money was in all their sacks. So they all were brought back to Joseph.

Joseph told them that he would retain only Benjamin, and the rest could return to their father. Judah told Joseph that if they returned without Benjamin, their father would die because he had already lost one son. Judah begged Joseph to retain him instead and allow Benjamin to return to their father. It had been Judah's suggestion that they sell Joseph to the caravan. Now it was Judah who would give himself up for Benjamin.

At this, Joseph could no longer hide his identity from his brothers. He sent all the servants out and revealed himself to his brothers with tears. At first, the brothers were in disbelief. Then, as reality set in, they became terrified. And rightly so.

But Joseph assured them with a miraculous confession of faith:

And now do not be distressed or angry with yourselves because you sold me here, for God sent me before you to preserve life. For the famine has been in the land these two years, and there are yet five years in which there will be neither plowing nor harvest. And God sent me before you to preserve for you a remnant on earth, and to keep alive for you many survivors. So it was not you who sent me here, but God. He has made me a father to Pharaoh, and lord of all his house and ruler over all the land of Egypt. (Genesis 45:5–8)

Incredible! Joseph had twenty-plus years to dwell on the wickedness his brothers inflicted on him. Imagine how bitterness could have taken root in Joseph's heart, especially when he suffered as both a slave and a prisoner. Although the Bible is silent about his heart during those years, there likely were times when his anger consumed him. As a human, he must have been caught in the loop of replaying his brothers' sins over and over again.

Joseph's perspective protected him from unrestrained anger. He was freed from the loop of replaying his brothers' wickedness. Instead, God gave him a new way to reflect on what happened. He remembered it very differently.

At this time, Joseph had both righteous judgment and authority to execute justice on his brothers, and they knew it. But instead of condemning them, Joseph forgave them and promised to take care of them and their families. He directed them to bring Jacob and all their families and belongings back to Egypt. When Pharaoh learned what was happening, he added to the gifts sent to Canaan and promised Joseph's family the best of the land.

What a glorious reunion for the family of Jacob! They were not only blessed with being together again, but they were richly provided for.

MIRACLE OF FORGIVENESS

Some time later, Jacob died. And Joseph's brothers feared once again. After all, they knew how much Joseph had wanted to be reunited with his father. Perhaps Joseph had been kind to them simply to see his father again. The brothers had good reason to fear Joseph.

But Scripture records a miracle of forgiveness known not only to Christians but many in the world as well. When forgiveness defies human reasoning, people take notice. Forgiveness is not natural to sinful people. It is a sacred act that even the world recognizes requires divine action. Forgiveness as God grants can only be described as a miracle.

The brothers expected Joseph to hate them and pay them back for the evil they had done. They even conspired to say that Jacob wanted Joseph to forgive them. Then they prostrated themselves before him, making themselves his servants.

One would think that in repentance they would be more honest about what Jacob said. But when any of us become desperate for mercy, we will do almost anything to save ourselves.

But Joseph once again forgave with an incredible confession of faith:

Do not fear, for am I in the place of God? As for you, you meant evil against me, but God meant it for good, to bring it about that many people should be kept alive, as they are today. So do not fear; I will provide for you and your little ones. (Genesis 50:19–21)

"Am I in the place of God?" Joseph recognized that only God could rightly judge his brothers and withhold forgiveness. Joseph had experienced the rich blessings of God despite his suffering, and he knew by faith that God used his suffering for extraordinary good. Joseph's amazing faith empowered him to forgive as God forgives. His fear of God revealed itself in his declaration. His trust in God enabled him to perform a divine act. His love for God compelled him to give his brothers the undeserved gift of mercy and grace. Joseph credited God for the forgiveness he gave his brothers.

Do such people exist today? Perhaps a more appropriate question is, does the God of Joseph still work divine acts through believers today?

FORGIVENESS AS A CONFESSION OF FAITH

Remember Gladys Staines, whose husband and two young boys were cruelly murdered?

People throughout India mourned that such a crime could be committed since Hindus typically are people of peace. But in a Hindu society where caste locks one into a lifetime of a certain status, people constantly strive for justice and improvement in their standing. The men who killed Graham and his boys were captured, tried, and sentenced. The leader was given the death sentence, and the others were sentenced to life in prison. A reporter who interviewed Gladys wanted to know if she felt that justice had been served.

TED

I had the privilege of meeting Gladys in person years later when she returned to Australia so that her daughter could attend medical college. There are two miracles in this story: first, what Gladys declared by her faith; and second, that a Hindu news report accurately recorded what she said.

As far as the sentence that the men received, Gladys said she had no comment, for God establishes authority, including government, which executes justice for society. Gladys reflected what Paul wrote in Romans 13 about another non-Christian government.

Then Gladys declared that she had forgiven the killers and held no bitterness. She explained that forgiveness brings healing, and India needed healing from hatred and violence. She went on to say that one should not mix up forgiveness and consequences.

The reporter was flabbergasted. He questioned if Gladys had forgotten how they murdered her husband and two little boys. Gladys had not forgotten, but she remembered it differently. She told me that every time she saw young men in their twenties, she thought of her sons who would have been those ages today. Clearly, she missed her husband and children. But as she reflected on the death of her family, she remembered that she forgave those who killed them.

She told the reporter she forgave them because her heavenly Father forgave her through Christ. She added that what India needs for healing is forgiveness and not retribution. Her confession of faith quickly spread throughout India and the world. News reporters came from all over—London; Paris; Toronto; New York; Washington, DC; and more—to interview this woman and verify this incredible story. Forgiveness as God forgives is truly divine. When it happens, it is a newsworthy event.

Gladys turned down most interviews. She exudes a quiet, unassuming personality. I found that there is not a bitter bone in her body.

She told me more than what was reported in the news about the case.

Graham prayed that all of India would become Christian. Following his death and the brutal murders of their sons, Gladys's forgiveness impacted lives throughout the land. It was reported that hundreds of thousands of Indians converted to Christianity because of her testimony. Graham's prayer was answered through his own death, the murders of his sons, and the resulting forgiveness expressed by his wife.

About two weeks before the murders, Gladys's personal devotions challenged her to give what she possessed to the Lord. She said, "Lord, I give You all I own." Then she laughed, because as a poor missionary she owned few worldly goods. Then she said, "But Lord, I could never give You my family." Saying that, she wept. She understood that she was making her family an idol. Convicted in her heart, she then said, "Lord, if You want to take my family, I freely give them to You."

I was awed by Gladys's confession of faith. Her identity was clearly found in Christ. She feared God most of all. She loved her Lord more than anything. She trusted Christ above all.

As I talked with her, I told her about my work in reconciliation. I shared that the most difficult work I do is help Christians who struggle to forgive. I also told her that I used her story to inspire others.

That's when she broke down and cried. And then she said to me, "Why do people find this story so sensational? Isn't forgiveness what Christians do?"

Oh, my friends! Such a simple statement, yet so hard to live. She acted in a similar way to Joseph when he declared, "Am I in the place of God?" God has certainly given Gladys a special measure of faith. But the Holy Spirit lives in all who believe and are baptized, and He grants us life and faith in Jesus.

Most of us have not suffered the pain of having our family murdered or being sold by our siblings into slavery. Sadly, I've met people who have experienced such trauma. Regardless, we have all experienced suffering because of evil committed against us. We know what it means to be betrayed by someone we loved and trusted, to have our reputation maligned, and to be personally hurt or have someone we care about be bullied or physically hurt. Many have experienced abuse in different forms—physical, sexual, emotional, mental, or spiritual.

As a result, it is very human for our hurt to give birth to anger, wrath, malice, hatred, and unforgiveness. Our bitterness keeps us in a loop of replaying the hurtful deeds over and over again, nursing our grudges and inflaming our anger. Our desire for justice on our terms fuels our rage.

But we have a Savior who experienced all the pain and hurt our sinful world can give. He experienced sickness, death, and wickedness among His family and friends. He was tempted as we are, and yet He did not sin. He was betrayed by His closest friends at the time of His greatest need. He was unjustly tried and convicted in an illegal trial. He suffered a painful, shameful, lonely death. He experienced being forsaken by God. He died. For me. For you. For the whole world.

He died and rose again for us so that we would be given an undeserved gift: forgiveness from God. He paid the full punishment of our sins so we would be declared righteous before God. He died so that we would be called children of God. He rose again so that we would know that we, too, will rise again and live with Him in eternity.

Based on the promises of Scripture, I can assure you that you are forgiven, even in your struggle to forgive or in your desire to be forgiven.

> For our sake He made Him to be sin who knew no sin, so that in Him
> we might become the righteousness of God. (2 Corinthians 5:21)

Receive God's precious, undeserved, heavenly gift. Focus on what He has done and is doing for you today. Then ask Him to help you give the gift you have received. Pray that you will not put yourself in the place of God. Forgive as the Lord has forgiven you.

HOW DOES THIS APPLY TO ME?

1. What amazes you most about the stories of Joseph and Gladys?

2. In the account about Joseph, with whom do you most relate? Why?

3. Some offenses take many years to work through. What comfort does the lifelong story of Joseph and his brothers give you?

4. What do you think God wants you to learn in your suffering?

5. How do you think your response to your situation affects others?

6. What did you observe about what led Joseph and Gladys to forgive the unforgivables in their lives?

7. Write a prayer asking God for help in your struggles. Include thanksgiving for the gift of forgiveness that is yours in Christ Jesus. Consider praying for those who have hurt you, or those who hurt someone you love, or those who haven't forgiven you. As you pray, place your trust in God for strength to live as His child.

PRAYER TEMPLATE

(See chapter 3, "How Should I Pray?")

INTRODUCTION

REFERENCE TO GOD'S WORK

PETITION

RESULT

CONCLUSION

CHAPTER 5

WHO'S THE NINEVITE IN YOUR LIFE?

If we persist in our demands
And seize control from others' hands,
  We have not long to wait
Until relationships of heart
With kindred spirits drift apart,
  And love devolves to hate.

When hate destroys all love and trust
Which then in shambles in the dust
  Lie trodden to the ground,
Repair the damage we have done;
Restore our love through Your dear Son;
  Let trust again rebound.

MARK

One of the participants I interviewed was Logan. He and his wife were newly married and living in a fixer-upper home. Logan had spent many hours rebuilding their bathroom. In the middle of a wintry night, Logan woke up to a blizzard and ran into the bathroom. There was a hole in the celling that he had not yet patched, and the snow was dumping in. He quickly woke up his wife to help him cover the hole. He was yelling at her to give him this or hold that.

She did not appreciate being yelled at and decided to go for a drive to clear her head. Logan took her car keys and refused to return them to her. "No, you can't go drive. It's a blizzard outside. Wait until the blizzard is over. I don't want you to die."

His wife was determined to have her way. She stormed across the road to the police station and reported that her husband wouldn't let her leave the house. The police arrested him for entrapment.

In the midst of the storm, Logan and his wife got distracted. They sinned against each other and refused to forgive each other because each felt self-righteous in their reactions to the situation. Their unforgiveness had them drowning in the waters of their self-justification, which resulted in anger, hate, bitterness, and thoughts of revenge. This continued for over a year. If you asked either one how married life was, they would retell the story of the blizzard. Each would make the case that their reaction was justified and their spouse was wrong.

Logan said, "My biggest thing was I felt so entitled. I was so full of myself that I was too good to admit what I had done wrong. I was too good to apologize to her for hurting her. I was too good to acknowledge that we had become people who scream for everything." Logan had judged his wife a Ninevite, someone not deserving of mercy and forgiveness.

WHAT IS A NINEVITE?

A Ninevite is a citizen of Nineveh, an ancient Assyrian city of Upper Mesopotamia (modern-day northern Iraq) that served as the capital of Assyria around the time of Jonah. But in Jonah's context, a Ninevite was an evil enemy of Israel, deserving of God's wrath and punishment.

The Hebrews detested this wicked city. Nineveh's residents worshiped idols and had a reputation for cruelty. Nineveh was known for its savage treatment of its enemies, including Israel. They sometimes skinned enemies alive and hung their skins on their city walls as a warning to adversaries.

Thus, it is no surprise that Jonah wanted nothing to do with calling the Ninevites to repentance. In righteous indignation, he judged them as evildoers who deserved God's condemnation.

WHAT RIGHT DOES GOD HAVE TO FORGIVE AS HE PLEASES?

Or what right does Jonah have to withhold God's forgiveness as he pleases? God was much more merciful and gracious than His prophet.

God called Jonah to preach repentance to Nineveh, but Jonah decided to run away from God. He boarded a ship for Tarshish to escape from the presence of the Lord.

So foolish, you might say. But don't we do the same thing when God calls us to go and be reconciled with someone we label a Ninevite? We may not physically run away, but we try to escape from God's direction when it doesn't fit our plans. Denial seems like such a good idea at the time.

God caused such a terrible storm on the sea that the sailors on Jonah's ship were terrified. Desperate, they cried out to their gods and threw cargo into the sea. Meanwhile, Jonah was sleeping in the inner part of the ship. The captain woke him: "What do you mean, you sleeper? Arise, call out to your god! Perhaps the god will give a thought to us, that we may not perish!" (Jonah 1:6).

The mariners then cast lots to learn who to blame for their peril, and the lots fell on Jonah. They demanded to know who he was and from where he came. Jonah responded, "I am a Hebrew, and I fear the Lord, the God of heaven, who made the sea and the dry land" (v. 9). He also told them he was running away from God. This report generated great fear among the men.

They asked what they could do to appease God. Jonah told them to throw him into the sea. The sailors resisted at first, trying to row harder. But the storm intensified. Praying to God for what they were about to do, they tossed Jonah overboard. Immediately, the sea became calm. The men feared and worshiped the Lord. By faith, they received God's blessing.

As he was drowning, Jonah repented and prayed for deliverance. Sometimes, we fail to go to God immediately, thinking we can do okay on our own. Only when we realize how helpless we are do we turn to Him.

God saved him by sending a fish to swallow him up. Jonah remained in the belly of the fish three days and three nights. Not what we would call a cozy safe haven!

Jonah prayed to God from the belly of the fish, praising Him for his rescue. He recounted his cries for mercy and thanked God for redemption. Jonah's faith is evident since many words of his prayer were taken from the book of Psalms.

After three days, the Lord spoke to the fish, and it spit Jonah out onto dry land.

Finally, he obeyed God's call. The repentant Jonah went to Nineveh to preach repentance to his enemies. Jonah spent three days crossing the large city, warning the Ninevites of impending disaster.

The people believed God and repented. The king clothed himself with sackcloth and sat in ashes. He issued a proclamation for a citywide fast, decreeing that all be covered with sackcloth and call out mightily to God: "Let everyone turn from his evil way and from the violence that is in his hands. Who knows? God may turn and relent and turn from His fierce anger, so that we may not perish" (Jonah 3:8–9).

God listened to their cry for mercy, forgave them, and relented from destroying them. Jonah's worst fears came true, and he was exceedingly unhappy.

Jonah wanted to decide who received God's forgiveness and who didn't. After the Ninevites repented and God forgave them, Jonah complained, "O LORD, is not this what I said when I was yet in my country? That is why I made haste to flee to Tarshish; for I knew that you are a gracious God and merciful, slow to anger and abounding in steadfast love, and relenting from disaster" (4:2).

Jonah understood God's character. He knew that if the people repented, God would forgive them. Jonah did not want the Lord to show mercy to Nineveh. That's why he had run away from God's call.

Jonah was so upset that he prayed, "Therefore now, O LORD, please take my life from me, for it is better for me to die than to live" (v. 3).

This is the same guy who prayed that God would save him from drowning after trying to run away from God. One might assume that since Jonah trusted God who was gracious and merciful to him, he would want others to benefit from that same loving God. Not so. Although Jonah wanted God to be gracious and merciful to him, he didn't want God to be gracious and merciful to Israel's enemy. Jonah believed that he was more worthy than the Ninevites.

God confronted Jonah's sinful attitude: "Do you do well to be angry?" (v. 4).

At this, Jonah went out of Nineveh and made a booth where he could sit and watch what would become of the city. He still hoped for its destruction.

TED

Now, if I were God, I would have granted Jonah what he asked. I'd zap him and watch him die! Such an ingrate doesn't deserve God's steadfast love.

But wait! Does not God see me as that same kind of unthankful wretch? Haven't I at times been just as sinful as Jonah or the Ninevites in God's eyes? And yet, my loving Father forgives me again and again, although I have personally experienced His loving favor while wishing condemnation for those I hate. Like Jonah, I have felt I was more worthy of God's steadfast love than someone I considered more wicked than me.

God continued to deal with Jonah through steadfast love. He raised a plant over Jonah to provide shade from the burning sun. That made Jonah "exceedingly glad" (4:6) because of his personal comfort. But the next day, God sent a worm to attack the plant, causing it to wither. A scorching east wind and hot sun beat down on Jonah so that he became faint.

> And [Jonah] asked that he might die and said, "It is better for me to die than to live." But God said to Jonah, "Do you do well to be angry for the plant?" And he said, "Yes, I do well to be angry, angry enough to die." (vv. 8–9)

It seems that whenever Jonah didn't get what he wanted, he felt like dying. Hmmm . . . I wonder, is that like anyone I know?

> And the LORD said, "You pity the plant, for which you did not labor, nor did you make it grow, which came into being in a night and perished in a night. And should not I pity Nineveh, that great city, in which there are more than 120,000 persons who do not know their right hand from their left, and also much cattle?" (vv. 10–11)

Jonah forgot who was God. It wasn't him.

THE IDOLATRY OF WITHHOLDING FORGIVENESS

In his prayer in the belly of the fish, Jonah declared, "Those who pay regard to vain idols forsake their hope of steadfast love" (2:8). In other words, anyone who worships false gods forfeits God's mercy and grace.

What was Jonah's false god? And what did he risk losing for his idolatry?

Jonah broke the First Commandment by making himself god. He wanted to determine who received God's forgiveness and who would not. Jonah wanted the privilege of judging people he considered more evil than himself, and then he wanted them condemned. He thought if he ignored God's command to preach repentance to the Ninevites, then they would not have opportunity to repent and God would therefore obliterate them. Jonah was a god wannabe.

When he didn't get his way, he repeatedly wanted to die. Over and over again, Jonah tried to play god.

When we put ourselves in the place of God, we risk losing God's love and mercy for us. We act as if we don't need God's love and forgiveness because we claim ourselves righteous on our own merits. Those who believe that they are righteous on their own don't need a Savior. They justify themselves, thinking they are better than others. And those who declare themselves righteous essentially reject the gift of God's forgiveness. They reject Jesus' blood and His righteousness.

While many may agree that certain people seem less evil than others, God doesn't view His creatures that way. He demands perfection from all. Because no one can meet His standard, He judges each one sinful and worthy of eternal punishment. But because He loves all, He sent His Son to die for all. God forgives everyone through Jesus Christ. Not so with people. We categorize some sins as worse than others. Certainly, there are wicked acts that hurt people more than other sins. But in God's judgment, all sin, even what we consider minor, deserves God's punishment. Christ died for all sin, including those sins we consider minor and those we declare significant. God forgives all sins through Jesus.

If we take issue with God's mercy and grace, we set ourselves up to be god. We want to determine who is a Ninevite and who deserves God's wrath and condemnation. We want to be god.

The book of Jonah instills hope for the child of God who forgets who really is God. By his confession, Jonah knew that God was gracious and merciful, slow to anger, and abounding in steadfast love. Yet, Jonah put himself in the place of God.

God cared for Jonah and showered him with mercy again and again, despite his repeated sin of trying to replace God. This gives us immense hope. Just as God repeatedly showed mercy to an ungrateful Jonah, we have hope that He does the same for us.

How often have we wanted God to nail our opponent and yet forgive us? Nevertheless, He continues to love and forgive us. And not only us—His love is also for those we name Ninevites.

Yes, God forgives the unforgivable. Repeatedly. Constantly. According to His gracious will, He forgives. Christ laid down His life so all the Ninevites of the world might be saved through Him. And that includes you and me.

STOP PLAYING GOD

One day Logan's father talked to him about the situation. "Are you too good to admit that you were wrong, that you would lose your relationship with your wife, the person you've been dating for how many years? [Are] you willing to lose that relationship because you're so entitled?"

In Logan's arrogance, he judged his wife as wicked. He got so distracted by his entitlement to being right that he could not see the gift of forgiveness in Christ. He was stuck in the loop of unforgiveness and felt the only way out was through justifying himself.

In time, Logan came to understand how much God had forgiven him. And it was God's love for him that moved Logan to forgive his wife. Logan said,

> We finally started trying to love each other instead of hating each other. If Christ was able to forgive everything, all the stupidness, then you should be able to forgive the other person for acting out of anger. If you forgive somebody truly, you're no longer thinking that the person is going to harm you. We fought for each other.

Who is the Ninevite in your life? And who is the Jonah? For which of these did Christ die?

> For the love of Christ controls us, because we have concluded this: that one has died for all, therefore all have died; and He died for all, that those who live might no longer live for themselves but for Him who for their sake died and was raised. (2 Corinthians 5:14–15)

HOW DOES THIS APPLY TO ME?

1. With whom can you most relate in the book of Jonah? Explain your answer.

2. What tempts you to play the role of god, either in your own life or in dealing with others?

3. Logan said, "My biggest thing was I felt so entitled. I was so full of myself that I was too good to admit what I had done wrong. I was too good to apologize to her for hurting her. I was too good to acknowledge that we had become people who scream for everything." Reflect on a conflict from your life that gave rise to anger. Pride often underlies anger. As you think back to that situation, describe how your sense of entitlement or pride may have influenced your thinking.

4. How can confessing your pride or desire to be god lead to healing in your relationship with God? How might that lead to healing in your relationship with others?

5. Write down what makes it most difficult for you to forgive someone who has hurt you deeply. Then write a prayer asking for God's help in removing those obstacles. Include a petition of thanksgiving for your God who is merciful and gracious, slow to anger, and abounding in steadfast love. Ask Him for a heart that reflects how He has been toward you.

PRAYER TEMPLATE

(See chapter 3, "How Should I Pray?")

INTRODUCTION

REFERENCE TO GOD'S WORK

PETITION

RESULT

CONCLUSION

CHAPTER 6

HOW DOES ANGER GIVE OPPORTUNITY TO THE DEVIL?

When resentment fuels my anger,
  Bitterness engulfs my mind.
If I'm heedless of the danger,
  Wrath and hate crowd close behind.
Can I claim, "I love You, Lord!"
Contrary to Your own Word
When by blatant misbehavior
I deny I love my neighbor?

Break for me this endless cycle;
  Evil thoughts spawn evil deeds.
By the prodding of the devil
  One sin to another leads.
Free me from his grip of wrath,
Set me on Your righteous path,
Make of me a new creation,
Grant forgiveness and salvation.

MARK

One of my research participants was Joyce. Her husband farmed with his father and brother. When his father died, Joyce and her husband were denied any chance to buy the land they had worked for so many years. The will had been changed. Only her husband's brother was given opportunity to buy the land. Joyce's anger grew into bitterness, and she coped with the situation by drinking alcohol. She described the moment her malice took over: "I sat outside at the firepit and cried and cried. Then I went in the house and got everything they [her brother-in-law's family] gave me and burned it. Everything, yeah. Which I never regretted."

Anger itself may not be a sin. It's what we do with our anger that can get us into trouble. Anger that is not dealt with quickly burns into a fiery wrath that is not easily extinguished.

Paul warns against anger that lasts more than a day: "Be angry and do not sin; do not let the sun go down on your anger, and give no opportunity to the devil" (Ephesians 4:26–27).

Feed anger, and it will grow out of control. Unbridled anger transforms into a bitterness that is not easily quenched. Bitterness and unforgiveness are inseparable. As Paul reminds us, anger that lasts past sunset gives opportunity to the devil. Anger tempts us to all kinds of sin.

The Bible cautions against a quick temper and warns us to avoid people who are angry:

A man of quick temper acts foolishly, and a man of evil devices is hated. (Proverbs 14:17)

Make no friendship with a man given to anger, nor go with a wrathful man. (Proverbs 22:24)

The Scriptures contrast what suppresses anger with what can incite it: "A soft answer turns away wrath, but a harsh word stirs up anger" (Proverbs 15:1).

THE FRUIT OF ANGER

Anger fuels unforgiveness. Dwell on it, stir it up inside you, replay the offense over and over again in your mind, and your anger justifies condemning the offender. You declare who are the Ninevites in your life, and you wish, even pray, for God to unleash His wrath against them.

Anger bears fruit. But notice that anger is not identified as fruit of the Spirit: "The fruit of the Spirit is love, joy, peace, patience, kindness, goodness, faithfulness, gentleness, self-control; against such things there is no law" (Galatians 5:22–23).

People who live in the Spirit exhibit the Spirit's fruit. They learn to deal with their anger quickly lest it give the devil a foothold. Instead of anger, fruit of the Spirit includes love, patience, kindness, gentleness, and self-control. The fruit of the Spirit strengthens us to resist long-term anger and instead show love, kindness, and gentleness to those who sin against us.

Anger produces different fruit. Jealousy, strife, fits of anger, rivalries, dissensions, divisions, and envy are listed among the works of the flesh (see vv. 20–21). And no wonder! Jealousy, rivalries, and envy lead to hatred. Strife, dissensions, and divisions lead to separation. Fits of anger lead to all kinds of destructive behaviors—even murder. All are opportunities for the devil. All keep you from forgiving.

Recall the very first murder. Cain's jealousy and long-term anger led him to murder his brother. Cain's anger began in his heart. The Lord warned him, "Why are you angry, and why has your face fallen? If you do well, will you not be accepted? And if you do not do well, sin is crouching at the door. Its desire is contrary to you, but you must rule over it" (Genesis 4:6–7).

God admonished Cain to rule over his anger because sin was crouching at the door. Anger not only results in harming others. The person hurt first and longest is the person who is angry. Anger produces fruit that maims and kills its owner—emotionally, physically, and spiritually.

Ah, but I haven't killed anyone, you might justify. My anger is under control. And I have a right to be angry!

Looking into the heart, Jesus associated anger with murder.

You have heard that it was said to those of old, "You shall not murder; and whoever murders will be liable to judgment." But I say to you that everyone who is angry with his brother will be liable to judgment; whoever insults his brother will be liable to the council; and whoever says, "You fool!" will be liable to the hell of fire. (Matthew 5:21–22)

Anger leads to hatred, and John equates hatred with murder: "Everyone who hates his brother is a murderer, and you know that no murderer has eternal life abiding in him" (1 John 3:15).

A fruit of anger is murder, beginning in the heart. It's an opportunity for the devil that leads to even more sin.

ANGER A VIRTUE?

For several years, our society has embraced anger and encouraged it. Don't get what you want? Then you have a right to be angry. We have been desensitized to the danger of anger.

TED

Anger has become a new virtue in the United States. Our world often views anger as something to embrace. We are influenced to think that anger produces good results. I listened to a news reporter interview a psychologist who said that anger leads to positive change. In other words, anger produces good.

She isn't alone in her views. Many believe that anger produces positive change in policy. That's why you should protest in anger—never mind that some protests result in violence and destruction of property. It's all worth it if it leads to change in policy. Or if it gets new people elected. Or if attitudes in our world change. The message? Anger is good for the community.

That's not how the Bible describes anger. Instead of it resulting in good, James declares, "The anger of man does not produce the righteousness of God" (1:20).

Scripture tells us that anger leads to strife and sin. "A man of wrath stirs up strife, and one given to anger causes much transgression" (Proverbs 29:22).

Embracing anger with an expectation of good is dangerous ground.

WHAT ABOUT RIGHTEOUS ANGER?

What about "righteous anger"? Is there such a thing as righteous anger for humans?

Certainly, God can have righteous anger. When His creatures sin against His commands, He has a right to be angry.

But how does our just God handle His anger?

The LORD is merciful and gracious, slow to anger and abounding in steadfast love. He will not always chide, nor will He keep His anger forever. He does not deal with us according to our sins, nor repay us according to our iniquities. (Psalm 103:8-10)

As our heavenly Father considers our sin and rebellion against Him, what do we hope will last longer? Thank God, He is merciful and gracious! "For His anger is but for a moment, and His favor is for a lifetime" (Psalm 30:5).

No one can claim to have righteous anger more than God. And yet, His anger lasts only a moment, and His favor for a lifetime.

If we want to claim righteous anger, can we who deserve God's wrath but receive His mercy demand more from those who sin against us? If we do, we are like Jonah, making ourselves to be above God.

BITTERNESS, A DANGEROUS HEART DISEASE

Unresolved anger evolves into bitterness and imprisons the unforgiving heart. Nursing a grudge and rehashing it repeatedly leads to heart disease. Even if it lies somewhat hidden, over time it slowly erodes your spiritual health.

Hebrews describes what happens when anger takes root in one's heart: "See to it that no one fails to obtain the grace of God; that no 'root of bitterness' springs up and causes trouble, and by it many become defiled" (12:15).

Note the clear connection between failing to obtain the grace of God and the root of bitterness growing in our hearts. Focusing on the hurt and the offender in anger takes our eyes off Jesus, the author and perfecter of our faith (see v. 2). The longer we nourish bitterness, the more our spiritual health deteriorates. We fall further and further from living in the grace of God.

Those with this kind of heart disease are more prone to get upset over things others say or do. Bitterness leads to more bitterness.

Terrible side effects arise from this disease.

First, bitterness is infectious. Others become defiled. They encourage the anger and adopt it as their own. They join in the cause for their own form of justice. Bitterness breeds more wrath. You can see this occur in angry protests, where individuals on their own would never resort to violence. But as a part of an angry mob, they give in to criminal acts, destroying property and attacking people.

Second, some decide to avoid the angry person. They tire of the rants and becoming recipients of the anger. The result? The bitter person becomes isolated, lonely, and even paranoid. All this leads to depression and despair.

Worst of all, untreated heart disease can separate you from God.

Paul speaks of bitterness and its end result:

"Their throat is an open grave; they use their tongues to deceive."
"The venom of asps is under their lips." "Their mouth is full of curses
and bitterness." "Their feet are swift to shed blood; in their paths
are ruin and misery, and the way of peace they have not known."
"There is no fear of God before their eyes." (Romans 3:13–18)

Left unchecked, bitterness gives birth to ruin and misery. Peace is not found
in their demand for justice. People lose their trust in Christ, and there is no fear
of God. True peace is lost.

John describes another fruit of bitterness:

For this is the message that you have heard from the beginning, that
we should love one another. We should not be like Cain, who was
of the evil one and murdered his brother. And why did he murder
him? Because his own deeds were evil and his brother's righteous.
Do not be surprised, brothers, that the world hates you. We know
that we have passed out of death into life, because we love the
brothers. Whoever does not love abides in death. Everyone who
hates his brother is a murderer, and you know that no murderer
has eternal life abiding in him. (1 John 3:11–15)

Hatred is a fruit of bitterness. And what is the implication of that?

If anyone says, "I love God," and hates his brother, he is a liar; for he
who does not love his brother whom he has seen cannot love God
whom he has not seen. And this commandment we have from Him:
whoever loves God must also love his brother. (1 John 4:20–21)

Anger, bitterness, hatred, unforgiveness—these all lead to spiritual, emotional, and physical suffering. Left untreated, they can lead to death.

MARK

Barbara was another participant in my study. She described the anger she
developed against her husband when he quit his job to start a rental business
with a friend. The rental business did not work out, and they found themselves
in a deep financial hole. She told her husband, "Yes, I'm angry with you. You
caused all this. I told you this wouldn't work. It's not working. A blind man
could see this wouldn't work."

She substituted an avoidance approach for forgiveness. She no longer wore her wedding ring, she stopped talking to him, and she made him sleep in the basement. She nurtured her bitterness, and her health deteriorated.

"I was sitting there with my dad and my neck was starting to hurt. I tell you I felt absolute depths of despair. We're in so deep financially. He doesn't have a job, he's drinking, and it's all on me."

Barbara lost hope for the future. She gave up on the marriage. Unforgiveness stole any joy she had. Through her bitterness, she could only see her husband's sin and how it negatively impacted her.

"The anger I felt—I think that was one of the lowest points. I remember my neck kept hurting. And that was, of course, the day I put my dad in the nursing home. Driving back I was just like, I just hope everything's over soon. I just hope I die in a car accident. I was praying for that because I can't keep doing this."

Then she learned she had shingles. Bitterness creates its own stress on one's health, physically, emotionally, and spiritually.

Bitterness born out of unforgiveness is a dark hole of despair that will negatively impact your well-being. Unforgiveness put Barbara's life at risk.

WHAT'S THE ALTERNATIVE?

God instructs us to replace our bitter heart condition with a new heart. Consider Paul's words to the Romans:

Bless those who persecute you; bless and do not curse them. Rejoice with those who rejoice, weep with those who weep. Live in harmony with one another. Do not be haughty, but associate with the lowly. Never be wise in your own sight. Repay no one evil for evil, but give thought to do what is honorable in the sight of all. If possible, so far as it depends on you, live peaceably with all. Beloved, never avenge yourselves, but leave it to the wrath of God, for it is written, "Vengeance is Mine, I will repay, says the Lord." To the contrary, "if your enemy is hungry, feed him; if he is thirsty, give him something to drink; for by so doing you will heap burning coals on his head." Do not be overcome by evil, but overcome evil with good. (Romans 12:14–21)

Doctor's orders for renewed health? Bless instead of curse. Live in harmony. Set aside personal pride. Do not repay evil for evil. Live peaceably with all. Leave vengeance to the Lord. Instead, be good to those who hurt you. Do not be overcome by evil, but overcome evil with good.

From Ephesians 4:31–32, we also read: "Let all bitterness and wrath and anger and clamor and slander be put away from you, along with all malice. Be kind to one another, tenderhearted, forgiving one another, as God in Christ forgave you."

Replace bitterness and its accompanying temptations with kindness, tenderness, and forgiveness.

WHAT HOPE IS THERE FOR ME?

For people caught in the loop of unforgiveness, it may seem hopeless. How can anyone do what God expects when the hurt is so deep, the offense is so unjust, and the anger seems so right?

Our hope is not found in feeding the anger and nourishing the bitterness. It is not found in focusing on the sin of others, no matter how great their sin or how deep the hurt. That focus only leads to more despair because it obscures the One who is our only hope.

Hope is found only in Him who took all our anger, wrath, bitterness, malice, and hatred to the cross. He sacrificed His blood for you and me. He paid the ultimate price so that we could live a life free from bitterness and unforgiveness. God forgives your anger, bitterness, and unforgiveness.

> The LORD is merciful and gracious, slow to anger and abounding in steadfast love. He will not always chide, nor will He keep His anger forever. He does not deal with us according to our sins, nor repay us according to our iniquities. (Psalm 103:8–10)

> For while we were still weak, at the right time Christ died for the ungodly. For one will scarcely die for a righteous person—though perhaps for a good person one would dare even to die—but God shows His love for us in that while we were still sinners, Christ died for us. Since, therefore, we have now been justified by His blood, much more shall we be saved by Him from the wrath of God. For if while we were enemies we were reconciled to God by the death of His Son, much more, now that we are reconciled, shall we be saved by His life. More than that, we also rejoice in God through our Lord Jesus Christ, through whom we have now received reconciliation. (Romans 5:6–11)

Wretched man that I am! Who will deliver me from this body of death? Thanks be to God through Jesus Christ our Lord! . . . There is therefore now no condemnation for those who are in Christ Jesus. (Romans 7:24–25; 8:1)

BUT HOW CAN I OVERCOME BITTERNESS?

Repent, and believe the Gospel. Confess your anger and bitterness to God. Receive the forgiveness won for you through Christ. Pray for God's strength through His forgiveness to overcome the temptation to go back to your anger.

Our anger and its fruit originate in the heart. To cleanse the heart of its disease, we confess our sin and trust in Christ's forgiveness for healing. The repentant heart bears fruit of the Spirit. In the words of David, "Create in me a clean heart, O God, and renew a right spirit within me" (Psalm 51:10).

Overcoming bitterness begins with repentance and receiving God's forgiveness. Although He has a right to be angry with our sinful anger and bitterness, God forgives the repentant sinner: "Whoever conceals his transgressions will not prosper, but he who confesses and forsakes them will obtain mercy" (Proverbs 28:13).

God's favor, mercy, and grace overflow into our hearts. Focusing on the cross of Christ, we are strengthened to put away the sins of our flesh and live the life of a redeemed child of God. "He Himself bore our sins in His body on the tree, that we might die to sin and live to righteousness. By His wounds you have been healed" (1 Peter 2:24).

HEALING FOR JOYCE

Joyce was stuck in an angry cycle of bitterness toward her brother-in-law after he stole the farm from her and her husband. She described her cognitive looping this way: "I'm very analytical and I try to figure everything out in my brain and then make it work. And there was no making it work. I couldn't get past that they had actually done that."

Joyce remained in her cognitive spiral of trying to rationalize her way to forgiveness. But she could never make sense of it all. Her calculations brought her to the conclusion that her husband's family were unjust people whom she did not need to forgive.

Unfortunately, Joyce was pulled into a vortex of anger and bitterness that sucked the life out of everything and everybody around her. Around and around she went, spiraling out of control. The more she thought about the situation, the more angry she felt. The more angry she felt, the more she sought out alcohol to escape from her bitterness. And when she saw her brother-in-law and his family or someone would ask about the situation, she would start the cycle all over again.

The endless cycle of bitterness only caused her to turn inward. She tried coping mechanisms such as deep breathing, journaling, mindful meditation, and physical exercise to help reduce negative emotions and slow down the dark storm. But such techniques could not pierce the darkness of sin.

The angry cycle of unforgiveness fed on itself until one day the light of Christ came piercing through the darkness of her anger and bitterness. Jesus said:

I am the light of the world. Whoever follows Me will not walk in darkness, but will have the light of life. (John 8:12)

As long as I am in the world, I am the light of the world. (John 9:5)

I have come into the world as light, so that whoever believes in Me may not remain in darkness. (John 12:46)

Joyce realized that no matter how hard she tried, she could not forgive. Forgiving as God forgives was not something she could do on her own. Forgiveness comes from Jesus Christ, who had already forgiven her. Jesus had forgiven her anger and bitterness. Jesus had forgiven her gossip and slander. Jesus had forgiven her murderous thoughts.

Joyce said, "I learned that God forgives me, and if He forgives me for my huge sins, how dare I think that it's not right to forgive them for that sin."

Joyce learned this from her pastor who patiently cared for her and spoke God's Word into her dark, coiling road. Forgiveness freed her from the spiraling vortex of anger and hate. No longer was she sinfully ruminating on the ungodly actions of her brother-in-law and his family. The light of Christ penetrated that darkness of unforgiveness and brought the light of forgiveness.

People struggle with the darkness of sin and often call out to God to take the darkness away. However, God does something very different. He does not take the darkness away. He walks us through the darkness into the light of Jesus Christ (John 8:12).

HOW DOES THIS APPLY TO ME?

Consider the situation where you are struggling to forgive. Then answer these questions.

1. How long have I been angry?

2. What kinds of opportunities has my long-term anger or bitterness given to the devil?

3. At whom or what has my anger been directed?

4. How am I justifying my anger?

5. Read Galatians 5:22–23. How does my spirit of anger compare with the fruit of the Spirit? Which fruit of the Spirit is most difficult for me in this situation?

6. Write a prayer of repentance, confessing your sins of anger before God. Consider confessing these sins out loud to your pastor or a spiritually mature friend, asking them to proclaim God's forgiveness to you. (See the section "Finding the Right Words" in chapter 16 for ideas on how your friend can declare forgiveness to you.)

PRAYER TEMPLATE

(See chapter 3, "How Should I Pray?")

INTRODUCTION

REFERENCE TO GOD'S WORK

PETITION

RESULT

CONCLUSION

CHAPTER 7

WHAT'S THE KEY TO OVERCOMING UNFORGIVENESS?

Lord, when I look within
 I find a special place
That hoards an unforgiven sin
 Which I have not erased.

I cannot shed its pow'r
 To bring myself release;
I beg You, Jesus, in this hour
 Come, bless me with Your peace.

My will must be undone;
 My gaze has been on me.
Now fix my focus on Your Son
 Who died to set me free.

TED

I know a man named Gene. He was born to an unwed mother in the early 1950s. At that time, there was more shame associated with that situation than there is today.

Gene's mother never married. Imagine how difficult it must have been for her as a single mother at that time! They were poor. At first, Gene didn't know any different, and he grew up in a loving home.

But one day some of the kids in the neighborhood said they couldn't play with him anymore. When Gene asked why, they told him their mothers wouldn't let them because of who he was. Gene says, "Do you remember the first word you looked up in the dictionary? The first word I looked up was *bastard*. That's why the mothers didn't want their kids playing with me."

Gene began to put things together. The reason he couldn't have a new bike or other toys like his friends was that his family was poor. And they were poor because Gene didn't have a father. He asked his mother who his father was, but she wouldn't talk with him about that. Gene began to be angry at the father he never knew.

He had constant reminders of who he was—a boy without a father. When he wanted to secure his first job, he had to apply for a Social Security number. He completed the form and got a copy of his birth certificate, which simply had a line through the space for "father." He and a few friends went to the Social Security office together.

When he submitted his forms to the clerk, she questioned, "Who's your father?"

"I don't know," he said. "You can see that the line is blank."

Loud enough for his friends to hear, she demanded, "Take this back home and have someone complete it. You can't get a number until it's properly filled out."

Once again, Gene was reminded he was without a father.

Anger burned inside him. Although he grew up in the church, he became angry at God. How could a loving God allow him and his mother to live in such a condition? As a teen, he stopped attending worship.

Unforgiveness will separate you from God.

CONSEQUENCES OF UNFORGIVENESS

Because of our human nature, we rarely think about the consequences of our own unforgiveness. In our hurt, our shame, or the injustice we have suffered, we focus our thoughts on how we have been wronged.

We were created with a sense of right and wrong, although that has been tarnished by sin. It's natural for us to want justice, especially when we have been mistreated or see someone we love being mistreated.

Our inner desire for justice turns our attention to the offender. We want offenders to pay for the wrongs they have caused. We condemn them in our hearts and devise what consequence they should suffer. The more shame or hurt we endure, the greater our anger grows. Often the offender does not suffer the punishment we think ought to be delivered. Unforgiveness is one punishment no one can deny us. And many around us support our feelings and encourage unforgiveness. After all, it's part of justice, right?

Unforgiveness may cause some pain for the offender. But its greatest harm is done to the one withholding forgiveness.

Consider a person who lived a lifetime of unforgiveness. She was abused physically and emotionally. Orphaned as a young child, she ended up being passed around to different relatives. Her bitterness grew as she was mistreated by more people. She ended up in a marriage of physical abuse. In divorce she was saddled with raising her children without outside support.

A relative asked her to visit him in the hospital as he lay dying. He asked for her forgiveness for the way he had talked about her. She refused to forgive him. Instead, she condemned him to hell. She left the hospital with resignation but no peace.

She learned never to forgive. For days and weeks, she would dwell on an offense, embellishing the hurt and feeding her bitterness. She lived in the loop of unforgiveness. Small offenses matured into monstrous hurts. She blamed God and resented many throughout her life. Bitterness destroyed most of her relationships among family and friends. She expected to be hurt or taken advantage of, so she coped by mistrusting nearly everyone. Left with few friends and family, she experienced fear, paranoia, and loneliness. It's understandable why she self-medicated with alcohol. In the end, the consequences of a lifetime of unforgiveness increased her suffering, and her addiction to alcohol ultimately ended her life.

Allowing unforgiveness to dwell in your heart subjects you to an unending cycle of anger, fear, and loneliness. It may begin with a single major offense by one person. But just like a whirling tornado destroys more property and picks up more rubbish, unforgiveness against one person sucks in more offenses by more people. It leads to more personal trauma in one's heart, and that individual is more susceptible to increasing pain in life.

HOW CAN I ESCAPE THE LOOP OF UNFORGIVENESS?

Focus is key.

When caught in a loop of unforgiveness, the focus is primarily on me and how I am hurt or unjustly suffering. My attention is only on how I have been hurt by that person, fanning the flames of anger and malice. Even if I don't outwardly act on my feelings, my heart keeps the coals of unforgiveness burning hot. My thoughts relive the offense, feeding the anger. My words retell the offense to others, and I look for validation of my feelings. Some who care about me will reinforce my justification, not realizing that their "comfort" hurts me even more.

When we look to the Bible for direction from our Creator, we see that focus is the key to escaping the loop of unforgiveness.

The writer of Hebrews 11 commends the heroes of the Old Testament for their faith in the Messiah. All those heroes were sinners. All of them fell short of the glory of God. Each one committed significant sins that are recorded in Scripture for all to see since their time. Yet, they are commended for their faith in God's promised Savior. They looked ahead with hope to the fulfillment of God's promise.

The writer of Hebrews then turns our attention to the sinners of today. We are directed to follow the example of the "great cloud of witnesses," those heroes we commend from the past, looking to Jesus for strength to run the race of life in the face of challenges.

Therefore, since we are surrounded by so great a cloud of witnesses, let us also lay aside every weight, and sin which clings so closely, and let us run with endurance the race that is set before us, looking to Jesus, the founder and perfecter of our faith, who for the joy that was set before Him endured the cross, despising the shame, and is seated at the right hand of the throne of God. Consider Him who endured from sinners such hostility against Himself, so that you may not grow weary or fainthearted. (Hebrews 12:1–3)

The message to those of us today struggling to live as children of God? Fix your eyes on Jesus, the author and finisher of our faith. Instead of fixating on yourself and how you were mistreated and hurt, fix your eyes on Jesus. Rather than reliving the painful offenses over again, look to the One who suffered for those hurts by dying on the cross and despising the shame. Instead of murdering the offender in your heart, which influences your words and actions, focus your thoughts on Jesus. Remember how He unjustly suffered and died in your place to pay the full price for your sins. In return He gives you His righteousness.

Jesus knows what it's like to be betrayed by your most trusted friends. He experienced injustice by church leaders, mobs, and government officials. While enduring physical pain and a shameful execution, He suffered the mental anguish of being forsaken by His heavenly Father. And yet, He prayed for all those who put Him on the cross, including sinners like you and me: "Father, forgive them, for they know not what they do." Jesus focused on His assignment, given by His Father. He took our place on Calvary so that we might become the forgiven children of God.

Remember Joseph and his focus when he came face to face with the brothers who concocted evil ways to get rid of him. He could have focused on all the pain and suffering he endured because of their deeds. He might have fixated on the deep hurt they caused their father in lying about Joseph's demise. He could have reflected on how evil his brothers were. While the Bible is silent about the thoughts he harbored toward his brothers during his darkest days, he may have even murdered them in his heart.

But when the day came and he revealed himself to his brothers, he chose a different focus. He credited God for sending him to Egypt. Notice his focus in proclaiming forgiveness to his brothers after their father's death:

Do not fear, for am I in the place of God? As for you, you meant evil against me, but God meant it for good, to bring it about that many people should be kept alive, as they are today. So do not fear; I will provide for you and your little ones. (Genesis 50:19–21)

First, he acknowledged that he is not God. For God is the ultimate judge, and He is merciful and gracious, slow to anger and abounding in steadfast love. Next, Joseph confessed that God used their evil intentions to send Joseph to Egypt, where he would be elevated to a high place of authority to save many lives.

Who of us today would have blamed Joseph for justly punishing his brothers? He had both the authority and right to do so. Yet, his focus was not on retribution. His focus was not on the suffering and hurt they caused him, his father, and his youngest brother. Joseph focused on God, who had shown great mercy and grace to him. In turn, Joseph shared the gifts God had given him with those who had hurt him so deeply.

REMEMBERING YOUR FORGIVENESS THROUGH CHRIST

Replace the dangerous looping of unforgiveness by remembering your own forgiveness in Christ.

Peter provides insight for living the life to which we are called as children of God. It's based on remembrance.

> His divine power has granted to us all things that pertain to life and godliness, through the knowledge of Him who called us to His own glory and excellence, by which He has granted to us His precious and very great promises, so that through them you may become partakers of the divine nature, having escaped from the corruption that is in the world because of sinful desire. (2 Peter 1:3–4)

Notice that living the Christian life requires divine power. We sinners cannot on our own strength live the way that God expects. We need divine intervention. God knows that. So He grants us His power through His "precious and very great promises."

What's the greatest and most precious promise of God? Forgiveness through the atoning work of Jesus Christ. "If we confess our sins, He is faithful and just to forgive us our sins and to cleanse us from all unrighteousness" (1 John 1:9). Those in Christ are no longer condemned by their own sins: "There is therefore now no condemnation for those who are in Christ Jesus" (Romans 8:1).

It is through God's "precious and very great promises" that we may become partakers of the divine nature. Forgiving as God has forgiven us is not possible in our sinful nature. It requires divine power, and Scripture tells us that God grants us that power.

This divine power enables us to escape from "the corruption that is in the world because of sinful desire." We can escape the trap of focusing on ourselves and protecting our own pride. We can escape the looping of sinful judging and condemnation. We can escape the consequences of unforgiveness—not on our strength, but on the divine nature that God gives through His promises.

Peter gives further instruction:

For this very reason, make every effort to supplement your faith with virtue, and virtue with knowledge, and knowledge with self-control, and self-control with steadfastness, and steadfastness with godliness, and godliness with brotherly affection, and brotherly affection with love. (2 Peter 1:5–7)

Look again at Peter's list. Supplement

- your faith with virtue.
- virtue with knowledge.
- knowledge with self-control.
- self-control with steadfastness.
- steadfastness with godliness.
- godliness with brotherly affection.
- brotherly affection with love.

Compare that list with Paul's fruit of the Spirit: "But the fruit of the Spirit is love, joy, peace, patience, kindness, goodness, faithfulness, gentleness, self-control; against such things there is no law" (Galatians 5:22–23).

Fruit of the Spirit is from our divine nature, given us by God through His precious and great promises. Our works reflect the faith in our hearts. What or whom we truly fear, love, and trust is revealed in how we respond to others, whether they treat us with kindness or offenses.

Peter then reminds us of what happens when our life reflects more of our faith in Christ than our sinful nature: "For if these qualities are yours and are increasing, they keep you from being ineffective or unfruitful in the knowledge of our Lord Jesus Christ" (2 Peter 1:8).

But a key insight is given when Peter identifies the underlying reason why some are unable to live the Christian life. They have forgotten the most precious and great promise. "For whoever lacks these qualities is so nearsighted that he is blind, having forgotten that he was cleansed from his former sins" (v. 9).

Forgetting I am cleansed of my former sins means that I have become nearsighted and blind. I lack the qualities that Peter lists and that Paul describes as fruit of the Spirit. Instead of on Christ and His cross, my focus is on me and the pain and injustice I have suffered. My failure to fix my eyes on Jesus means that I fixate on those who have sinned against me. I forget how I have sinned against my almighty, holy, all-knowing God. I minimize my own sin compared with the sins I have experienced from others, and in so doing, I minimize the justifying work that Jesus has done for me.

REMEMBRANCE LEADS TO HEALING

The key to overcoming unforgiveness is to remember how forgiven you are in Jesus Christ.

Gene struggled in his teen years. After high school graduation, he went to work for Kmart. One day a friend recognized him in the store. They exchanged greetings, and then she said, "We haven't seen you in church for a while."

"I know. But I work some Sundays."

"How about this Sunday?"

"Well, I'm not working, but I'd feel funny going back to church after being gone so long."

"How about if I stopped by to pick you up? You can go with me."

"Okay."

Because of the gentle restoration of a kind friend, Gene started going back to worship. One day his pastor approached him.

"Gene, how would you like to teach children in our Sunday School?"

"Who, me? I've not taught before. I wouldn't know what to do."

"We have classes to prepare our teachers, and you'll have materials to guide you. I've seen the way you interact with children, and I think you'd make a great teacher."

"I'll give it a try."

Soon Gene found himself surrounded by little children as he taught them lessons about Jesus and how He went around the countryside healing and forgiving people. But then Gene realized he was a hypocrite. How could he teach about a forgiving Jesus when he himself couldn't forgive his earthly father and even resented his heavenly Father? He decided to resign as a Sunday School teacher.

But before he quit teaching, he had one more lesson to teach—the Passion of Christ. As he was preparing his lesson, he came across these words of Jesus on the cross: "Father, forgive them, for they know not what they do" (Luke 23:34).

Gene cried out loud, "I can't forgive him! I don't want to forgive him! I hate him! God help me!"

That's when God healed Gene. Gene realized that Jesus prayed for him on the cross: "Father, forgive Gene, for he doesn't know what he is doing."

Gene also realized that Jesus prayed for his earthly father. Jesus died for them both and rose again. Gene and his father were both forgiven by God.

Gene experienced a peace like he'd never had before. He forgave a man he'd never met but had hated for most of his life. His battle of unforgiveness was over.

One day Gene's mother approached him. "I want to tell you something. I want to tell you who your father is. He came to see me last night. He's dying from cancer. Here is his name and telephone number."

Imagine the emotions that Gene must have felt! For years he hated a man without a name, but now he had a name and contact information. What would Gene say to him?

Gene took a few days to pray and think about what they might talk about. He confirmed that he had forgiven his father, but Gene had some questions. He picked up the phone and dialed the number. But the man had left town for cancer treatment, and he died before he could return home. Gene never met his father, but he learned that the man had married another woman and had three children.

TED

In 1989, my father died from cancer. And that's when I learned that I have an older brother named Gene. I and my sister and younger brother could not believe that my father had an older son that he had ignored all these years.

Then I learned that nearly all my extended family knew the secret. My mother knew before she died. All four of my grandparents knew. My aunts and uncles knew. Many of my cousins knew. But no one told us four children for more than thirty years.

I became angry at my own relatives. I felt betrayed. How could they live as if this never happened? Gene and I attended the same high school (a few years apart). I shopped often at the Kmart where he worked. Gene even thought about applying for a job with my dad's company where I worked. We attended sister churches in the same town.

One weekend, Gene, my sister, younger brother, and I went on a retreat with our families to a hot springs resort to get to know one another better. The four of us siblings met alone one afternoon to talk without our spouses or children. We three younger siblings asked Gene why he didn't hate us. Wasn't he jealous of us? We had both a father and mother. He had no father. He grew up poor and often did without. We didn't experience that. We three all had opportunity to attend college. He didn't. Why was he not angry with us?

Gene explained that if he had met us years earlier, he would have hated us. But then he told us his story of how God healed him while he was teaching Sunday School. Gene remembered that he was forgiven, and that enabled him to forgive a father he never met. Gene held no resentment toward us.

That was a life-changing event for me. Gene reminded me how forgiven I am in Christ. I learned to forgive my relatives for what I considered decades of betrayal.

WHAT RESEARCH REVEALED ABOUT REMEMBERING CHRIST'S FORGIVENESS

MARK

The research participants narrated their well-rehearsed stories with great detail and emotion. As I listened to them describe the transgressions and the broken relationships, I felt drawn in by the intensity of each saga.

Midway through their descriptions of the events, they often slowed down and reverently remembered something. In the midst of the stormy stories of transgression, they remembered something that should never have been forgotten.

They remembered the forgiveness of Christ.

As a Christian bystander, it is easy to be harsh and judgmental. How could a Christian forget about Jesus?

Yet, the people of Israel seemed to forget what God had done for them and forget what God promised to do for them. The Israelites worshiped other gods (see Exodus 32:1–24; Numbers 25:1–3), and they complained against God and fantasized about how better it was being slaves in Egypt (see Exodus 16:3; 17:3; Numbers 11:4–6).

Circular thinking leads us back into the darkness of sin, and we tend to forget God and His promise of forgiveness.

But God never forgets His people.

Can a woman forget her nursing child, that she should have no compassion on the son of her womb? Even these may forget, yet I [God] will not forget you. (Isaiah 49:15)

Hide not Your face from me. Turn not Your servant away in anger, O You who have been my help. Cast me not off; forsake me not, O God of my salvation! (Psalm 27:9)

For I am sure that neither death nor life, nor angels nor rulers, nor things present nor things to come, nor powers, nor height nor depth, nor anything else in all creation, will be able to separate us from the love of God in Christ Jesus our Lord. (Romans 8:38–39)

The research participants benefited by having another Christian remind them of God's forgiveness for them and for their adversary. One participant said, "God gave His Son to die and suffer for my sins. I could've saved myself a year or maybe two years of total torture and pain if I would've just went right to the cross." She had forgotten about Christ's forgiveness and lived in the misery of unforgiveness. But when she was reminded of the work of Jesus on the cross, everything changed.

Another participant said, "I know because of Christ I can forgive. Because I can't forgive, but with Him, in Christ, I can forgive." Remembering the forgiveness of Christ changed everything for him.

Two common themes appeared among the research participants. First, all of them provided an articulate description of the transgression. Second, all of them were able to forgive their transgressor when they remembered what God had done for them through Jesus Christ.

Remembering Christ's forgiveness changes everything. Christ's forgiveness pierces the darkness of sin and interrupts the endless and hopeless cycle of living in the darkness of unforgiveness.

DIVINE POWER

How do I overcome the power that unforgiveness holds over me?

To forgive as God forgives is impossible—with our own strength. To do a divine work, such as forgiving as God forgives, requires divine power.

Paul reminds us: "I can do all things through Him who strengthens me" (Philippians 4:13).

The key to overcoming unforgiveness is to focus on what God has done for you through Christ. Remember that you have been cleansed from your past sins.

Christ died for you. He rose again for you. He ascended into heaven for you. He is coming again with power and glory for you.

Paul tells us how we can do the divine work that God calls us to do:

For the love of Christ controls us, because we have concluded this: that one has died for all, therefore all have died; and He died for all, that those who live might no longer live for themselves but for Him who for their sake died and was raised. (2 Corinthians 5:14–15)

What compels us to do divine work? The love of Christ.

Why? Because He died for all. He paid the full price for the sins of the whole world.

What is the result? We might no longer live for ourselves but for Christ who for our sake died and was raised again.

Remembering how forgiven we are in Christ empowers us to live as children of God.

Peter also declares, "He Himself bore our sins in His body on the tree, that we might die to sin and live to righteousness. By His wounds you have been healed" (1 Peter 2:24).

We die to the sin of unforgiveness and live to righteousness by remembering that Jesus died for us. We are healed by the wounds Christ suffered on the cross.

Remember Gene's cry to God? "I can't forgive him! I don't want to forgive him! I hate him! God help me!"

Gene's prayer was a cry in faith. When we acknowledge our weakness and inability to forgive, we submit ourselves to God's mercy and grace. We confess our sinful desires to be like God, and He forgives. We confess naming someone a Ninevite, and God shows His mercy to both the Ninevite and us. We remember God's most precious and great promise: He who repents and believes is saved. You are forgiven.

HOW DOES THIS APPLY TO ME?

1. How long have you suffered with unforgiveness?

2. What consequences has bitterness in your heart caused you so far?

3. What will be the long-term effects of unforgiveness in your heart?

4. The First Commandment is "You shall have no other gods before Me" (Exodus 20:3). This means that we should fear, love, and trust in God above all things. Yet we often put ourselves and other things above God.

   IF YOU ARE STRUGGLING TO FORGIVE

   Reflect on how you have sinned against this commandment, especially in your thoughts toward the person who has hurt you.

   ▶ How have you attempted to make yourself god, making your thoughts, your desires, your ideas more important than God's?

   ▶ How has pride affected your struggle to forgive?

   ▶ How has your love for God not been evident in how you love your enemies?

   ▶ What or whom do you fear most of all? (An answer other than God gives insight about your false gods.)

   ▶ Whom are you trusting for justice in the offenses against you or others you love? (An answer other than God gives insight about your false hope.)

IF YOU ARE ANGRY OR UNFORGIVING TOWARD SOMEONE WHO HAS NOT FORGIVEN YOU

Reflect on how you have sinned against the First Commandment in your thoughts toward the unforgiving person. (For more on this, see chapter 13, "What If Others Won't Forgive Me?")

▶ How have you attempted to make yourself god, making your thoughts, your desires, your ideas more important than God's?

▶ How has pride affected your demand to be forgiven?

▶ How has your love for God not been evident in how you love your enemies?

▶ From whom do you most desire affirmation, acceptance, or love? (An answer other than God gives insight about your false gods.)

▶ Whom are you trusting for the forgiveness you seek? (An answer other than God gives insight about your false hope.)

5. Pray out loud the following prayer of repentance, or write one that fits you better.

    Heavenly Father, I praise and thank You for the many blessings You give me, but especially for the gift of forgiveness through Jesus Christ, Your Son. You are a God who has been merciful and gracious to me. I deserve Your wrath and punishment, but You forgive me because Jesus paid the full price for me. O God, You know how I want to live as Your child and to forgive as You have forgiven me. But such a divine work is impossible with my own strength. God, help me! Help me remember how forgiven I am in Jesus. You have promised that Your Holy Spirit lives within me. Empower me by Your great and precious promises to do that which I cannot do on my own. Help me forgive _____ as You have forgiven me. Give me peace that surpasses all understanding. Help me heal from the deep hurts. Grant me relief from my suffering. And God, as You have shown mercy to me, show mercy also to _____. I ask this in the name of Jesus, who died and rose again for me. Amen.

6. Look up these passages and read them aloud. What comfort does each one give you in response to your reflections in the above questions?

    ► Psalm 103:11–14   ► Ephesians 1:7–10

    ► John 3:16–17   ► Philippians 4:7

    ► Romans 8:1

CHAPTER 8

WHAT IF THEY DON'T REPENT?

How difficult is it to offer a gift
  To someone who will not receive it!
The Gospel to those who in sin are adrift
  Seems futile—they will not believe it.
  Have mercy upon us, O Jesus.

Rely on the wisdom that comes from above
  And offer without fear or favor
The peace of forgiveness in truth and in love
  That flows freely from the Savior.
  Have mercy upon us, O Jesus.

MARK

My family and I had moved into a new home, and my wife was excited about decorating the house. Our two boys would share a room with a bunk bed. Before we moved them into their room, we painted the walls and planned to put a decorative border along the top of the wall. We took the boys to a local shop and let them pick out the border. They chose one with airplanes flying against a blue sky. I stood there in disbelief when I found out how much this nine-inch piece of paper was going to cost. But my wife insisted this was going to be great.

We went home and began the process of attaching the border to the wall. But the border did not stick to the wall because we had not let the paint cure long enough. Ugh! All that expensive border was wasted. After waiting the appropriate time for the paint to cure, we purchased more overpriced border and tried again. Finally, we stood in the doorway of the boys' bedroom and admired our work. Our sons moved into their new room. We ended the day feeling a sense of accomplishment.

When I arrived home from work the next day, my wife met me at the door.

"Now don't get mad."

Just hearing those words, I was mad. I didn't even know what I was mad about. But it had to be horrifying. I walked up to the boys' room to discover that they had climbed on the top bunk and ripped off, as far as they could reach, all that expensive border. I was angry, and I let the boys know it. I went on and on about how much that cost and how much time we spent attaching it to the wall. I shouted, "We even let you pick out the border design! What were you thinking?" I yelled, screamed, and said a lot of words no godly person should say, especially a pastor. I exploded like a volcano.

When I had come to the end of my tantrum, my oldest son, who was ten at the time, looked up at me and said, "Dad, I think you need to repent."

Repent? *Repent?!* That stirred up my anger even more! I should not be the one to repent, I thought. You boys are the ones who need to repent! Look what you did! Do you know how much money that cost me, how much time we spent trying to make this room look nice?

I had no plans of repenting. I was not the one who needed to repent. The boys needed to repent.

REPENT?

John the Baptist paved the way for Jesus with the message, "Repent, for the kingdom of heaven is at hand" (Matthew 3:2). Repenting is acknowledging that you have sinned against God and against your neighbor.

A repentant person is sorry for what he has done. She shows contrition, remorse. When a person repents, he first expresses contrition. The psalmist demonstrates the depth of sorrow in this way: "The sacrifices of God are a broken spirit; a broken and contrite heart, O God, You will not despise" (51:17). "Out of the depths I cry to You, O LORD! O Lord, hear my voice! Let Your ears be attentive to the voice of my pleas for mercy!" (130:1–2).

More important, a repentant person believes in the Gospel. That is why John the Baptist points to Jesus when he calls upon people to repent. It is Jesus who forgives the sins of sorrowful people. The apostle Paul says, "Therefore, since we have been justified by faith, we have peace with God through our Lord Jesus Christ. Through Him we have also obtained access by faith into this grace in which we stand, and we rejoice in hope of the glory of God" (Romans 5:1–2).

King David expressed contrition for committing adultery with Bathsheba and murdering Uriah. But he also believed the good news of the prophet Nathan: "The LORD also has put away your sin; you shall not die" (2 Samuel 12:13). In contrast, Jesus' disciple Judas was sorry for his sin but did not believe the good news of forgiveness. "When Judas, who had betrayed Him, saw that Jesus was condemned, he was seized with remorse and returned the thirty pieces of silver to the chief priests and the elders. 'I have sinned,' he said, 'for I have betrayed innocent blood'" (Matthew 27:3–4 NIV). Judas showed remorse and attempted to make satisfaction for his sin, but he did not trust in the forgiveness of Christ. Jesus indicated this when He said to the disciples, "But there are some of you who do not believe" (John 6:64).

Repentance of sin comprises two parts: (1) contrition and (2) faith that one's sin has been forgiven through Jesus Christ. After Jesus had risen from the dead, He appeared to His disciples and said, "Thus it is written, that the Christ should suffer and on the third day rise from the dead, and that repentance for the forgiveness of sins should be proclaimed in His name to all nations, beginning from Jerusalem" (Luke 24:46–47).

MARK

God's desire, according to the Ten Commandments, is that I do not misuse His name, that I do not murder others with my words, that I do not slander or speak poorly about others. When I spoke words of anger to my sons, I broke God's Commandments. I sinned against God, and I sinned against my boys. I was not disciplining my sons in love—I was punishing them out of anger.

Nonetheless, I was initially unwilling to repent of these sins. I was not sorrowful and did not see any need to be forgiven. Yes, I know that Jesus preached the same message as John the Baptist: "Repent, for the kingdom of heaven is at hand" (Matthew 4:17). And Peter also proclaimed, "Repent and be baptized every one of you in the name of Jesus Christ for the forgiveness of your sins, and you will receive the gift of the Holy Spirt" (Acts 2:38). I am well versed in what the Bible says about me being a sinner and needing to repent. Yet, repenting is not easy. It's not my nature to repent. My sinful flesh wanted to self-justify rather than receive Christ's forgiveness.

WHAT LEADS TO UNREPENTANCE

Several factors can lead one to resist repentance.

Take Saul, for example. King Saul disobeyed God by failing to completely destroy the Amalekites and all their possessions. Instead, Saul allowed his people to plunder the best sheep and oxen of the Amalekites for themselves.

God was displeased with Saul and told Samuel, "I regret that I have made Saul king, for he has turned back from following Me and has not performed My commandments" (1 Samuel 15:11). King Saul had sinned against God.

Yet, Saul did not acknowledge his sin. Nor was he willing to repent of it. When Saul greeted Samuel, he said, "Blessed be you to the Lord. I have performed the commandment of the Lord" (v. 13). Samuel asserted that Saul did not follow the commands of the Lord, pointing out that he could hear the cries of the Amalekite sheep and oxen. God had commanded Saul to destroy everything that belonged to the Amalekites, including livestock.

Instead of repenting, Saul defended himself and tried to justify his disobedience. Saul explained that the sheep and oxen were spared so they could be used to make sacrifices to the Lord (see v. 15).

Samuel rejected the excuse and addressed Saul's sin again. This time Saul shifted the blame to his people:

I have obeyed the voice of the Lord. I have gone on the mission on which the Lord sent me. I have brought Agag the king of Amalek, and I have devoted the Amalekites to destruction. But the people took of the spoil, sheep and oxen, the best of the things devoted to destruction, to sacrifice to the LORD your God in Gilgal. (vv. 20–21)

Although Samuel called him to repent, Saul responding by making excuses and blaming others.

When my son suggested that I repent, I did the same thing. I justified my sinful behavior by pointing out that I was responding to their sinful behavior. I justified my anger because I wanted to make sure they would never do it again. Like Saul, I was unwilling to repent because I did not believe I had done anything wrong, and I could provide a suitable explanation for my behavior.

What makes it so difficult to repent? Consider five unholy factors.

IT IS DIFFICULT TO REPENT

...BECAUSE I CLING TO MY SIN.

God made man and then made woman from man and said, "Therefore a man shall leave his father and his mother and hold fast [cling] to his wife, and they shall become one flesh" (Genesis 2:24). It is God-pleasing for a man to cling to his wife. Throughout Scripture, marriage is a union between a man and a woman that should not be broken. This is God's command. So, if a married man or woman decides to cling to someone else, they have committed adultery. That one has sinned against God and against his or her spouse.

Anna, a research participant, was married eighteen years to her husband who served in active-duty military. They were living near her family and friends until the military decided to reassign him eight hundred miles across the country to a different base. Anna packed up the house and moved with her children to a new home to be with her husband. She said, "I unpacked it all, had everything ready for when he finally did arrive." But her husband never spent a night in their new home.

He had met someone else and was having an affair. Her husband stopped holding fast, or clinging, to his wife and decided to break God's commandment. Of course, he asserted lots of excuses and blamed Anna for many things. But he was unwilling to repent of his sin. He was so invested in his new relationship that, Anna said, "He paid to move us back and get us out of his way."

When someone refuses to repent, he is choosing to cling to the sin that he has committed. When confronted with his sin, he feels no sorrow or remorse. He has no intent to turn away from the sin. In fact, he plans on indulging in the sin.

The psalmist says, "My soul clings to the dust; give me life according to Your word!" (119:25). Jonah also reflected, "Those who cling to worthless idols turn away from God's love for them" (2:8 NIV). We either cling to our sinful ways or we cling to God for mercy. Those who cling to their sin die in their sin, but those who cling to God inherit eternal life.

...BECAUSE I FEAR OTHERS MORE THAN I FEAR THE LORD.

We often think of fear as being terrified or scared of something. People are afraid of spiders, snakes, heights, or germs. Biblically, the word *fear* can refer to people who are frightened, but it can also be used toward the person or things in which you place your trust. When the angel of the Lord appeared to the shepherds to proclaim the birth of Jesus, the angel assured them, "Fear not, for behold, I bring you good news of great joy that will be for all the people" (Luke 2:10). It would be correct to say that the angel was saying, "Do not be terrified by my appearance and do not trust in yourselves. Trust in the Word of God that I am speaking to you."

MARK

Sometimes we are more concerned with what others think about us than what God's Word has to say. It may be difficult to repent because we think others will see repentance as weakness or a failure. The Bible calls this idol "fear of man" (Proverbs 29:25). We fear what others think of us more than we fear God. Saul feared that others might view him as a failed king. I feared that others might view me as a failed father.

Sin tends to lead us to fear and trust in our own ability by making excuses and blaming others. We forget about God. We neglect to fear or trust in God, who promises to forgive a repentant person.

If someone doesn't repent, it may be that she fears and trusts in herself or others more than she fears and trusts in the Lord. And when confronted with her sin, she chooses to trust in her own ability to handle the situation rather than being refreshed by the Lord's forgiveness (e.g., Acts 3:19). She trusts in her own justification rather than in Jesus' cleansing blood.

Paul says, "You were bought with a price; do not become bondservants of men" (1 Corinthians 7:23). We either fear and trust in ourselves and others, or we fear and trust in the Lord.

Proverbs 29:25 declares, "The fear of man lays a snare, but whoever trusts in the LORD is safe."

Those who fear and trust in themselves and others are trapped in sin that leads to death. But those who fear and trust in God live eternally with Him.

...BECAUSE I WANT TO AVOID CONSEQUENCES.

Sin brings consequences. After Adam and Eve sinned, they could no longer stay in the Garden of Eden, they would have to work the land, and women would have pain in childbirth (Genesis 3). After Moses struck the rock with his staff, he was not allowed to enter into the earthly Promised Land of Canaan (Numbers 20:1-13).

There are two kinds of consequences that result from sin—earthly consequences and eternal consequences. Adam and Eve and Moses endured earthly consequences for sinning against God. But they did not suffer eternal consequences.

Sin produces both earthly and eternal consequences. Some people avoid admitting sin because they think they can escape the consequences of their actions. They fear the earthly consequences but often forget the eternal consequences. For example, someone who broke a contract, stole money from an employer to pay for credit card debt, or hit another car while backing out of a parking space might attempt to cover up the transgression to avoid suffering the consequences. To avoid earthly consequences, they hide the sin by lying, blaming others, manipulating, and a plethora of other means. They forget that clinging to unrepentance bears eternal consequences.

If they don't repent, it may be that they are more terrified of earthly consequences than eternal consequences. When confronted with their sin, they strive to avoid the earthly consequences, unaware of the eternal consequences.

Repenting means acknowledging that you have sinned and you need the forgiveness of Christ. A repentant person turns away from the transgression and turns toward Christ. God freely grants the gift of forgiveness to all who trust in Jesus Christ for their salvation. Yes, there may be earthly consequences, but those who repent will never endure eternal consequences. Peter says, "Repent and be baptized every one of you in the name of Jesus Christ for the forgiveness of your sins, and you will receive the gift of the Holy Spirit" (Acts 2:38). And "Repent therefore, and turn back, that your sins may be blotted out, that times of refreshing may come from the presence of the Lord" (3:19–20). Adam and Eve and Moses endured earthly consequences for their sinful actions, but in repentance (that is, confession and faith) they turned away from their sin and turned to God.

Those who do not repent die in their sin and suffer eternal consequences. But those who repent do not perish but have eternal life.

. . . BECAUSE I WANT TO BE IN THE PLACE OF GOD.

A conflict arose between a pastor and the principal of the church's parochial school. The reconciler met with each party separately to prepare them for mediation and to help address their sin. The principal was able to identify her sins, and she repented.

But the pastor declared, "Look, I know I am a sinner, but I haven't done anything wrong."

During the mediation the pastor constantly made the case that he had not sinned against the principal. He refused to confess anything. Nevertheless, the pastor presented great detail about how the principal had sinned.

Jesus said,

Why do you see the speck that is in your brother's eye, but do not notice the log that is in your own eye? Or how can you say to your brother, "Let me take the speck out of your eye," when there is the log in your own eye? You hypocrite, first take the log out of your own eye, and then you will see clearly to take the speck out of your brother's eye. (Matthew 7:3–5)

When people refuse to address their own sin but are eager to point out the sins of others, they put themselves in the place of God. Such persons assert authority to judge others for their sin but do not believe they have done anything wrong.

It is tempting to sit in the place of God. But God tells us, "Be still, and know that I am God. I will be exalted among the nations, I will be exalted in the earth!" (Psalm 46:10). Who alone can claim, "I am God"?

Note the significance of "I am." God instructed Moses to tell the Israelites who sent him: "Say this to the people of Israel: 'I AM has sent me to you'" (Exodus 3:14). In the Gospel of John, Jesus declared, "I am the bread of life; whoever comes to Me shall not hunger, and whoever believes in Me shall never thirst" (John 6:35). He also said, "I am the light of the world. Whoever follows Me will not walk in darkness, but will have the light of life" (John 8:12). Christ claimed, "I am the door. If anyone enters by Me, he will be saved and will go in and out and find pasture" (John 10:9). Only God can truthfully claim, "I am God."

Sometimes we act as if we are the great "I am." We can either put ourselves in the place of God or acknowledge that God is God. Those who put themselves in the place of God die in their sins. But those who trust in the God who says "I am" will have life.

. . . BECAUSE I DON'T BELIEVE I NEED CHRIST'S FORGIVENESS.

A rich young man once approached Jesus and said, "Good Teacher, what must I do to inherit eternal life?" (Mark 10:17). Jesus referred him to the Ten Commandments, but the self-confident man replied, "Teacher, all these [Commandments] I have kept from my youth" (v. 20). Jesus looked at him with love and responded, "You lack one thing: go, sell all that you have and give to the poor, and you will have treasure in heaven; and come, follow Me" (v. 21). But the rich man was disheartened by Jesus' words and went away sad because he had great possessions.

A person who believes in Christ's forgiveness knows that there is no way he can keep all the Commandments, and it is foolish to trust in himself. Yet, the rich man is an example of a person who does not repent because he does not think he needs Christ's forgiveness. His confidence (that is, his faith) is based on himself and his wealth. He has no need for Christ—not only foolish but also damning!

Jesus invites, "Follow Me." Even the disciples found it difficult to follow Jesus at times and tried to rely on themselves instead. A man brought his demon-possessed son to the disciples of Jesus, but they were unable to drive out the demon. Jesus instructed, "All things are possible for one who believes," and He commanded the demon to come out of the boy (Mark 9:23, 25). When the demon obeyed, the disciples were perplexed, asking, "Why could we not cast it out?" (v. 28).

The disciples trusted primarily in themselves. They trusted their own ability to drive out the demon. In contrast, the father who sought help for his son spoke in faith when he exclaimed, "I believe; help my unbelief!" (v. 24). The father trusted in Jesus.

Those who refuse to repent choose to hold on to their sins. They reject Jesus, who can forgive. And when confronted with their sins, they turn inward. So tragic!

Those who believe they do not need Christ's forgiveness retain their sins and its consequences. But those who believe in Christ's forgiveness escape condemnation and receive life.

THE CRUX OF THE MATTER

Pilate faced his most crucial moment when he had to decide what to do with Jesus. He sought to punish Jesus and release Him, but the chief priests, rulers, and people joined with one voice, "Away with this man, and release to us Barabbas" (Luke 23:18). Pilate tried again, hoping the crowd would change their minds. But they kept shouting, "Crucify, crucify Him!" (v. 21).

Pilot gave in to their demands and handed Jesus over to be crucified.

The people cried out, "Crucify Him!" But on the cross, Jesus pleaded, "Father, forgive them, for they know not what they do" (v. 34).

MARK

Standing in the doorway of my sons' room with anger spewing from my mouth, I had cried out my own version of "crucify him!" But my son cried out for forgiveness. To this day I have no idea why they thought it was a good idea to rip the high-priced border off the wall. Still, my boys' sins did not justify my sin. This was a critical moment in our relationship. The crux of the matter was this: would I repent for my sin in this conflict?

SPEAK THE TRUTH IN LOVE

When Saul tried to evade responsibility for his sin, notice how Samuel approached the unrepentant king. Samuel did not ignore or abandon Saul. He did not gossip or slander Saul. Samuel clearly stated Saul's sin with the hope that he would repent. Eventually Saul did repent, confessing his fear of man (see 1 Samuel 15:24–25).

MARK

By God's grace, I repented and restored the relationship with my sons. Yet, it does not aways end up that way.

Anna wanted her husband to repent so that their marriage could be restored. But her husband refused to repent, retaining his own sins. How do you unhitch from an unrepentant person?

UNHITCHING FROM AN UNREPENTANT PERSON

A pickup truck is a powerful vehicle that can pull a camper. The camper has no power on its own. Wherever the pickup truck goes, so goes the camper.

Anna's husband was like a pickup truck, and she was like the camper. She was hooked up to him, and wherever he went, whatever he did, impacted her. His unrepentance impacted her. Anna did not want to forgive him because he did not deserve it. Her refusal to forgive her unrepentant husband kept her hooked up to him.

With time and pastoral care, Anna forgave her unrepentant husband. This might shock some people. Surely, we should not forgive someone who has not repented. Would our Lord do that?

Since we are to forgive as God forgave us, let's explore His forgiveness in relation to repentance. When does God forgive us? He forgives when we confess (see 1 John 1:9). He forgives through the word of His absolution (see 2 Samuel 12:13). His forgiveness is given in the Lord's Supper (see Matthew 26:26–28). We receive forgiveness when we are baptized (see Acts 22:16). God forgives us while we are yet sinners (see Romans 5:8).

His forgiveness even predates our actual sin. We were forgiven when Jesus died on the cross (see 1 Peter 2:24). The promise of our redemption was given to our first parents in the Garden of Eden (see Genesis 3:15). We were chosen in Christ before the foundation of the world, that we should be holy and blameless before Him (see Ephesians 1:4).

In other words, God granted forgiveness before we were born—before we could repent. The giving of His forgiveness is not dependent on our repentance.

But why does repentance matter? Those who do not repent (contrition and faith) reject the forgiveness that is theirs in Christ Jesus. Jesus made this clear when He said, "Whoever does not believe is condemned already, because he has not believed in the name of the only Son of God" (John 3:18). In other words, receiving forgiveness is dependent on repentance.

God's truth is simply amazing. The granting of forgiveness is not dependent on repentance. God's forgiveness is for all people. Jesus did not come to earth to suffer, die, and rise again for only a few. He did this gracious act for all people (see John 3:16). But not all benefit from this forgiveness. Those who do not repent demonstrate that they do not believe they need Jesus' righteousness. They therefore retain their sin and its condemnation.

Thus, when we forgive others who have not repented, we forgive as God forgave us. However, those who sin against us do not receive the benefit of that forgiveness unless they acknowledge their need of it. They receive the gift when they repent.

Anna forgave her husband because forgiveness is a gift. Because she had received her own forgiveness in Christ, she could offer her husband the gift of forgiveness even though he had not repented. By forgiving him, she was able to unhook herself from him.

Her husband did not want the gift. He did not want her forgiveness or Christ's. He did not believe he had done anything wrong. Instead, he clung to his sin of adultery. He continued to drive down the road of unrepentance. He chose to retain his own sins.

When we forgive an unrepentant person, we unhitch ourselves from them. They no longer are dragging us through their life, taking us places we don't want to go. When we forgive, it gives us an engine of our own, so that instead of being dragged by them, we can now drive up alongside of them. We come alongside them to encourage repentance and faith in the forgiveness of sin.

You don't want to go down that person's dirt road, and you don't have to. You don't want to side with their accomplices, and you don't have to. You don't want to drive through a blinding blizzard, and you don't have to. When you have forgiven them and unhitched yourself from them, you can choose the moments you want to travel with them. And when you ride up alongside them, you are like Samuel. You can speak the truth in love about their sin and encourage them to repent. Calling sinners to repent prepares them to receive the gift that is already theirs in Christ Jesus.

However, remember who you are and who God is. It is not your job to make them repent.

Paul admonished Timothy with these words: "And the Lord's servant must not be quarrelsome but kind to everyone, able to teach, patiently enduring evil, correcting his opponents with gentleness" (2 Timothy 2:24–25).

We are not to be quarrelsome. As the Lord's servants, we are called to be kind, exercise patience, and gently correct those who need to repent, in the hope that *God* will bring them to repentance. Read the next part of the passage: "God may perhaps grant them repentance leading to a knowledge of the truth, and they may come to their senses and escape from the snare of the devil, after being captured by him to do his will" (vv. 25–26). As children of God, we correct with kindness, patience, and gentleness. We do not quarrel. We bring God's message to the unrepentant, but we cannot make anyone repent. We wait on God to grant them repentance.

As we wait on God, we make every effort to live at peace with them:

Repay no one evil for evil, but give thought to do what is honorable in the sight of all. If possible, so far as it depends on you, live peaceably with all. Beloved, never avenge yourselves, but leave it to the wrath of God, for it is written, "Vengeance is mine, I will repay, says the Lord." (Romans 12:17–19)

So what do you do when someone is not ready to repent? As far as it depends on you, live at peace with them. Forgive them in the name of Christ. Give them the gift of forgiveness and wait on the Lord.

The granting of forgiveness is not dependent on repentance, but the receiving of forgiveness is dependent on repentance and faith. If they don't repent, you forgive them in the name of Christ and pray that they will repent. If they refuse to repent, they will not receive forgiveness; but if they repent, they will receive the gift of forgiveness earned by Jesus Christ.

WHEN TO PROCLAIM FORGIVENESS

When we grant forgiveness, we may or may not announce that forgiveness to the unrepentant person. Speaking that forgiveness depends on the context. The goal is the other person's restoration to God. The question is not whether you should forgive but rather when you should proclaim it to the person. What will be most helpful to bring about their repentance and confirm their faith in Jesus? Sometimes, announcing forgiveness breaks the unrepentant heart. At other times, the pronouncement may be withheld to assist in their repentance.

Anna decided to speak forgiveness to her husband and told him that she had forgiven him for committing adultery. Because he was unrepentant, he did not receive the gift, and he remained in his sin. But her forgiveness unhitched her from him and put her in a different position. No longer was she like a camper, being dragged around by him to places she did not want to go. She was now free to decide when she would come alongside him and encourage him with God's Word.

Anna could have used their kids as a weapon against her husband, but she said, "I didn't want to be the reason that the kids were mad at their dad." She wisely understood that if she punished her husband this way, she would be hurting her children. When she forgave him, she was able to treat him as a person for whom Christ died. She did not wait for him to repent. She was proactive in speaking Christ into his life.

Sometimes people will say, "I will not forgive her until she has fully repented." Consider the implications of such a position. First of all, who alone can see into another's heart? Only God! (See Psalm 44:21; Jeremiah 17:10; Hebrews 4:13.) If I stipulate that forgiveness is dependent on fulfilling *my* demands, I am playing God! I am declaring that I know how much repentance is in his or her heart. Furthermore, forgiveness cannot be merited. Forgiveness is a free gift, and it cannot be earned by any action of mankind, including the act of repenting.

Repentance does not earn forgiveness. Repentance receives forgiveness.

But if someone openly and continually refuses to repent, especially after much admonition, the church has responsibility to act, for that person's eternal welfare is at stake.

WHEN SHOULD FORGIVENESS INTENTIONALLY BE WITHHELD?

Jesus gave to His church the special authority to forgive sins or withhold forgiveness. On the evening of the day Jesus rose from the dead, He appeared before His disciples who were gathered in a locked room and said, "Peace be with you" (John 20:19). Jesus then commissioned them for this special authority. "He breathed on them and said to them, 'Receive the Holy Spirit. If you forgive the sins of any, they are forgiven them; if you withhold forgiveness from any, it is withheld'" (vv. 22–23).

This is called the Office of the Keys, since forgiveness is the key to unlocking heaven. Withholding forgiveness locks, or closes, heaven. It is also referred to as church discipline or excommunication. One who is under this discipline is restricted from receiving Communion until she repents because one who receives Communion without faith brings harm to herself.

The church exercises this austere authority when one of its members demonstrates open unrepentance. In effect, the church determines that the unrepentant person is acting as if he does not believe in Christ's forgiveness for his sins. With open unrepentance, this person retains his own sin and its consequence. In other words, he retains his judgment to hell. Such a determination is not made lightly or quickly. It requires love, patience, and repeated admonition (see Matthew 18:15–20).

When the church exercises the Office of the Keys, the purpose is not to punish this person or to encourage the congregation to shun her. We exercise church discipline to help the sinner realize the seriousness of her unrepentance in order to lead her to repentance and faith (see Matthew 12:20; Acts 3:19). Another purpose is to prevent her from leading others into sin (see Matthew 18:6; 1 Corinthians 5:6).

Declaring that a church member is a nonbeliever is a serious allegation. It means the difference between heaven and hell. Thus, if a person is concerned that someone is so unrepentant that he has forfeited his faith, the concerned person should seek the help of the church.

In Matthew 18:15–20, Jesus instructed believers individually and corporately how to proceed in such instances:

> If your brother sins against you, go and tell him his fault, between you and him alone. If he listens to you, you have gained your brother. But if he does not listen, take one or two others along with you, that every charge may be established by the evidence of two or three witnesses. If he refuses to listen to them, tell it to the church. And if he refuses to listen even to the church, let him be to you as a Gentile and a tax collector. Truly, I say to you, whatever you bind on earth shall be bound in heaven, and whatever you loose on earth shall be loosed in heaven. Again I say to you, if two of you agree on earth about anything they ask, it will be done for them by My Father in heaven. For where two or three are gathered in My name, there am I among them.

The context of this section of Scripture is about restoring the lost. It includes the parable of the lost sheep and the parable of the unforgiving servant. The Office of the Keys is not about getting rid of a problem sinner. It is about restoration.

Only one sin warrants church discipline: open and persistent unrepentance. We do not exercise church discipline just because someone has committed a particularly heinous sin. All who repent, even of "great" sins, receive Christ's forgiveness. Rather, the church exercises discipline when someone denies their faith by refusing to repent after being admonished.

Remember, though, that forgiveness does not necessarily remove earthly consequences. When a serious sin hurts others, the offender often endures consequences even though they are forgiven. (For more on this, see chapter 10, "Does Forgiveness Release Consequences?")

The authority of the church to forgive or withhold forgiveness must be exercised with all soberness. Jesus authorized this discipline to bring back the errant and protect the flock. It's about saving a sinner from eternal damnation.

THE NONBELIEVER

How does forgiveness work with a person who is not a Christian and does not repent? The nonbeliever is unable to repent of sin in the same way that a child of God repents. Christian repentance is based on contrition and faith in Jesus. While a nonbeliever may express sorrow for what he has done, he does not believe that Jesus died and rose again for the forgiveness of his sin. His repentance is incomplete, and he does not benefit from Christ's forgiveness.

This should not stop you from forgiving the nonbeliever. Remember, the granting of forgiveness is not dependent on repentance, but the receiving of forgiveness is dependent on repentance and faith. You can speak forgiveness to a non-Christian with the hope that she will become a child of God and have faith in Jesus who grants forgiveness.

The granting of forgiveness to unrepentant and unbelieving people does not mean they become Christians or that they enjoy the gift of Christ's forgiveness. But it does clearly speak the Gospel into their lives with the hope that they will become Christians and repent. At times the Holy Spirit uses that opportunity to work faith in a person who receives the incredible, undeserved gift of forgiveness.

While hanging on the cross and suffering the sins of the world, Jesus saw the Roman soldiers who mocked Him, spit on Him, beat Him, and nailed Him to the cross. He saw the religious leaders who initiated and sought His crucifixion. He saw the crowd who cried, "Crucify Him!" And He sees us, whose sin put Him on the cross. Nevertheless, Jesus said from the cross, "Father, forgive them, for they know not what they do" (Luke 23:34).

Jesus granted forgiveness to everyone by His death on the cross. The granting of His forgiveness did not mean that everyone repented and received the forgiveness. But Jesus was clearly speaking the Gospel into the lives of all sinners with the hope that they would repent and believe in the forgiveness that His death and resurrection brought into the world.

Jesus told His disciples, "You have heard that it was said, 'You shall love your neighbor and hate your enemy.' But I say to you, Love your enemies and pray for those who persecute you, so that you may be sons of your Father who is in heaven" (Matthew 5:43–45).

The persecuted Jesus modeled for His disciples what He had taught them earlier to do—love your enemies and pray for them. From the cross, Jesus prayed for those who put Him there, and He prayed that they repent and believe that they are forgiven. While the crowds cried out, "Crucify Him," Jesus cried out, "Forgive them."

A Roman centurion at the cross said, "Truly this man was the Son of God!" (Mark 15:39). One of the thieves hanging next to Jesus said, "Jesus, remember me when You come into Your kingdom" (Luke 23:42). Through the preaching of Peter after Jesus' resurrection and ascension, "those who received his word were baptized, and there were added that day about three thousand souls" (Acts 2:41). All these people were unrepentant nonbelievers who became repentant believers because the Gospel was spoken into their lives.

Not everyone at the cross or listening to the apostles repented and became a believer. Not everyone to whom you speak forgiveness will repent or become a Christian. We can't make people repent and believe in Jesus. But we can speak the Gospel into their lives with the hope that the Holy Spirit will lead them to repent and believe in Jesus.

Stephen was doing just that when the religious leaders decided to drag him out of the city and stone him to death. As the stones pelted his face, his chest, and his back, Stephen prayed, "'Lord Jesus, receive my spirit.' And falling to his knees he cried out with a loud voice, 'Lord, do not hold this sin against them.' And when he had said this, he fell asleep" (Acts 7:59–60).

Stephen spoke the Gospel into the lives of unrepentant and unbelieving people with the hope that they might repent and believe in the forgiveness of Jesus Christ. One in the crowd witnessing Stephen's murder was a man named Saul, who "approved of his execution" (Acts 8:1). By the grace of God, we know that Saul became Paul (Acts 9), one of the most well-known apostles of the Gospel of Jesus Christ.

HOW DOES THIS APPLY TO ME?

1. Consider situations when you were frustrated or angry that someone was not repenting.

2. Reflecting on 2 Timothy 2:24–26, who were you trying to be when you pressured someone to repent?

3. What would be a godly approach when working with an unrepentant Christian?

4. What would be a godly approach when working with an unrepentant nonbeliever?

5. Write a prayer thanking God that He reconciled you to Him while you were still a sinner. Ask God to help you be patient with someone who is unrepentant and to look for the best way to minister to the person, including sharing the Gospel. Include a petition for someone you know who is unrepentant.

PRAYER TEMPLATE

(See chapter 3, "How Should I Pray?")

INTRODUCTION

REFERENCE TO GOD'S WORK

PETITION

RESULT

CONCLUSION

CHAPTER 9

WHAT IF I HAVE FORGIVEN BUT STILL FEEL HURT OR ANGRY?

When angry emotions well up in our hearts,
Our sense of serenity quickly departs.
Firm on the foundation of faith we rely;
Our trust in our feelings we wisely deny.

Alice described the transgression in this way: "The sin was betrayal of a friend who was caught up in an emotional affair with my husband. Yes, a betrayal of a good friend." The friend worked for her husband as an office assistant. Alice's husband did not initially realize the intent of the friend until another office worker discussed it with him. When he was made aware of what was going on, he fired the office assistant and told Alice what took place.

Alice talked with her pastor about the situation, and her pastor arranged for a mediation between the two couples. Both couples were members at the same church and participated in many church activities. The mediation was not easy, but Alice was able to forgive her friend for the emotional affair.

THE EFFECT OF EMOTIONS ON FORGIVENESS

Alice had forgiven her friend. She now expected to feel good about it, but she didn't. She still felt hurt and angry. The emotions of hurt and anger welled up inside her every time she saw her friend at church. It would have been easier for Alice not to forgive her friend. At least the unforgiveness would account for her feelings of hurt and anger. But what do you do when your feelings do not match the words of forgiveness you spoke to the offender?

We do not live in an emotionless world. Every thought, word, and action is flavored with emotion. We experience positive emotions of happiness, joy, gratefulness, serenity, excitement, amusement, and love. We also face negative emotions of anger, sadness, fear, disgust, depression, and anxiety.

God created us as emotional people. It is important that we not demonize emotions. Instead, think of emotions as a way to gauge what is going on inside our hearts. Biblically speaking, the heart is the core of a person's beliefs. What comes out of your heart determines how you feel, think, speak, and act. Whatever our hearts are set on reveals where we are placing our hope, and our emotional responses to other people also reflect this.

The problem is that we often seek hope outside of Jesus Christ. Alice had forgiven her friend. But the hurt and anger she felt indicated that she was still struggling with the ability to forgive. When God forgives, absolution takes place right away. Jesus took upon Himself our sins when He suffered and died on the cross. However, we may need time to sort through our emotions before we are able to forgive someone. Negative emotions tend to lead us back to unforgiveness.

Although Alice had forgiven her friend, she started to second-guess herself when she felt hurt, angry, betrayed, and resentful. Alice said, "I question myself—have I really forgiven? It changed everything. At church, you know we're in ministry together. It made other relationships awkward, and that still bothers me a little bit, even though I've forgiven."

It's natural to have negative emotions about the person who hurt you. But do not place your hope in those emotions. Negative emotions may tell us that we have not fully worked through all the aspects of the transgression.

Alice was wise to seek out her pastor to further work through the emotions she was experiencing. With his help, she realized that her emotions of hurt and anger were a result of feeling out of control. Alice had hoped that the relationship with her friend would go back to the way it was before the transgression. But every time she saw her friend at church, feelings of hurt and anger came from her heart as she grieved the fact that the relationship would never be the same. Alice had placed her hope in her ability to forget the sin rather than forgive it. As a result, Alice saw her friend as a threat rather than a forgiven child of God.

The negative emotions caused Alice to slip from forgiving to unforgiving. Alice could only see the offense. She wanted relief from the emotional pain but found herself in a loop of reliving the event without Christ. The hurt and anger she felt when recalling her friend's sin caused Alice to despair—she had no hope that the situation would get better. While she initially forgave her friend, her emotions drove her back into the despair of unforgiveness.

Despair is giving up hope. It is a form of imprisonment. Despair can't see the light at the end of the tunnel. It is blinded by the various negative emotions. Despair doesn't look to Jesus. Despair can only see the transgression that caused the broken relationship and the feelings of hurt.

> But this I call to mind, and therefore I have hope: The steadfast love of the LORD never ceases; His mercies never come to an end; they are new every morning; great is Your faithfulness. "The LORD is my portion," says my soul, "therefore I will hope in Him." (Lamentations 3:21–24).

Hope is not found in facts, physical strength, good deeds, or our emotional state. Hope is always found outside of us in the promises of God. Our emotions can indicate when we are in despair, but our emotions cannot save us from despair. We cling to God in the midst of despair, and we hope in His salvation.

The psalmist said, "My soul clings to the dust; give me life according to Your word!" (119:25). And Moses said, "But you who held fast to the LORD your God are all alive today" (Deuteronomy 4:4). Those who cling to the dust, those who cling to themselves and their negative emotions, remain in despair. But those who cling to the Lord will be able to find emotional peace.

Emotions do not determine our salvation. This may be difficult to accept when we rely so heavily on how we feel about things. But remember, our emotions are a gauge to tell us something about our heart. Emotions do not determine the truth of Christ's forgiveness. Emotions simply help us reveal where we have put our hope.

Emotions cannot save us from despair. Likewise, emotions cannot bring us hope. Often people try to rely on their emotions to bring them hope, but this false hope will only bring more anger, depression, sadness, fear, and anxiety. Alice was caught in an emotional loop of despair that overshadowed her hope in the forgiveness of Christ.

HOW MANY TIMES SHOULD I FORGIVE?

That's a question asked by many throughout the ages, including Jesus' disciples.

Then Peter came up and said to [Jesus], "Lord, how often will my brother sin against me, and I forgive him? As many as seven times?" Jesus said to him, "I do not say to you seven times, but seventy-seven times." (Matthew 18:21–22)

Peter had a limited understanding of forgiveness and failed to grasp the width and depth of forgiving in the name of Christ. Jesus died once and for all (Romans 6:10). He does not need to be re-sacrificed on the cross over and over. But we need to hear the proclamation of that forgiveness over and over. Why? Because our sinful hearts trust our emotions more than our God.

Put yourself in Alice's shoes, struggling with her emotions of anger and betrayal of a good friend. You also might ask, "How many times must I forgive?" Jesus says, "You forgive and forgive, just as I forgive you again and again." The psalmist reminds us, "As far as the east is from the west, so far does He remove our transgressions from us" (103:12).

Forgiveness challenges us when we continue to feel emotional hurt from the transgression. But this provides opportunity to pray and seek out pastoral guidance. Alice realized that her emotions were rooted in a desire for the offense to disappear and for things to go back to the way they were before the sin. Since this desire did not materialize for her, it became an idol in her life that made it difficult to treat her friend as a forgiven child of God. Unchecked emotions can cause us to remain in despair and only see the sin without forgiveness. But when we cling to the cross of forgiveness, we have hope in Jesus, whose blood gives us peace.

When emotions lead us to despair, we focus only on the sin, discounting forgiveness. But by fixing our eyes on Jesus, we can overcome the despair.

> Therefore, since we are surrounded by so great a cloud of witnesses, let us also lay aside every weight, and sin which clings so closely, and let us run with endurance the race that is set before us, looking to Jesus, the founder and perfecter of our faith, who for the joy that was set before Him endured the cross, despising the shame, and is seated at the right hand of the throne of God. Consider Him who endured from sinners such hostility against Himself, so that you may not grow weary or fainthearted. (Hebrews 12:1–3)

Jesus was arrested, flogged, nailed to a cross, and left to die—a despairing sight. One of the fellow criminals hanging next to Jesus joined in with those who mocked Him and said, "Are You not the Christ? Save Yourself and us!" (Luke 23:39). The scene on Calvary looked hopeless. Yet, in the midst of death, God was at work.

Forgiven children of God can have hope when struggling in the darkness of emotions by turning our focus to Jesus.

LIVE BY FAITH AND NOT BY EMOTIONS

The Pharisees complained when they saw Jesus' disciples eating food without first ceremonially washing their hands. They challenged Jesus, expecting Him to direct His disciples to follow the tradition of the elders. Instead, Jesus rebuked the Pharisees by quoting Isaiah: "This people honors Me with their lips, but their heart is far from Me; in vain do they worship Me, teaching as doctrines the commandments of men" (Matthew 15:8–9).

Peter asked Jesus to further explain what He said to the Pharisees. He answered,

> Do you not see that whatever goes into the mouth passes into the stomach and is expelled? But what comes out of the mouth proceeds from the heart, and this defiles a person. For out of the heart come evil thoughts, murder, adultery, sexual immorality, theft,

false witness, slander. These are what defile a person. But to eat with unwashed hands does not defile anyone. (Matthew 15:17–20)

Jesus was teaching that we should be less concerned about traditions and practices created by church leaders and more concerned with matters of the heart. The devastation of despair and hopelessness that results in unforgiveness comes from within a person. The emotional hurt and anger that Alice experienced was not imposed on her from someone outside of herself—it came from her heart.

The unchecked emotions of her heart led her to live according to those emotions and not according to faith in Christ.

Living according to our emotions becomes a roller-coaster ride. One moment you are on top of the world and your blood is pumping with excitement. Then in a blink of an eye, you are hurtling down into a barrel roll of despair. Around and around the track you go, feeling nauseous from the endless looping of emotions with no way to get off. Living by way of your emotions proves foolish. The proverb says, "The way of a fool is right in his own eyes, but a wise man listens to advice" (Proverbs 12:15). It may seem right to rely on your emotions, but soon you will pass out from the superficial promises of peace that never materialize.

The wise person listens to counsel from God's Word. The psalmist says, "How can a young man keep his way pure? By guarding it according to Your word. With my whole heart I seek You; let me not wander from Your commandments!" (119:9–10). God's Word remains a foundation that does not shift with changing times or emotions. God's Word is the only peace that can calm our hearts and help us live by faith.

When David committed adultery with Bathsheba, he experienced an array of emotions. The foolish David initially lived according to his emotions and ignored God's Word. But in repentance, David became wise by listening to the Word of God proclaimed by Nathan.

David's prayer reflected his change of focus: "Create in me a clean heart, O God, and renew a right spirit within me. Cast me not away from Your presence, and take not Your Holy Spirit from me. Restore to me the joy of Your salvation, and uphold me with a willing spirit" (Psalm 51:10–12).

God says in Ezekiel, "I will give you a new heart, and a new spirit I will put within you. And I will remove the heart of stone from your flesh and give you a heart of flesh. And I will put My Spirit within you, and cause you to walk in My statutes and be careful to obey My rules" (36:26–27).

On an emotional roller coaster? Fix your eyes on Jesus. Live by faith in Him, and God will give you a new heart that enables you to live at peace with those who have sinned against you. Live by faith in Christ Jesus. He will calm the emotions that might drive you back to unforgiveness.

When you feel hurt and emotions well up even after you have forgiven someone, do not fear. Remember God's promises: "Fear not, for I am with you; be not dismayed, for I am your God; I will strengthen you, I will help you, I will uphold you with My righteous right hand" (Isaiah 41:10).

God has provided for you His Word that is not sinking sand but a solid foundation (see Matthew 7:24–27).

HOW DOES THIS APPLY TO ME?

1. Identify emotions that you struggle with after forgiving someone.

2. How are these emotions affecting your decision to forgive?

3. Read the following passages. What comfort do you find in each one?
    ▶ Isaiah 43:1–4
    ▶ Matthew 11:28–30
    ▶ Psalm 103:1–5, 11–13
    ▶ 1 Peter 2:24
    ▶ Romans 5:6–8

4. Write a prayer that God will strengthen your faith in His promises for you and decrease the hurt and anger and other emotions that haunt you. Thank Him for His forgiveness and the invitation to lay your burdens at the foot of Jesus' cross. Pray for those who sinned against you. Ask God to give you a gracious way to think about them.

PRAYER TEMPLATE

(See chapter 3, "How Should I Pray?")

INTRODUCTION

REFERENCE TO GOD'S WORK

PETITION

RESULT

CONCLUSION

CHAPTER 10

DOES FORGIVENESS RELEASE CONSEQUENCES?

The civil law must be obeyed:
A debt incurred must be repaid.
To those who would the law defy
The consequence soon applies.
  Have mercy, Lord.

God's holy Law is higher still;
We must obey His perfect will.
They who transgress its height or breadth,
The consequence then is death.
  Have mercy, Lord.

Praise be to Christ for grace and love,
The perfect gift from God above,
Forgiveness and salvation free:
Our consequence eternally.
  Have mercy, Lord.

In chapter 4, we related the story of Gladys, the Australian missionary in India whose husband and boys were murdered.

Although Gladys forgave the men who committed the crimes, the government convicted and sentenced them. The leader received the death penalty. The others were sentenced to life in prison.

When asked if she thought the sentence provided justice, Gladys said she had no comment. She told the reporter that God establishes authority, including government, which executes justice for society. Gladys reflected what Paul wrote in Romans 13 about another non-Christian government.

Then Gladys declared that she forgave those who killed her husband and sons. She went on to say that one should not mix up forgiveness and consequences.

WHAT CONSEQUENCE IS RELEASED IN FORGIVENESS?

Not all consequences are released in forgiveness. But with God's forgiveness, the most significant consequence of all is wiped away.

The consequence of sin is eternal separation from God. "The wages of sin is death" (Romans 6:23a).

But in the forgiveness of Christ, the consequence of eternal death is taken away. "But the free gift of God is eternal life in Christ Jesus our Lord" (Romans 6:23b).

Those who believe that Christ died and rose again for the forgiveness of their sins are saved from God's wrath.

For God so loved the world, that He gave His only Son, that whoever believes in Him should not perish but have eternal life. For God did not send His Son into the world to condemn the world, but in order that the world might be saved through Him. Whoever believes in Him is not condemned, but whoever does not believe is condemned already, because he has not believed in the name of the only Son of God. (John 3:16–18)

The Good News of the Bible is that the consequence of hell has been paid in full through Jesus' death and resurrection. When Jesus proclaimed from the cross, "It is finished" (John 19:30), He declared that our debt from sin was paid in full. The consequence of being separated from God has been satisfied for us.

Those who believe in Jesus are no longer condemned to eternal death.

"Death is swallowed up in victory." "O death, where is your victory? O death, where is your sting?" The sting of death is sin, and the power of sin is the law. But thanks be to God, who gives us the victory through our Lord Jesus Christ. (1 Corinthians 15:54–57)

With Christ's forgiveness, we sinners who believe in Jesus have been fully justified. "There is therefore now no condemnation for those who are in Christ Jesus" (Romans 8:1).

Does forgiveness relieve consequences? Yes! God's forgiveness clears us of the sentence of eternal death!

However, forgiveness does not eliminate all consequences.

CAN FORGIVENESS AND CONSEQUENCES COEXIST?

When we sin, earthly consequences often follow, even for the forgiven.

Adam and Eve experienced consequences for their sin, even though God promised redemption through a Savior. They were evicted from the garden, they encountered hard labor, they felt pain from the sorrows of life, and they died.

Consider Moses, who directly disobeyed God. When the children of Israel needed water in the wilderness of Zin, God directed Moses to speak to the rock in Kadesh, and He promised it would produce water for the people. But instead, "Moses lifted up his hand and struck the rock with his staff twice, and water came out abundantly, and the congregation drank, and their livestock" (Numbers 20:11).

God pronounced judgment on Moses with a severe consequence: "Because you did not believe in Me, to uphold Me as holy in the eyes of the people of Israel, therefore you shall not bring this assembly into the land that I have given them" (v. 12).

Just before the people entered the Promised Land, God restated His judgment of Moses:

That very day the LORD spoke to Moses, "Go up this mountain of the Abarim, Mount Nebo, which is in the land of Moab, opposite Jericho, and view the land of Canaan, which I am giving to the people of Israel for a possession. And die on the mountain which you go up, and be gathered to your people, as Aaron your brother died in Mount Hor and was gathered to his people, because you broke faith with Me in the midst of the people of Israel at the waters of Meribah-kadesh, in the wilderness of Zin, and because you did not treat Me as holy in the midst of the people of Israel. For you shall see the land before you, but you shall not go there, into the land that I am giving to the people of Israel." (Deuteronomy 32:48–52)

Was Moses forgiven? Yes! New Testament evidence of His forgiveness was revealed when he appeared with Jesus and Elijah on the Mount of Transfiguration. Yet, God disciplined Moses with a severe earthly consequence.

Imagine leading the huge assembly of Israel for forty years in the wilderness. It was often a thankless job with a congregation that grumbled and complained against Moses. At long last, he was able to view the Promised Land where his congregation would dwell, but he was kept from going with them.

Moses was prevented from entering the earthly Promised Land (consequence), but he died and entered the heavenly promised land (forgiveness). Moses experienced both God's forgiveness and earthly consequences.

Consider King David, a man blessed by God who misused his authority to commit adultery, murder, and denial. The prophet Nathan proclaimed God's forgiveness to David. God granted mercy to David—he did not suffer all the potential earthly consequences: "David said to Nathan, 'I have sinned against the LORD.' And Nathan said to David, 'The LORD also has put away your sin; you shall not die'" (2 Samuel 12:13).

God showed mercy to the king. He did not remove David from his throne, and He allowed David to live. But there were harsh consequences for David's transgressions. Nathan delivered God's message with the consequences.

"Why have you despised the word of the LORD, to do what is evil in His sight? You have struck down Uriah the Hittite with the sword and have taken his wife to be your wife and have killed him with the sword of the Ammonites. Now therefore the sword shall never depart from your house, because you have despised Me and have taken the wife of Uriah the Hittite to be your wife." Thus says the LORD, "Behold, I will raise up evil against you out of your own house. And I will take your wives before your eyes and give them to your neighbor, and he shall lie with your wives in the sight of this sun. For you did it secretly, but I will do this thing before all Israel and before the sun." (2 Samuel 12:9–12)

Moreover, there was another consequence more painful for David. "Nevertheless, because by this deed you have utterly scorned the LORD, the child who is born to you shall die" (v. 14).

Was David forgiven by God? Yes! Nathan announced God's forgiveness in verse 13: "The LORD also has put away your sin."

But David experienced earthly consequences:

- The sword never departed from his house.

- David witnessed the calamity and suffered the shame and humiliation of his own son sleeping openly with his wives.

- David and Bathsheba's son died, even though David prayed in sackcloth and ashes for mercy.

At the same time, David was shown mercy in his consequences. He did not die, and he did not lose his position of king. Most of all, he was forgiven by God.

Although David's sins were many and public, God kept His promise that the Messiah would come from David's descendants. Bathsheba gave birth to another son, Solomon. The Savior of the world descended from this son of David.

Sin often results in natural consequences, even when there is forgiveness.

- Cheating on one's taxes may result in penalty and interest.

- Yelling at someone you love and attacking their character may result in a broken relationship.

- Betrayal of love or friendship results in mistrust and possible separation.

- Negligence of property or relationships may result in loss.

- Embezzling from your employer will result in guilt, shame, termination, and possible criminal penalties.

- Criminal acts often result in prosecution.

Consequences impact not only the offender but often many around him too.

- The reputation of a family or company may be harmed when someone in their midst sins.

- A person injured in an accident caused by another endures pain and may not fully heal or may even die.

- Someone may suffer years of mental anguish because of emotional harm or damaged reputation on social media.

- The offender's family may suffer humiliation or loss of income or financial well-being.

- When someone dies because of an offense, many are left grieving the loss.

- Annual celebrations and other gatherings may be impacted by the feelings surrounding the harm caused.

A fruit of sin is suffering. We all suffer the consequences of sin in our world. Some suffering is because of others' sins against us. Some of the suffering is because of our own sin.

Because of these consequences, some feel that forgiveness should be withheld as another consequence.

Yet, with our God, He does not withhold forgiveness for those who seek it. He freely forgives because Jesus' blood was shed for that sin and the consequences that many endured.

On the other hand, just because forgiveness is granted does not necessarily mean that earthly consequences will not apply.

MUST CONSEQUENCES ALWAYS BE APPLIED?

Our God is a God of mercy. Even with earthly consequences, He often shows mercy.

The LORD is merciful and gracious, slow to anger and abounding in steadfast love. He will not always chide, nor will He keep His anger forever. He does not deal with us according to our sins, nor repay us according to our iniquities. (Psalm 103:8–10)

God often shows mercy to the sinner. Consider Jesus' parable of the prodigal son in Luke 15:11–32.

The younger son demanded his share of his inheritance while his father was alive. The father gave that son his portion, and the son traveled to a country far away where he squandered his entire inheritance in wild living. When the money ran out, he was desperate and took a humiliating job feeding pigs (an unclean animal for a Hebrew). In poverty and hunger, he remembered that his father's servants had more than enough to eat. He came to his senses (repentance) and planned to return home and beg to be a servant. He acknowledged that he no longer deserved to be called a son.

What did the son deserve? He had suffered some consequences already, but certainly he should lose his family privileges, right? He wasn't even worthy to be a servant of his father, let alone be considered a son.

But while he was still a long way off, his father, who had been watching for him, ran out to embrace and kiss him. The son confessed to his father. The father showed incredible mercy. He clothed him with a robe and shoes, and he placed the family ring on him, designating him as a son. Then the father threw a celebration banquet for him.

Talk about getting out of consequences!

Not everyone was happy about the father's mercy. The older brother brooded when he learned what was happening. He was angry and refused to join the celebration. He likely felt his younger brother did not deserve mercy. He was jealous that, as the "good" brother, their father didn't give him a goat to celebrate with his friends.

It is true that the younger son did not deserve mercy. Mercy is not earned—it is a gift.

The father could have shown anger with his elder son and refused to see him. But he showed compassion also for his angry son. Just as he did with the younger, the father went out to his older son to show him love.

Jesus told this parable in response to the Pharisees and the scribes who grumbled, saying, "This man receives sinners and eats with them" (Luke 15:2).

When mercy is shown, or when someone does not suffer the consequences we think she deserves, we, too, can sulk and be angry with God or the authorities who made the decision. We act like the older brother, resentful that our heavenly Father is not more generous to us and more judgmental toward those who we believe deserve His condemnation.

When we do that, we forget who we are and who God is. We need to ask, "Am I in the place of God?" We have declared someone a Ninevite, and we have judged and condemned the sinner. We want that person to suffer and not benefit from God's mercy. (See chapters 4 and 5.)

So when should one show mercy, and when should one with authority apply consequences? Before making such a decision, let's consider the reasons for consequences.

WHAT IS THE PURPOSE OF CONSEQUENCES?

Consequences do not diminish forgiveness, nor does forgiveness remove all the consequences. Consequences can serve several purposes.

- Consequences may be necessary to provide restitution.
- Consequences may be a form of discipline.
- Consequences can provide an example or warning to others.
- Consequences may protect a sinner from further temptation.
- Consequences may be necessary to protect others from harm.

RESTITUTION

When I harm someone or her property, I need to do what I can to make the person whole again. When driving, if I crash into your car, I pay to have the damage to your car repaired. If I hit a golf ball through your window, I pay to replace the glass. I make you whole again.

God prescribes restitution:

And the LORD spoke to Moses, saying, "Speak to the people of Israel, When a man or woman commits any of the sins that people commit by breaking faith with the LORD, and that person realizes his guilt, he shall confess his sin that he has committed. And he shall make full restitution for his wrong, adding a fifth to it and giving it to him to whom he did the wrong." (Numbers 5:5–7)

In Luke, we see how Zacchaeus promised to make restitution for those he harmed: "Zacchaeus stood and said to the Lord, 'Behold, Lord, the half of my goods I give to the poor. And if I have defrauded anyone of anything, I restore it fourfold'" (Luke 19:8).

Making monetary restitution—a consequence of his pattern of stealing and misusing his authority as a tax collector—was done of his own accord as a fruit of his repentance. Note Jesus' response. "Jesus said to him, 'Today salvation has come to this house, since he also is a son of Abraham. For the Son of Man came to seek and to save the lost'" (vv. 9–10).

Restitution is an appropriate consequence that is not negated by forgiveness.

DISCIPLINE

The root of the word *discipline* is from the Latin word *disciplina*, which means "instruction and training." A disciple is a learner and follower. The purpose of discipline, therefore, is for correction and training. According to Scripture, applying discipline is evidence of love. "Whoever spares the rod hates his son, but he who loves him is diligent to discipline him" (Proverbs 13:24).

God Himself disciplines those whom He loves.

And have you forgotten the exhortation that addresses you as sons? "My son, do not regard lightly the discipline of the Lord, nor be weary when reproved by Him. For the Lord disciplines the one He loves, and chastises every son whom He receives." (Hebrews 12:5–6)

The Bible goes on to indicate the implication of not disciplining:

It is for discipline that you have to endure. God is treating you as sons. For what son is there whom his father does not discipline? If you are left without discipline, in which all have participated, then you are illegitimate children and not sons. (vv. 7–8)

Sometimes we think that being merciful means withholding discipline. But if the motivation for discipline is love, then the purpose is to teach and yield blessings for the one who endures it. "For the moment all discipline seems painful rather than pleasant, but later it yields the peaceful fruit of righteousness to those who have been trained by it" (v. 11).

Just as children need discipline to learn from their errors, adults may also need to be disciplined for their learning to avoid future harm to themselves and others. If no discipline is applied when appropriate, the offender will not learn and will likely repeat the offense.

For example, what would happen in a society where crimes have no consequences for the offender? No one would learn the lessons of the pain caused by committing crimes.

Discipline is a form of love and concern for the one who sinned.

EXAMPLE OR WARNING

When someone commits a sin known to others, a consequence serves as an example or warning to others. Without a consequence, others learn that such sin can be committed without negative ramifications. In other words, people are encouraged to repeat another's sin because it bears no personal consequence.

Paul warned the church in Corinth about this danger when the congregation failed to discipline one of its members who was known to be living in sexual sin:

Your boasting is not good. Do you not know that a little leaven leavens the whole lump? Cleanse out the old leaven that you may be a new lump, as you really are unleavened. For Christ, our Passover Lamb, has been sacrificed. (1 Corinthians 5:6–7)

In a case where a church employee embezzled church funds, the congregants were divided on what to do. Some felt that as Christians they should simply forgive and forget. Others wanted to prosecute to the fullest extent of the law. Neither extreme view was godly. After some biblical teaching and prayer, the congregation decided unanimously that there needed to be both forgiveness and consequences. The concern was raised that since this was a public offense against the entire body, there needed to be consequences. Otherwise, people would learn by example that stealing was acceptable. The church decided that criminal prosecution was not necessary in this case because the employee expressed repentance and promised to pay back what was taken. If he went to prison, there would be little opportunity to make restitution. In addition, he had a family who depended on him.

Thus, they developed a plan that incorporated forgiveness, consequences, and mercy. Forgiveness was proclaimed. Consequences included restitution and counseling. The employee lost his position because it required him to handle cash. However, the church wanted the employee's children to be covered by health insurance, which was one of the benefits lost when he lost his job. As an act of mercy, the church established a fund to make certain that his children would not go without health care. And the church decided not to prosecute.

Acts 5:1–11 provides another biblical example of consequences that served as a warning to the early church. Ananias and Sapphira sold a piece of property to give all the proceeds to the church. But they secretly kept back some of the proceeds. When Peter confronted them, they maintained the lie. They claimed a right to their sin, and they died as a consequence. The result? "Great fear came upon the whole church and upon all who heard of these things" (v. 11).

The consequences they suffered served as a warning not to lie to the Holy Spirit.

PROTECT A SINNER FROM FURTHER TEMPTATION

In the example above about embezzlement, the employee was terminated because his position required him to handle cash. Since this had been a significant part of his sin, it would have been unwise to leave him in a place where he would be tempted again. The loss of his job protected him from being tempted in the same way again.

Think of a recovering alcoholic. Part of recovery necessitates that the person make lifestyle changes to eliminate factors that contributed to the addiction. For example, she may need to find new friends who don't socialize in bars. She may need to find ways to avoid places where alcohol is readily available. A consequence of alcohol addiction is that one must avoid the people and habits that tempt one to drink.

In the Lord's Prayer, Jesus taught us to pray, "And lead us not into temptation, but deliver us from evil" (Matthew 6:13). Removing a person from further temptation is another way to show care, even though it is a consequence.

The apostle Paul admonished the Thessalonians to avoid those situations that would tempt them to sin:

> For this is the will of God, your sanctification: that you abstain from sexual immorality; that each one of you know how to control his own body in holiness and honor, not in the passion of lust like the Gentiles who do not know God; that no one transgress and wrong his brother in this matter, because the Lord is an avenger in all these things, as we told you beforehand and solemnly warned you. For God has not called us for impurity, but in holiness. Therefore whoever disregards this, disregards not man but God, who gives His Holy Spirit to you. (1 Thessalonians 4:3–8)

PROTECT OTHERS FROM HARM

A person who has been repeatedly arrested for driving while intoxicated may be incarcerated for some time. This consequence protects others from being injured or killed by his drunk driving.

When a person sexually abuses children, the abuser is often imprisoned and not allowed to be around children alone again. This protects other children from being harmed.

Consequences are necessary to separate those who physically abuse others in domestic disputes.

Consequences are necessary when others need protection.

WHEN SHOULD I REQUIRE CONSEQUENCES AND WHEN SHOULD I SHOW MERCY?

This is a difficult question. Both consequences and mercy may be appropriate. God applies both in our lives, as He applied both in the lives of the saints who went before us.

In many cases, consequences are determined by someone other than the offended. For example, the consequences of a criminal act are determined by a court. The discipline of a child may be determined by a parent rather than another child who was hurt. In other words, God has placed people in authority to determine appropriate consequences.

When others have the authority, we must take care not to avenge ourselves when we are dissatisfied with the outcome. We may play an appropriate role in advising the authorities (such as a victim witness). However, if others have the God-given authority, we must not take it upon ourselves to carry out justice.

But there are situations when we as the hurting party will have the authority to decide what consequences should be applied and what mercy should be shown. When you are suffering at the hands of others, it is difficult to make a godly decision on what is best for the offender, for you as the hurting party, and for society in general. Sometimes people are too willing to show mercy when the offense requires some consequence. Other times people are so hurt they want the offender to feel pain.

If you find yourself in a situation where you have the proper authority to render judgment or show mercy, we recommend that you work with a spiritually mature person to guide you in considering your options. When we are hurting, our emotions can cloud better judgment. The counsel of a spiritually wise friend can benefit you and others involved.

To know wisdom and instruction, to understand words of insight, to receive instruction in wise dealing, in righteousness, justice, and equity; to give prudence to the simple, knowledge and discretion to the youth—Let the wise hear and increase in learning, and the one who understands obtain guidance, to understand a proverb and a saying, the words of the wise and their riddles. (Proverbs 1:2–6)

And, of course, pray for God's guidance:

Do not be anxious about anything, but in everything by prayer and supplication with thanksgiving let your requests be made known to God. And the peace of God, which surpasses all under-standing, will guard your hearts and your minds in Christ Jesus. (Philippians 4:6–7)

DIFFERENCE BETWEEN LOVING CONSEQUENCES AND RETRIBUTION

Consequences are applied out of love for the offender and all those affected. When we apply consequences for godly purposes, they will benefit the offender, the offended, and society. Consequences are a natural outcome of sinful actions.

The difference between godly consequences and sinful retribution is vengeance. Vengeance is a form of making oneself god, causing pain for the offender out of hurt and anger rather than exercising godly consequences out of love. Vengeance is taking justice into your own hands and acting out of hurt and anger. God warns against vengeance: "Beloved, never avenge yourselves, but leave it to the wrath of God, for it is written, 'Vengeance is mine, I will repay, says the Lord'" (Romans 12:19).

God contrasts vengeance with what He calls us to do. "To the contrary, 'if your enemy is hungry, feed him; if he is thirsty, give him something to drink; for by so doing you will heap burning coals on his head.' Do not be overcome by evil, but overcome evil with good" (vv. 20–21).

To punish someone out of vengeance is to act in God's place; it is to be overcome by evil. In vengeance and anger you sin against God and others. And that sin will come with its own consequences.

HOW DOES THIS APPLY TO ME?

IF YOU ARE THE OFFENDED

1. Begin with forgiveness. If you have not yet done so, forgive the person in your own heart. See the other chapters in this book for help on forgiveness.

2. Guard against taking vengeance. If you are tempted to act out of vengeance, review chapter 6, "How Does Anger Give Opportunity to the Devil?" Pray for God to protect your heart from desiring vengeance.

3. Having forgiven the person, determine your role in applying consequences.

    ▶ What is your role in determining consequences?

    ▶ If you do not have authority to determine consequences, how can you best support the authorities who have the power to judge?

    ▶ If you do have authority to determine consequences, seek spiritually wise counsel to guide you in applying mercy and consequences that will benefit all affected.

4. Write a prayer for God's help for you in this situation. Include praying for the offender, yourself, and others who are affected. Pray for personal peace, patience, and understanding, whatever the outcome. Thank God for the mercy shown you in your life and ask that He grant you a gracious and merciful heart.

IF YOU HAVE AUTHORITY TO DETERMINE CONSEQUENCES BUT ARE NOT THE ONE WHO WAS DIRECTLY IMPACTED

1. Seek to learn how all are affected, including the offended, the offender, and others.

2. Identify several options and weigh the godly benefits. Review the purposes of consequences in this chapter. Consider how consequences might affect the offender (especially restitution), the offended, and the community.

3. Only grant mercy where you have authority to do so. Render your decision based on justice, and if appropriate, the offended may grant mercy based on the just consequences.

4. Pray for God's wisdom and guidance. If appropriate, seek godly counsel. Pray for the offended, the offender, and others affected.

IF YOU ARE THE OFFENDER

1. Repent of your sin and confess to God and those you have hurt. Include your desire to make restitution and amend your sinful ways.

2. As you are able with God's help, make restitution.

3. Write a prayer seeking God's help in accepting the consequences, whether or not you believe them to be just. Pray for the authorities making the decision regarding your consequences. Pray for yourself, the offended, and others who are affected. Thank God for the forgiveness you have in Jesus Christ. Pray that those hurt may not be burdened with unforgiveness, and pray for your patience with them as they work through their unforgiveness.

PRAYER TEMPLATE

(See chapter 3, "How Should I Pray?")

INTRODUCTION

REFERENCE TO GOD'S WORK

PETITION

RESULT

CONCLUSION

CHAPTER 11

WHAT ABOUT ABUSE?

If someone seeks to cause us harm,
  To bully or molest us,
And there is cause for our alarm,
  Lord, by Your might protect us.
Help us abused to shun and flee
Nor fall into a trap where we
  Engage in such behavior.

There are many forms of abuse: sexual, physical, psychological, verbal, neglect, emotional, economic, and cultural. An abuser is someone who intentionally harms another person through aggressive, manipulative, neglectful, or violent behavior by taking advantage of others in order to satisfy the abuser's own sinful desires.

The abuser creates an environment where the victim is isolated and alone. The victim knows there will be consequences if she speaks to others about what is going on. The abuser consistently reminds his victims that they are worthless, unclean, and not acceptable. And the abuser provides warped comfort—"I am the only one willing to care for you. You should show me some appreciation."

The abuser makes her victims feel less than human by treating them as those who are less than human.

The abuser is wicked because he imposes evil on the victim with malice and with the intent to destroy the victim for selfish gain.

Later in this chapter we'll answer, "Is the abuser forgivable?" But first, we want to highlight important issues regarding abuse.

A DIFFICULT TOPIC

Abuse leaves deep wounds that penetrate the core of a person's identity. It is uncomfortable to talk about the horrors of abuse. Yet, the alternative—to ignore it—will only allow this evil sin to continue to destroy lives.

If you are a victim of abuse, seek professional help immediately. There are a variety of resources that can provide counseling, safe places to live, and legal assistance. There are also many national crisis organizations that provide confidential assistance (e.g., National Domestic Violence Hotline, National Child Abuse Coalition, Suicide Prevention Services, and National Teen Dating Abuse Helpline).

This chapter is not intended to address the multitude of issues related to abuse or to provide any psychological treatment. This chapter may accompany professional counseling or spiritual care to help people understand abuse from a biblical perspective.

God clearly denounces the evil of abuse. But God also speaks a word of peace into our lives: "And the peace of God, which surpasses all understanding, will guard your hearts and your minds in Christ Jesus" (Philippians 4:7).

God is here in the midst of abuse, providing help through the psychological and medical professions; through the support of friends, family, neighbors, and coworkers; and through pastors and others who provide spiritual care. God has not abandoned you, and there is hope.

For I know the plans I have for you, declares the LORD, plans for welfare and not for evil, to give you a future and a hope. (Jeremiah 29:11)

Be strong and courageous. Do not fear or be in dread of them, for it is the LORD your God who goes with you. He will not leave you or forsake you. (Deuteronomy 31:6)

For I am sure that neither death nor life, nor angels nor rulers, nor things present nor things to come, nor powers, nor height nor depth, nor anything else in all creation, will be able to separate us from the love of God in Christ Jesus our Lord. (Romans 8:38–39)

WHAT IF YOU ARE BEING ABUSED?

Being abused is not acceptable. And abuse is not limited to romantic relationships. People can be abused by coworkers, a boss, teachers, neighbors, friends, or care workers.

It may not always be easy to identify an abusive relationship. At some point in every relationship, we have probably mistreated another person with our words or actions. But when the mistreatment is chronic, malicious, and unrepented, it is often abuse.

These traits signal an abusive situation:

Feeling isolated—when a particular person tries to monopolize all your time and does not let you spend time with others. You may notice that this person is rude to your friends and family. You may feel like you don't have the freedom to socialize with friends and family outside of the relationship with this individual. You may feel that the person does not allow you to express your ideas or feelings.

No privacy—when a particular person wants to know where you are at all times. She may insist on tracking your phone. He may demand to know all your passwords to social media, medical records, email, and electronic devices. She may get angry when you don't return phone calls or reply to text messages. You may feel like you can't have any time alone without the other person being there or checking in with you.

Feeling it is all your fault—when a particular person blames you for everything that goes wrong and is unwilling to take responsibility for anything. You find yourself apologizing but never hearing the other person apologize. You may feel forced to confess things that are not sinful. You may feel as if you can't do anything right. He claims it is your fault for getting upset because he was just joking around or trying to have fun.

Feeling intimidated—when a particular person makes verbal, written, or physical threats to get her way. You may feel afraid to make decisions on your own without receiving the other person's permission. You may fear that she will find a way to destroy you, embarrass you, or shame you if you don't do what she wants.

Feeling controlled—when a particular person prevents you from doing things. He may not allow you to get a job, have your own checking account, make your own decisions, or choose your own clothing and food. You may feel like you can't have your own opinion or feelings without consulting him.

Feeling manipulated—when a particular person twists reality so that you begin to second-guess yourself. She might convince you that you have misunderstood or misremembered something. Taking this approach allows her to do inappropriate things without getting in trouble. You may feel as if she is getting what she wants at your expense.

HOW CAN A VICTIM BE PROTECTED FROM FURTHER HARM?

The victim of abuse should seek out professional counseling, which will assist in creating appropriate boundaries for any interaction with the abuser.

Abusers work hard to make victims feel as if they are incapable of making decisions. Setting boundaries puts the victim in the driver's seat. You can't control what the abuser will do, but you can control your response. Depending on the situation, the victim may decide to have no contact with the abuser, or the victim may choose limited or supervised contact. The victim will also need to make decisions about how to respond to phone calls, text messages, social media posts, and other items. Setting boundaries with an abuser will give the victim more control to make healthy and godly decisions.

Well-known experts Henry Cloud and John Townsend have written about setting healthy boundaries.[8] Their work is foundational to understanding how boundaries can help us live God-pleasing lives. Reading their book on boundaries

---

8   See Henry Cloud and John Townsend, *Boundaries: When to Say Yes, How to Say No to Take Control of Your Life* (Grand Rapids, MI: Zondervan, 2017).

in tandem with counseling will provide a strategic path for responding to an abuser.

Cloud and Townsend identify two extremes to avoid. The first is when a person has no boundaries at all. Think about a yard that surrounds a house. If the yard does not have a fence, there is no boundary. Good things and bad things can come into your yard because there is no fence to keep them out. Without a good boundary an abuser can come into your life whenever he wants and do whatever he pleases.

The second extreme is when a person has a mile-high wall built out of reinforced concrete. This boundary will not let anything come into her yard and won't let anything get out of her yard. This approach may protect a person from an abuser, but it will also isolate her from all the good that is in the world.

A healthy and godly boundary, according to Cloud and Townsend, will help you to take responsibility for yourself. A healthy boundary is a fence that clearly communicates what is acceptable and what is not acceptable behavior in your yard. You can see over or through the fence to talk with people. And the fence has a gate that you can open and shut to determine who can enter your yard.

Here are some examples of healthy boundaries that an abuser would need to respect, if the relationship is to continue:

- **The abuser would need to seek out counseling and pastoral care.**
- **The abuser would not demand that you act a certain way.**
- **The abuser may provide advice or opinions, but you will make decisions that are appropriate for your individual life.**
- **When the abuser gets angry and yells, you will leave the room and, if necessary, leave the residence or the relationship.**

These boundaries are like a fence—they clearly communicate to someone what is appropriate or godly and what is not appropriate or godly. But a fence can be ignored by an abuser. The abuser can jump over the fence or tear down the fence in order to get what she wants. Boundaries are only effective when others respect the boundary that you have set up. But a boundary itself will not change an abuser.

This is why some victims would rather build a mile-high wall surrounded by a moat that can only be accessed by means of a drawbridge. Such a boundary will most definitely keep abusers away unless they take extreme action to blow a hole in your wall. But it could also isolate you from healthy relationships.

Such isolation might encourage rumination and focus your attention so inward that it would be difficult for even God's Word to speak to your troubled heart.

Such a wall is not a good boundary because it will separate you from the joys of living life. But if the abuser is unwilling to respect your boundaries, you may need to create a safety plan.

Professional counselors are equipped to help you make a safety plan. Every situation is unique, and a counselor can help you design a safety plan to meet your individual needs. You should have a phone number of a local shelter and a go bag that would include some of these items:

- **Important documents (birth certificates; Social Security cards; driver's license; passports; marriage, divorce, or custody papers; health insurance cards; medical records; etc.)**
- **Cash and credit cards**
- **Medications**
- **Several sets of clothing**
- **Toiletries**
- **Keys to vehicles and house**
- **Electronics (tablets, phone, computer)**

WHAT IF YOU ARE ABUSING SOMEONE?

King Jehoiakim was a ruthless king who abused the people and only cared for himself. Jehoiakim rejected and destroyed the Word of God written on Jeremiah's scroll (see Jeremiah 36:22–23). This is what the Lord said of Jehoiakim: "They shall not lament for him, saying, 'Ah, my brother!' or 'Ah, sister!' They shall not lament for him, saying, 'Ah, lord!' or 'Ah, his majesty!' With the burial of a donkey he shall be buried, dragged and dumped beyond the gates of Jerusalem" (Jeremiah 22:18–19).

Jehoiakim heard the Word of God and intentionally refused to repent of his abusive behavior, and God cursed him.

If you are abusing someone, your actions are sinful. It is time to confess your sin and repent so that you will receive God's forgiveness.

Or do you not know that the unrighteous will not inherit the kingdom of God? Do not be deceived: neither the sexually immoral, nor idolaters, nor adulterers, nor men who practice homosexuality, nor thieves, nor the greedy, nor drunkards, nor revilers, nor swindlers will inherit the kingdom of God. And such were some of you. But you were washed, you were sanctified, you were justified in the name of the Lord Jesus Christ and by the Spirit of our God. (1 Corinthians 6:9–11)

Your acts of abuse are destructive. Paul says in 1 Corinthians that such acts deserve hell without ever seeing the glorious new creation of heaven.

But those who confess and repent of these destructive sins are washed, sanctified, and justified in the name of Jesus Christ. There is forgiveness for the abuser. There is forgiveness for you.

What good news it is to hear that such abusive sinful behavior is forgiven. However, it may be difficult to turn away from abusive behavior that has become so much a part of your identity. An abuser needs professional help from a mental health counselor to find ways to live a life that does not include abuse of others.

People who have been abused will be encouraged to create boundaries that will keep them safe from unwanted activities. Boundaries will clearly communicate what behavior is appropriate and what behavior is destructive. When boundaries are communicated to you, listen to what is being said and work toward following the boundaries. Respect the person's right to their own feelings, thoughts, and activities.

HOW GOD VIEWS ABUSE

God encourages people to stay away from the path of wickedness: "Do not enter the path of the wicked, and do not walk in the way of the evil. Avoid it; do not go on it; turn away from it and pass on" (Proverbs 4:14–15).

The path of the wicked leads to the depths of extreme darkness. "For they [the wicked] cannot sleep unless they have done wrong; they are robbed of sleep unless they have made someone stumble. For they eat the bread of wickedness and drink the wine of violence" (vv. 16–17).

God takes no joy in the wicked.

The LORD tests the righteous, but His soul hates the wicked and the one who loves violence. Let Him rain coals on the wicked; fire and sulfur and a scorching wind shall be the portion of their cup. (Psalm 11:5–6)

The way of the wicked is an abomination to the LORD, but He loves him who pursues righteousness. There is severe discipline for him who forsakes the way; whoever hates reproof will die. (Proverbs 15:9–10)

The psalmist directly lays out the fate of the wicked.

If a man does not repent, God will whet His sword; He has bent and readied His bow; He has prepared for him His deadly weapons, making His arrows fiery shafts. Behold, the wicked man conceives evil and is pregnant with mischief and gives birth to lies. He makes a pit, digging it out, and falls into the hole that he has made. His mischief returns upon his own head, and on his own skull his violence descends. (Psalm 7:12–16)

And Jesus says this about the unrepentant evil person:

I tell you, I do not know where you come from. Depart from Me, all you workers of evil! In that place there will be weeping and gnashing of teeth, when you see Abraham and Isaac and Jacob and all the prophets in the kingdom of God but you yourselves cast out. (Luke 13:27–28)

Abuse is a wicked and evil thing that is not tolerated by our God.

Yet, the abuser is forgivable.

IS THE ABUSER REALLY FORGIVABLE?

How can this be? How can God forgive such evil, such wickedness? How can God forgive an abuser?

All sin is evil and wicked before God. Paul reminds us,

"None is righteous, no, not one; no one understands; no one seeks for God. All have turned aside; together they have become worthless; no one does good, not even one." "Their throat is an open grave; they use their tongues to deceive." "The venom of asps is under their lips." "Their mouth is full of curses and bitterness." "Their feet are swift to shed blood; in their paths are ruin and misery, and the way of peace they have not known." "There is no fear of God before their eyes." (Romans 3:10–18)

Sin of any kind results in condemnation. "The wages of sin is death" (Romans 6:23a). Before God, all sin deserves eternal punishment. However, as we live in His creation, we consider some sins more heinous than others because people are so deeply harmed. Abuse causes significant harm to others and should never be tolerated.

Yet, God does not want the abuser to go to hell. "As I live, declares the Lord GOD, I have no pleasure in the death of the wicked, but that the wicked turn from his way and live; turn back, turn back from your evil ways, for why will you die, O house of Israel?" (Ezekiel 33:11).

Yes, "the wages of sin is death, but the free gift of God is eternal life in Christ Jesus our Lord" (Romans 6:23).

God wants all to be saved. Paul writes that God "desires all people to be saved and to come to the knowledge of the truth" (1 Timothy 2:4).

There is therefore now no condemnation for those who are in Christ Jesus. . . . For I am sure that neither death nor life, nor angels nor rulers, nor things present nor things to come, nor powers, nor height nor depth, nor anything else in all creation, will be able to separate us from the love of God in Christ Jesus our Lord. (Romans 8:1, 38–39)

Jesus will seek after all the lost sheep and the prodigal sons who followed the path of wickedness (see Luke 15:3–7, 11–32).

Jesus did not die for the righteous but for those who need His righteousness.

For one will scarcely die for a righteous person—though perhaps for a good person one would dare even to die—but God shows His love for us in that while we were still sinners, Christ died for us. Since, therefore, we have now been justified by His blood, much more shall we be saved by Him from the wrath of God. For if while we were enemies we were reconciled to God by the death of His Son, much more, now that we are reconciled, shall we be saved by His life. (Romans 5:7–10)

Jesus shed His blood for all sinners, including abusers. The abuser is forgivable.

CONSEQUENCES

God's forgiveness is for all people no matter what the sin. A repentant sinner who believes in the forgiveness of Jesus Christ will not suffer the eternal consequence of hell. However, there are earthly consequences for sin.

The Israelites complained that there was no food and water for the community. Moses spoke to the Lord on their behalf. The Lord told Moses, "Take the staff, and assemble the congregation . . . and tell the rock before their eyes to yield its water" (Numbers 20:8). Moses went before the people and said to them, "'Hear now, you rebels: shall we bring water for you out of this rock?' And Moses lifted up his hand and struck the rock with his staff twice, and water came out abundantly, and the congregation drank, and their livestock" (vv. 10–11).

But this did not please the Lord. Moses rebuked the people, and he struck the rock with his staff instead of speaking to it. The Lord was displeased that Moses decided to put his own twist on God's command. The Lord said to Moses, "Because you did not believe in Me, to uphold Me as holy in the eyes of the people of Israel, therefore you shall not bring this assembly into the land that I have given them" (v. 12).

Moses died and was given eternal life (see Deuteronomy 34). God forgave him. However, God disciplined Moses because he did not trust Him when he provided water from the rock. Moses endured earthly consequences for his sin but not eternal consequences.

The abuser is a sinner who can repent and receive the gift of forgiveness and eternal life. Yet, the abusers need to accept the earthly consequences of their transgressions. These consequences may be imposed on them by the government, other authorities, or by the victim.

RECONCILIATION?

Should you reconcile with an abuser?

It depends.

A victim can forgive without being reconciled with the abuser. An abuser who is unwilling to confess and repent of any sin remains in his sin and will continue the abusive behavior. It is not possible to reconcile with a person who will not acknowledge her sinfulness.

However, if the abuser confesses and repents, there is hope that the relationship can be reconciled. But the relationship will never go back to a time when abuse was not an issue. The relationship will be different, and you will need to renegotiate how to live with each other. Engage the help of a third party who can mediate conversations and explore solutions for a new relationship. Safe boundaries and consequences for violating boundaries will need to be established.

It is unwise for a victim to meet with an abuser alone. It is very possible that the abuser will use this as an opportunity to continue abusive behavior. A professional third party can help both parties be accountable for their words and actions.

Jessica discovered that her disabled husband had been taken advantage of by her good friend from church. Jessica was angry but willing to forgive and participate in a mediation with the help of her pastor. While Jessica was able to forgive, it was difficult for her to trust her friend, and the relationship was never fully reconciled.

Her pastor provided this wisdom: "Instead of being on the same ship, you're on two ships now. You're sailing in the same ocean but not on the same ship. And it's not a friendship anymore, but you're still in a Christian community, but you're not on the same ship called friendship." The relationship between Jessica and her friend had changed.

Abuse changes every relationship that it touches, and it makes maintaining a relationship more difficult. Jessica said this about her relationship: "I don't want to pretend that everything is okay when it is not. Let's just go on our different ships. You take the speedboat and I'll take the canoe."

Jessica had forgiven her friend, but it was difficult for her to trust that friend again. Her friend was remorseful for what she did but not repentant. The friend continued to take advantage of Jessica's husband and seemed to have a difficult time turning from her sinful ways.

Peter asked Jesus, "'Lord, how often will my brother sin against me, and I forgive him? As many as seven times?' Jesus said to him, 'I do not say to you seven times, but seventy-seven times'" (Matthew 18:21–22).

It is loving to forgive. God showed His love for us in our forgiveness through Christ. And forgiveness has no limit. No matter how often we sin, forgiveness is ours in Jesus. Yet, we sometimes suffer earthly consequences for our sin.

As God had shown His love to her, Jessica showed love to her friend by forgiving her. But it would not have been loving for Jessica to allow her friend to continue abusing her husband. Jessica needed to set boundaries with her friend so that the abuse would not continue. They were still in the same ocean. They would see each other at church and see each other around town. But they were sailing in different ships to prevent further abuse from taking place.

HOW DOES THIS APPLY TO ME?

IF YOU FEEL THAT YOU ARE IN AN ABUSIVE RELATIONSHIP

1. Describe the abusive traits that you are experiencing.

2. Identify some specific boundaries that would be appropriate for your situation.

3. Set up an appointment to speak with a professional mental health counselor. Your pastor may be able to provide some referrals.

4. Pray for courage to address the abusive situation and for support from family and friends. Pray that the abuser would repent of his or her sinful ways and be receptive to professional help.

IF YOU ARE EXHIBITING POTENTIALLY ABUSIVE BEHAVIOR

1. Describe what you are doing to pressure someone to comply with your demands.

2. How have you threatened the other person? (E.g., "Do what I want or you will pay!")

3. Identify how you have not respected the boundaries of those you have abused.

4. Set up an appointment to speak with a professional mental health counselor. Your pastor may be able to provide some referrals.

5. Repent of your sin. Ask your pastor or a spiritually mature friend to hear your confession to God and proclaim God's forgiveness to you.

6. Write a prayer for the ability to confess your abusive behaviors. Pray that God will put people in your life who can professionally assist you and help you turn away from being abusive. Pray for the people that you have abused as they seek healing.

PRAYER TEMPLATE

(See chapter 3, "How Should I Pray?")

INTRODUCTION

REFERENCE TO GOD'S WORK

PETITION

RESULT

CONCLUSION

CHAPTER 12

WHAT IF I CAN'T FORGIVE MYSELF?

How can I forgive the sin
  Gnawing at my spirit
That my conscience deep within
  Grieves and cannot bear it?
My attempts to self-atone
  All end in disaster
When I think that I alone
  Am my lord and master.

Jesus came to rescue me
  From my self-made prison,
Set my soul and conscience free
  By His grace from heaven.
Long ago He paid the price,
  Long ago forgave me
Through His blood and sacrifice,
  Out from bondage saved me.

TED

While teaching at a Spanish-speaking pastors conference, I was asked by a professor to meet privately with a seminary student. Diego had been a good student but was recently failing. Apparently, he had become depressed. The professor had talked with Diego and knew what caused his depression, but he was unable to help Diego overcome his struggles.

Because Diego didn't know much English and I knew even less Spanish, I asked him who he would like to translate for us. He chose Juan, another student and close friend.

I asked Diego what was happening that led to his recent problems at school. He had become so depressed that he wasn't finishing assignments, and there were days when he stayed in bed and skipped class. I asked what was causing his depression.

"I can't forgive myself. And I don't qualify to study for the pastoral office."

I invited him to tell me more.

Diego told me his story. As a child before puberty, he was introduced to sexual activity. Over time, he participated in all kinds of sexual acts into his teen years. In his midteens, he became a Christian. He was so grateful to learn about Jesus that he committed his life to becoming a pastor. As a Christian, he stopped the physical sexual activity. But he was unable to give up internet pornography.

He was excited when he first started seminary, and his studies went well. But then he began to learn how abominable his sexual past had been before God. He also learned how sinful his pornography addiction was. He realized that he shouldn't be a pastor with his past and current struggles.

"So that's why I can't forgive myself."

"Do you believe that Jesus died for you and that God forgives you for Jesus' sake?"

"*Sí, pero* . . ." Yes, but . . . "I can't forgive myself."

I can't forgive myself. Over my years as a reconciler, I have heard this statement several times. Before I became a reconciler, I used the phrase myself. I went through a challenging time in my early business career when our local economy nose-dived. My two businesses and my personal investments were dependent on the real estate market, which had suffered its worst since the Great Depression. I was a young husband and father, so the guilt and shame of not being able to pay bills in the business and provide for my family led me into depression. I finally sought help from my pastor and told him the reason for my anguish. "I can't forgive myself."

What is at the root of the declaration "I can't forgive myself"?

My pastor startled me when he asked, "Is Jesus' blood not good enough for you?" I was miffed that he would question my faith, although I tried to cover up my reaction. I stalled for time.

"What do you mean?"

He helped me understand that by my self-condemnation I was rejecting the atoning work of Christ. I could say that I believed that Jesus died for me. But my declaration of not forgiving myself put my own forgiveness above God's. In essence, I attempted to be the god of my own life. If I didn't meet my own expectations, then I condemned myself and sought ways to punish myself for my failures. (Notice all the references to I, myself, and me?) In other words, I sinned against the First Commandment because I trusted in myself for justification more than God.

My pastor understood my heart issue. He was right. I confessed my sin to God of not trusting in Jesus' blood for my righteousness. I also confessed that I was not trusting in God for His provision. My depression was caused directly by shame and guilt that I assumed. I was nearsighted and blind, and I had forgotten how much I had been cleansed from my own sins (see 2 Peter 1:9).

Confessing my sin before God and hearing the proclamation by my pastor of the good news of Christ's forgiveness led to a healing of spirit and mind. My depression left me, although my financial condition had not changed. But my attitude made a complete turnaround (a description of repentance). I no longer looked to myself first for my financial situation—I trusted God for His provision. I no longer sought to condemn and punish myself because my shame and guilt had been paid for by the precious blood of the Lamb. I believed in the forgiveness of sins for me.

As I met with Diego, I recognized that he was struggling with a similar idol.

"Diego, do you know about Jonah in the Old Testament?"

"Sí."

"Why did Jonah try to run away from God when he was called to preach repentance to the Ninevites?"

Diego recounted Jonah's story. Jonah did not want the Ninevites to repent because he knew that God was merciful and gracious and would forgive them. Jonah wanted the Ninevites to be condemned, not forgiven.

"Diego, you remind me of Jonah."

"Jonah? How?"

"You have declared yourself a Ninevite, someone who does not deserve to be forgiven by God. By declaring you can't forgive yourself, you are denying yourself of the freedom of God's forgiveness. You are making your own forgiveness more important than God's. Like Jonah, you are making yourself out to be God. You have judged yourself unworthy of God's grace and mercy. While that is true, His forgiveness is a gift that you cannot earn. You are not trusting God in His justification for you. This is a sin against the First Commandment. Your trust is in your self-condemnation and not in God's love and forgiveness for you."

Diego was convicted. "I never thought of it that way. You're right. I'm trying to be 'god' and not trusting what God has done for me through Jesus."

"You also remind me of the apostle Paul."

"Paul? How?"

I asked Diego to read Romans 7:15–24 aloud from his Bible. Even though he read in Spanish, I could see that some verses connected with him:

> For I know that nothing good dwells in me, that is, in my flesh. For I have the desire to do what is right, but not the ability to carry it out. For I do not do the good I want, but the evil I do not want is what I keep on doing. Now if I do what I do not want, it is no longer I who do it, but sin that dwells within me. . . . Wretched man that I am! Who will deliver me from this body of death? (vv. 18–20, 24)

As he read the words "Wretched man that I am," he pounded his Bible with his finger.

"That's me! That's me! I am like Paul. I am that wretched man!"

"Now, read the first part of verse 25."

He read, "Thanks be to God through Jesus Christ our Lord!"

"Diego, I want you now to read Romans 8:1. But when it says, 'for those,' I want you to insert your own name, 'for Diego.'"

In his native language, he read, "There is therefore now no condemnation for [Diego] who [is] in Christ Jesus."

Immediately, Diego wept hard for minutes. The Gospel was doing its work to cleanse his sinful heart.

"Diego, read it again."

Once again, Diego read those words with his name inserted in the verse. He responded with more tears.

"Diego, can you read it a third time?"

This time, he was too spent to cry.

"Diego, do you believe that Jesus has died for all of your sins, including your past and current?"

"¡Sí! ¡Yo creo!" Yes! I believe!

"What about forgiving yourself?"

"It is not necessary! I have been forgiven by Christ!"

In confession of sin and faith in the Gospel, Diego gave up his attempt to be the god of his own life. He confessed his sin of breaking the First Commandment, and he clung to the good news that he was forgiven in Christ. He no longer forgot that he had been cleansed from his past sins. Now he remembered who he was—a forgiven child of God.

I talked with Diego about what happened to him years before. Clearly, he was a victim of childhood sexual abuse. What happened early in his life was not his fault. But he was responsible for his decisions later in life. Jesus died both for those sins committed against him as well as his own sins. Forgiveness through Jesus heals from both shame and guilt.

AM I IN THE PLACE OF GOD?

Not forgiving oneself is an attempt to play god. It minimizes Christ's atoning work on the cross and elevates one's personal forgiveness above God's. Those who say, "I believe that Jesus died for me, but I can't forgive myself," are trusting themselves for justification instead of God. Their confession of faith is in themselves more than God. They do not fear, love, and trust in God above all things, but rather fear, love, and trust themselves and their own works—good or bad—more than God.

To focus on forgiving oneself is to put yourself in God's place.

As I told Diego, not forgiving yourself is a similar sin to what Jonah did. You declare yourself a Ninevite, one whom you decide must be condemned rather than forgiven. You withhold God's forgiveness or convince yourself that your own forgiveness is more important than God's. You punish yourself with guilt. You take on shame that Jesus paid for on the cross. Although it may be unintentional, your attitude of making your own forgiveness primary in your life is a way to reject what Christ did for you. You put yourself in the place of God.

God knows our sinful nature is to act as if we are the gods of our own lives. Common phrases in our society reflect this attitude:

- I'm the god of my own destiny.

- If I don't look out for number one, who will?

- I'm the ruler of my own castle.

- I did it my way.

Each of these phrases illustrates how we by nature put ourselves in the place of God. We usually don't recognize the sin against the First Commandment, "You shall have no other gods before Me" (Exodus 20:3). But it's the most basic form of idolatry—making myself out to be God.

God knows that about us. He is more aware than we are of our nature to be self-absorbed, to think more highly of ourselves than we ought, to put ourselves in His place. Pride is a reoccurring sin for people.

Nevertheless, God condemned and punished His Son for our prideful idolatry. Jesus paid the price for our breaking the First Commandment, and God declares us righteous. "For our sake He made Him to be sin who knew no sin, so that in Him we might become the righteousness of God" (2 Corinthians 5:21).

OVERCOMING "I CAN'T FORGIVE MYSELF"

How do I get out of the loop of "I can't forgive myself"?

Repent and believe the Gospel. Confess your sin of elevating your personal forgiveness over God's. Confess your pride and lay down your idol of self-made god. Then believe the good news: "There is therefore now no condemnation for those who are in Christ Jesus" (Romans 8:1).

Replace trust in your own justification with trust in God's redeeming work for you:

[Jesus said,] "For God so loved the world, that He gave His only Son, that whoever believes in Him should not perish but have eternal life. For God did not send His Son into the world to condemn the world, but in order that the world might be saved through Him. Whoever believes in Him is not condemned, but whoever does not believe is condemned already, because he has not believed in the name of the only Son of God." (John 3:16–18)

When someone has experienced years of sexual abuse and then initiated his own actions, he has a lot of baggage to unload. I asked Diego if he wanted to confess out loud those sins which troubled him most and hear God's forgiveness proclaimed to him. He took the opportunity.

We went into the sanctuary and stood before the altar. I told the translator he was not needed, since I didn't need to know what Diego confessed and God knew Spanish. I read in English from a pamphlet of Bible passages on God's forgiveness, and Diego followed along with a Spanish version of the pamphlet.[9] Diego decided that he wanted his friend to stay, but I asked the translator not to translate what was confessed.

Diego prayed out loud his confession before God. He would say a few sentences, cry, and be silent. This was repeated multiple times. Finally, he looked at me. He was ready for good news.

I read several Bible passages that proclaimed God's forgiveness to him. I inserted his name into the verses. Diego followed along in his Spanish pamphlet. When we were done, we both prayed.

I was flying home the next day, and I wanted to leave Diego with some additional instruction for the future. Whenever a child is introduced to sexual activity, those first incidents often replay in the victim's mind. Diego had described such incidents to me, saying that they played like a movie over and over again in his mind when he tried to shake the memories. He was traumatized by his past, and these memories tortured him. He also wondered what to do when he was tempted to use pornography again.

God's Word is powerful and effective. I coached him to use Scripture in those spiritual battles. When those memories haunted him or he was tempted to use pornography, he could take out the pamphlet with the Scripture verses and read them aloud, inserting his own name. I suggested he save Romans 8:1 for the last verse each time. Diego agreed that he would do that.

I have not seen Diego again. But several years later, at an event where I was speaking, I met a woman who served as a missionary in Diego's country. And she gave me a message from him:

"Thank you, Ted. My depression was gone that night. I talked with my professors, and they allowed me to make up my missed work. I graduated and was ordained. Today I am a pastor who believes in the power of forgiveness."

---

9   This pamphlet, *Proclaiming God's Forgiveness*, is available in English and Spanish from Ambassadors of Reconciliation at AoRHope.org.

FREEDOM FROM THE PRISON
OF UNFORGIVENESS

Hank and his best friend were drafted into the Army and sent to Vietnam. Hank promised his friend's wife that he would watch over her husband and bring him home safe. It was a promise he could not keep. His friend was fatally wounded and died in his arms.

Hank never got over his guilt for not keeping his promise. When he returned home, he struggled to keep a legitimate job. He often turned to crime and was imprisoned multiple times over the years.

Brad met Hank through prison ministry. As he talked with Hank about life's struggles, he heard Hank declare, "I can't forgive myself." Hank had repeatedly condemned himself year after year as he sought relief from his torment. At first Brad tried comforting Hank that it wasn't his fault that his friend died in war. But it became clear that such reasoning provided no relief. Hank lamented that he could not keep his word to his friend's wife, and he regretted the many crimes he had committed since.

Brad realized that what Hank needed was assurance of God's forgiveness. He shared a simple devotion with Hank on not forgiving himself.[10] The devotion focused on how Jesus paid the price for all our sins, including guilt. Hank asked some questions, and Brad kept pointing back to what Jesus had done for Hank. He also encouraged Hank to read aloud several Bible verses that proclaimed God's forgiveness to him, inserting his own name.

After decades of self-disgust, Hank was healed by the powerful Word of God. He was freed from the prison of unforgiveness to which he had condemned himself. He learned to trust in the forgiveness of the cross and empty tomb. Hank was a redeemed child of God.

Brad gave him the booklet from which the devotion came, and Hank formed a Bible study group in prison to share the devotions with other inmates. They used one devotion a week for their study. Hank intentionally shared the love and forgiveness of Christ in each lesson.

---

10 The devotion told the story of Diego. It's one of forty-two devotions in the booklet *Forgiven to Forgive*, available from Ambassadors of Reconciliation at AoRHope.org.

HOW DOES THIS APPLY TO ME?

1. For what offenses have I struggled to forgive myself?

2. What is the ultimate root of my withholding forgiveness from myself?

3. By declaring "I can't forgive myself," whom am I trusting most for my justification?

4. Reviewing this chapter, what were the main components that led different people to learn how to overcome the attitude of "I can't forgive myself"?

5. If your unforgiveness of yourself is long-term and deep-seated, identify a mature Christian you can ask to read this chapter and help you work through your challenges.

6. Write a prayer of confession of sin and confession of faith in Jesus' forgiveness for you. Include a petition for outside help and direction when needed. If this chapter has helped you overcome your unforgiveness toward yourself, incorporate a petition of thanksgiving to God for His mercy and grace shown through Jesus Christ.

PRAYER TEMPLATE

(See chapter 3, "How Should I Pray?")

INTRODUCTION

REFERENCE TO GOD'S WORK

PETITION

RESULT

CONCLUSION

CHAPTER 13

WHAT IF OTHERS WON'T FORGIVE ME?

If I sin against another
  And transgress God's clear command,
I must beg them for forgiveness,
  Never making a demand,
But in faith and prayerful patience
  Hope the other's heart and mind
Will respond with love and mercy
  And forgiveness for me find.

But if they will not forgive me
  And respond with hardened heart,
If they shame me or reject me,
  What should be my proper part?
Lord, if I am bid defiance
  When forgiveness was my goal,
Help me place my full reliance
  On the One who makes me whole.

Ben and Sophia were newly married Christians. Ben was completing his undergraduate degree with the plan of attending the seminary and becoming a pastor. Sophia was teaching at an elementary school and looking forward to moving to the seminary with Ben within a year. They spent their nights together watching TV, with Ben studying and Sophia grading papers.

Sophia began talking with her co-teacher Jack about the challenges of being married to Ben and her feelings. Over time Sophia and Jack began to hang out together. On one occasion they ended up having sex with each other. Sophia regretted it, knew it was wrong, and quickly told Ben about it. She asked him to forgive her.

Ben reacted with anger, bitterness, and rage. How could his wife do such a thing? How could Jack take advantage of the situation? Why did God allow this to happen? After all, he was preparing to be a pastor.

Ben and Sophia sought out a pastoral counselor and attended many sessions. But Ben could not forgive her. Sophia promised it would not happen again. She pleaded with Ben for forgiveness. But after every counseling session, Sophia was disappointed that Ben could not forgive her.

What should Sophia do?

TRUST IN CHRIST'S FORGIVENESS

When you have asked for forgiveness but the person you hurt does not forgive, what can you do?

First and foremost, place your trust in Jesus for your forgiveness. Then seek the Spirit's help in responding to others. Remember how much He has forgiven you so you may be empowered to live as His forgiven child.

Regardless of your sin, God's promise of forgiveness is yours in Jesus Christ. "If we confess our sins, He is faithful and just to forgive us our sins and to cleanse us from all unrighteousness" (1 John 1:9).

Your righteousness is not found in your confession or good deeds or acceptance of others—it is found only in the sacrifice of God's Son for you. "For our sake He made Him to be sin who knew no sin, so that in Him we might become the righteousness of God" (2 Corinthians 5:21).

Your peace is not found in the forgiveness of people—it is found only in the atoning work of Christ. "Therefore, since we have been justified by faith, we have peace with God through our Lord Jesus Christ" (Romans 5:1).

Your hope is not found in the forgiveness of people—it is found only in the One who died and rose again for you. "May the God of hope fill you with all joy and peace in believing, so that by the power of the Holy Spirit you may abound in hope" (Romans 15:13).

Your salvation is not found in the saving grace of others—it is found only in the saving name of Jesus. "And there is salvation in no one else, for there is no other name under heaven given among men by which we must be saved" (Acts 4:12).

Freedom from guilt and condemnation is not found in the mercy of others—it is found only for those who are in Christ Jesus. "There is therefore now no condemnation for those who are in Christ Jesus" (Romans 8:1).

Sinners often struggle to forgive or refuse to forgive. Forgiveness from God is instantaneous and constant. But with people, the process of forgiveness takes time.

Do not expect nonbelievers to forgive as God forgives. Non-Christians are not capable of forgiving as God has forgiven because they have not yet received God's gift (see chapter 1, "What Is Unforgiveness?").

For Christians, they still struggle with their sinful nature. Many require time and patience to forgive, or they may not forgive at all. You should anticipate that some people hurt by your offense will not forgive for some time. Expect that others may not forgive at all.

Therefore, it is critical that even as you seek forgiveness from others, you fix your eyes on Jesus, trusting in His forgiveness and waiting on Him to move others to forgive you. While waiting for forgiveness from others, your focus on Jesus will strengthen you to avoid the pitfall of being unforgiving toward those who do not forgive you.

As sinners, we are all beggars. We can ask for mercy, but we have no right to demand it. Even a perfect confession does not deserve forgiveness. Forgiveness is a gift that is never deserved, and it cannot be earned or bought.

Should we demand forgiveness, we make ourselves to be a god, commanding others to give us what we want. We fall into a new sin, replacing the true God with a false one (ourselves) and putting ourselves over others, even those we have sinned against.

At first, we may not realize we are demanding forgiveness. Such an expectation begins in the heart. It begins with an attitude of entitlement. The thoughts of the heart then morph into words and actions. Our demand for forgiveness becomes a new sin against God and others. Our demand for forgiveness develops into an idol.

THE DEVELOPMENT OF AN IDOL

Sin breaks relationships. Wanting to be forgiven by others is a good desire because it restores relationships. But if we turn that desire into a demand, we begin to develop an idol.

An idol is anyone or anything we fear, love, or trust more than God. Not all fears, loves, or trusts are sinful. But they become sinful when we make them more important than God.

The Bible study *Conflict Resolution vs. Reconciliation* from Ambassadors of Reconciliation discusses how we develop an idol. Idols begin in our heart. We often develop idols of the heart without even realizing what is happening.

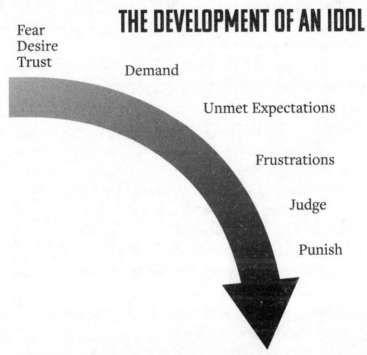

THE DEVELOPMENT OF AN IDOL

Fear
Desire
Trust

Demand

Unmet Expectations

Frustrations

Judge

Punish

End Result: Destruction or Death

An idol can begin with a godly fear, desire, or trust. But once we demand what we want, it begins to develop into a full-blown idol. We slide down a slippery slope, moving from desire to demand. When expectations are not met, our frustration increases, and we judge those who will not give us what we want. If they continue to refuse us, we punish them.

The devil promises good things—restored relationships, happiness, satisfaction, safety, success, fame, or special knowledge—if we turn our devotion away from God and devote ourselves to the idols of our hearts. But this is a great deception!

If left unchecked, idolatry results in the destruction of the idol and/or the person worshiping it. In other words, idolatry leads to death. Scripture describes this progression: "But each person is tempted when he is lured and enticed by his own desire. Then desire when it has conceived gives birth to sin, and sin when it is fully grown brings forth death" (James 1:14–15).

Consider a man who has committed adultery. He confesses to his wife and says, "Now, as a Christian, you have to forgive me." His desire for forgiveness becomes a demand. His expectations are not met when she refuses to forgive, and he becomes frustrated. He lashes out at her in anger, judging her as being unchristian for not forgiving him. Then he punishes her by telling their friends and family that she is a hypocrite for not forgiving him. What do you think the result will be if he does not repent of his attitude and actions? She may leave him and file for divorce. The very thing he desired is destroyed by his own slide into idolatry. His desire for a restored marriage ends in destruction of the marriage.

Not everyone is guilty of adultery and demanding forgiveness. But our own idols can lead to similar results.

Demanding forgiveness from another is an example of a desire turned idolatrous. The desire to be forgiven by others is godly. But it turns idolatrous when we believe that someone owes us forgiveness. When our expectations are not met (the person doesn't forgive), we become frustrated (angry!) and judge the unforgiving person. We seek ways to punish her—angry words, gossip, running away, and the like.

If we don't stop this developing idol, we risk death or destruction of the idol or ourselves. Our unforgiveness of the unforgiving person adds fuel to the fire. Our relationship sours even more. Our own hearts suffer from the bitterness that separates us from others. Eventually, our unforgiveness can separate us from God.

Moreover, idols demand sacrifice. We give up something good to satisfy the idols of our heart. Consider the unfaithful husband who demands forgiveness from his wife. What will he sacrifice to serve his idol? Integrity, relationships with family and friends, his own Christian witness, and eventually the hope for a restored marriage. What do we sacrifice when we are unforgiving toward those who won't forgive us?

AN UNGRATEFUL DEBTOR

There was a certain king who loaned a great sum to one of his servants. The servant owed so much money that he would never be able to pay it back in a lifetime. Because the servant could not pay the debt when due, the king planned to sell the servant and his family into slavery until the debt could be paid. The servant fell to his knees and begged the king to be patient. He promised to pay back what was owed and begged for more time. Surprisingly, the king had mercy and compassion on the servant. He knew that the servant could never pay back the debt in ten lifetimes. He forgave the debt and let the man go free.

Amazing! Unexpected! What good news! The king had every right to sell the servant and his family and imprison them, but he chose not to. He chose to forgive.

Jesus told this parable (Matthew 18:21–35) to illustrate the relationship between God (the king) and us (servants with debts too great to pay). We deserve eternal death in hell for our sins. We could prostrate ourselves and plead with God to give us more time so that we can try to pay off our debt. But no matter how hard we try, good deeds will never be able to pay off the debt of our sins. God knew that. So He gave His only Son, the King of kings and Lord of lords, to pay our debt in full. God has had mercy and compassion on us through Jesus Christ, who has forgiven our sins and set us free from condemnation in hell.

But then something bizarre takes place in the parable. The forgiven servant left the presence of the king and sought a fellow servant who owed him money—a tiny amount compared to what he had owed the king. He attacked his fellow servant, putting his hands around his neck and choking him, demanding, "Pay what you owe" (see Matthew 18:28).

The fellow servant was unable to pay the debt. He fell face down and begged for more time to repay the debt. Although this debt was miniscule in comparison to his own enormous debt to the king, the forgiven servant was unwilling to show any mercy or compassion to his fellow servant. He refused to give more time, let alone forgive the debt. He had his fellow servant thrown into prison until the debt could be repaid.

How horrendous! The king graciously forgave the huge debt of the servant and let him go free. But when the forgiven servant had the opportunity to do the same thing for a fellow servant, he refused to show any compassion. He refused to grant the same mercy that was given him.

The unforgiving servant was selfish, callous, and heartless. His reaction to his fellow servant was a stark contradiction to the king's response to him. It is astonishing that someone who had been forgiven so much was not willing to show the same mercy and compassion to someone indebted to him. His actions proved he was ungrateful for what he had received.

The ungrateful servant had an insufficient understanding and appreciation of forgiveness. He was willing to receive forgiveness for his huge debt but not willing to grant forgiveness for his neighbor's tiny debt. His eyes were fixed on the debt owed him rather than the love shown him by the king. He lost the opportunity to show similar love to his neighbor. His focus was on the money owed him. His focus become his idol.

Scripture teaches us where to focus:

> Let us run with endurance the race that is set before us, looking to Jesus, the founder and perfecter of our faith, who for the joy that was set before Him endured the cross, despising the shame, and is seated at the right hand of the throne of God. (Hebrews 12:1–2)

When we fixate on the debt of sin rather than on Jesus, we lose sight of God's love. We fail to appreciate the depth of God's forgiveness. We miss the joy of God's incredible gift. We forfeit the peace that passes understanding. And we fail to share that same love with our neighbor.

Fix your eyes on Jesus, and the love of God will fill your heart with a peace that surpasses all understanding (see Philippians 4:7). Your action to forgive those who don't forgive you is a manifestation of your gratitude for the King's mercy and love shown to you. However, your unforgiveness toward someone who doesn't forgive you demonstrates ungratefulness for the forgiveness shown you in Christ.

WHERE TO FIX YOUR EYES

Peter quickly learned the consequences of failing to fix his eyes on Jesus when he stepped out of the boat and walked to Jesus on the water. While Peter kept his eyes on Jesus, he walked on water. But as soon as Peter got distracted by the storm swirling around him, he became afraid and began to sink.

"Lord, save me," Peter cried out as he swiftly slipped away (Matthew 14:30). Jesus immediately reached out His hand, taking hold of Peter and rescuing the doubting and foolish disciple from the waters of death.

Peter initially doubted, along with his fellow disciples, that it was Jesus walking on the water. Shortly after, Peter doubted Jesus again when he feared the waves. Each time Peter lost sight of Jesus, Jesus reached out to save him.

Remember when Peter turned his back on Jesus just before His crucifixion? He outright denied he even knew Jesus: "I do not know the man" (Matthew 26:72). He even began to invoke a curse on himself and swear, "I do not know the man" (v. 74). This was the same Peter who, just hours earlier, had declared, "Even if I must die with You, I will not deny You!" (v. 35)!

Peter did not always have his eyes fixed on the Lord. He fixed his eyes on himself and his fears. He fixed his eyes on the storm. He fixed his eyes on the consequences of being associated with Jesus. Nevertheless, Jesus reached out to save Peter over and over again. Each time Peter benefited from the love of Christ. Empowered repeatedly by Jesus' love, Peter shared that love with others. Peter said, "Like newborn infants, long for the pure spiritual milk, that by it you may grow up into salvation—if indeed you have tasted that the Lord is good" (1 Peter 2:2–3). Peter's trust in the Lord often faltered because he became distracted. But when he stopped engaging in sin, which distracts, and started looking to Jesus for salvation, his heart was filled with the peace that surpasses all understanding.

The King makes forgiveness possible. We would not even be having this discussion if the king had simply thrown the unforgiving servant and his family into prison. But the King is merciful and compassionate. He sacrificed His Son, Jesus, so He could forgive the debt of sin. What the King does sets the stage for what all servants of the King may do for one another.

It seems so easy. Yet, for the unforgiving servant Ben, it was not easy. The emotions and feelings whirling inside him made it difficult to forgive his wife. The anxiety he felt over whether it might happen again. The shame he felt as someone studying to be a pastor. The fear of others finding out. The anger, the sadness, the betrayal, the fear, the confusion, the grief, the contempt, the hatred . . . All these emotions were eating him up from the inside out, and it was difficult for him to forgive.

He could not forgive because he was trusting in his own ability to tackle the mountain of emotion that was twisting his world inside out. He could not forgive because his trust was not first and foremost in God. Ben struggled with his own idols. Yet God had forgiven Ben's debt of sin many times over.

Ben had struggled with porn and having sexual conversations over the internet when he was in high school. Sexual pleasure outside of God's design for sex had become an idol for Ben. He knew this had the potential to keep him out of the ministry. However, Ben broke from the development of his idol. He confessed his sin to his pastor and was honest with seminary admissions personnel about his sinful struggles. To his surprise, the sin was forgiven. Repentance frees us from our false gods and restores our relationship to God.

Ben benefited from the love of God, but he struggled to share that love by forgiving Sophia.

How do you think Sophia responded when Ben was unable to forgive her?

HOW NOT TO REACT TO AN UNFORGIVING SERVANT

Sophia's desire for her husband's forgiveness turned into a demand and became an idol.

It began when Sophia expected her husband to forgive her. Her offense was serious, but she had confessed. God forgave her. Why shouldn't her husband?

Sophia tried pressuring Ben to forgive her. She attempted shaming him: "If you don't forgive me, God will not forgive you." She took a vocational approach: "How can you be a pastor if you don't forgive me?"

The expectation in her heart had become a demand.

Pressuring someone to forgive you will only drive him deeper into his emotional spiral. He will feel like his head is being squeezed in a vise. When the pressure becomes overwhelming, he will likely respond in sinful ways to relieve it.

When she didn't get what she wanted, Sophia judged her husband and decided to punish him. She began to gossip and slander Ben's reputation when she talked with her family and friends. She painted him as a hypocritical Goody Two-shoes. Do you think that helped her or her husband? Now who was struggling with unforgiveness?

Her desire turned into a demand, and she began sliding down the slippery slope of her own idolatry. She was making herself a god. Instead of trusting God and waiting on Him, she took matters into her own hands.

Sinning against the person who refuses to forgive you will fail. You simply give them more kindling for the fire they already have burning against you. But you also end up acting like an ungrateful servant, forgetting how much you've been forgiven by Christ.

Although her attempts to force Ben to forgive her were failing, Sophia continued down her slippery slope. She considered abandoning her husband. She threatened to divorce. She moved in with her parents for a month. She refused to talk to him until he forgave her. Unless she escaped from her idolatry, the relationship she wanted to restore would be permanently destroyed. If left unchecked, idolatry results in destruction or death. Not only would the relationship be ruined but both she and Ben would continue to be in spiritual danger.

Sophia was willing to sacrifice much to her idol of demanding forgiveness. In the end, she was willing to sacrifice the very relationship she wanted to restore! That's the irony of idolatry. It promises happiness, fulfillment, and security. But this is Satan's lie. If we continue to bow to our idol, we receive just the opposite.

If Sophia withdrew and abandoned Ben, he would be isolated from the hope of Christ that she could speak into his life. His friends might encourage him to remain unforgiving and do ungodly things that they think would help him. But sinful responses would only add to his suffering.

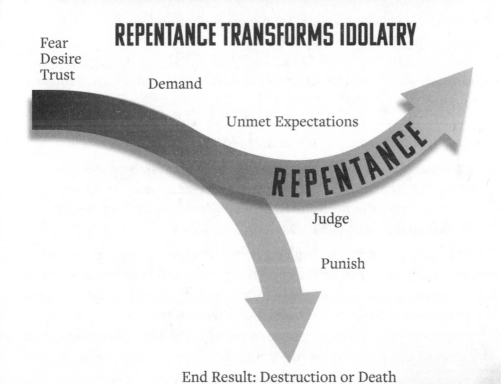

BREAKING IDOLS THROUGH REPENTANCE

REPENTANCE TRANSFORMS IDOLATRY

Fear
Desire
Trust

Demand

Unmet Expectations

REPENTANCE

Judge

Punish

End Result: Destruction or Death

God calls us to repent of our sin, including the idols of our hearts. Through repentance, we break the development of the idol. We exchange our worship of our false gods for the worship of the true God. Repentance transforms idolatry.

The way to flee from our idols and turn toward God is this: Repent! Confess your sins to God and believe in His forgiveness for you! Wait on Him. He knows what you need and what you want. He wants you to fear, love, and trust in Him most of all, and He will provide you what you need most.

Repentance breaks the slide into idolatry and leads us to healing.

HOW TO RESPOND TO AN UNFORGIVING SERVANT

Sophia was blessed to have godly people speak into her life and give her biblical guidance on the best approaches to encourage Ben to forgive her. These people showed grace to the one who had forgotten how much she had been forgiven (see 2 Peter 1:9).

Sophia was encouraged to be patient with Ben and allow him the space he needed to work through the emotions of the situation. This may be one of the most difficult things to do. It may seem there is no end in sight, and it may seem as if nothing is happening. But do you really know if or how the Holy Spirit is working in someone's heart?

Consider how long Noah floated in the ark. Recall how long the people of Israel were in slavery and how long they wandered in the wilderness. Remember how long Abraham waited for Isaac to be born. Consider how long it took God to send the Messiah who was promised to Adam and fulfilled in Jesus.

You might feel like crying out to the Lord with the psalmist:

How long, O Lord? Will You forget me forever? How long will You hide Your face from me? How long must I take counsel in my soul and have sorrow in my heart all the day? How long shall my enemy be exalted over me? (13:1–2)

Being patient with an unforgiving person does not guarantee she will forgive you. But it does provide the opportunity for her to forgive you. Moreover, it provides an opportunity for you to remember how forgiven you are in Christ and to forgive the person who struggles to forgive you!

In some cases, forgiveness may come quickly. Remember the woman at the well who promptly went into town and told everyone, "Come, see a man who told me all that I ever did. Can this be the Christ?" (John 4:29). She experienced Christ's forgiveness in her first conversation with Him.

Recall the criminal hanging next to Jesus on the cross who said, "Jesus, remember me when You come into Your kingdom." Jesus replied, "Truly, I say to you, today you will be with Me in paradise" (Luke 23:42–43). The thief experienced forgiveness from Jesus just before he died.

God forgives immediately. But people, even Christians, often need time.

Sophia had a choice: be bitter, demanding, punishing, and unforgiving toward Ben, or be patient, loving, and forgiving toward him. Forgiving an unforgiving servant is not easy. Such a person does not deserve it, and he does not appear to benefit from God's gift of forgiveness. But forgiveness is the lifestyle of a Christian.

Sophia needed to forgive Ben so that she would not end up bitter and unforgiving toward him. Granting forgiveness is not dependent on repentance. God promised to send a Savior before anyone repented of sin (Genesis 3:15). Jesus came into this sinful world to fulfill that promise, offering us forgiveness through His sacrifice. But receiving that forgiveness depends on repentance and faith. Ben is a child of God, and the gift of forgiveness is his through Jesus Christ. But if he does not repent of being an unforgiving servant, he will forfeit the peace that comes from the forgiveness of sins (see Jonah 2:8).

Sophia confessed her own unforgiveness and repented of her idolatrous sin. She broke free from the idolatry of demanding forgiveness. She was forgiven in the name of Jesus Christ. God was patient with her. He promises not to use that sin against her. He will not use that sin to kick her out of His kingdom. He will not use that sin to punish her with the eternal damnation of hell. She stands before God and Ben as forgiven in the Lord. She need not fear eternal consequences for her sin.

But she still needed to bear the earthly consequences of her sinful behavior. Ben lost his trust in her. To rebuild that trust, Sophia needed to consistently live out her faith. She needed to be transparent with Ben, to be honest about her relationships, finances, emotions, struggles, and dreams. She could not stretch the truth or allow Ben to believe things that were not true. When Sophia repented and lived out her faith, it produced fruit. She was honest with Ben, which gave him opportunity to trust her again.

Sophia wanted to reflect the patience shown her by God. She did not abandon Ben. She returned and remained with him every day, loving him and forgiving him for his unforgiveness. She prayed for her husband and with him. She gave him the space he needed to work through the emotions that trapped him as an unforgiving servant. She commended him to the Lord's care, trusting in the Holy Spirit to work on Ben's heart.

By God's grace, Ben was able to forgive his wife within two years. A Christian friend encouraged him and spoke God's Word into his life. Ben remembered the great debt of his own sin that God had forgiven. He no longer wanted to be an unforgiving servant, imprisoning his wife for sins that God had already forgiven. The day Ben forgave his wife was a day of peace that surpassed all human understanding for both of them. Not only was Ben reconciled with God, but he was now also reconciled with his wife. He thanked God that she did not abandon him but was patient with him and desired a reconciled relationship through the forgiveness of Jesus Christ. Her patient forgiveness helped him heal. In return, her prayers to be forgiven by him were answered.

If Sophia had clung to her idolatry, she likely would have lost what she desired most. By repenting of her own sin and forgiving Ben, she demonstrated her trust in God.

When you wait on the Lord to change the heart of an unforgiving person, what joy when one day they are able to forgive!

But what happens if the person who refuses to forgive us has rejected the gift of forgiveness from the King and remains imprisoned in their unforgiveness?

DEMANDING FORGIVENESS

TED

I know a man who betrayed and deeply hurt three of his closest friends. His sin was also a criminal offense that landed him in prison.

He confessed his sin directly to each of the three friends before he was imprisoned. One of the three forgave him. But two refused.

I visited Ernie a few times in prison. During one of my visits, he complained to me about the two friends who had not forgiven him. Then he said, "They better not pray the Lord's Prayer because they will be praying judgment on themselves." He was referring to the petition "forgive us our trespasses as we forgive those who trespass against us."

His arrogance shocked me. I had seen Ernie's contrition, and we had talked about his sin and confession a few times. He knew that he deserved to be in prison. He acknowledged that he did not deserve God's forgiveness, and he was grateful that God and the one friend had forgiven him. Others who knew him also assured him of their support. Nevertheless, he judged the two who had not forgiven him.

I chastised him. I reminded him that he had no right to demand forgiveness from those he wounded. His expectations had crossed the line. His good desire for forgiveness developed into an idol.

Was there an element of truth in his assessment of his friends? Certainly. If they remained unforgiving toward Ernie, they were in danger of harming their own spiritual health. However, Ernie was in no place to judge these fellow Christians after what he had done to them. His demand for their forgiveness (in his heart and in his private conversation to me—he did not communicate this to his former friends) was idolatrous. His callous attitude toward them ignored his own sin and the horrendous pain it caused them.

Instead, I urged him to pray. First, he should confess to God his sin of demanding forgiveness when his offense was so awful. Next, pray for his friends that God would release them from bitterness and they may not be harmed further. Finally, ask God for patience to wait and hope in Him.

I didn't know it at the time, but Ernie resented my rebuke. He didn't tell me because he looked forward to my visits, and he didn't want me to stop visiting him in prison.

A year later, Ernie confessed his sin of judgment toward his friends and his resentment toward me. He told me that he thought of my admonition every night before he went to sleep. God used that exhortation to work on his heart. Ernie had commended his friends to God for His care and love, and he no longer judged them for their unforgiveness. Of course, I assured him of God's forgiveness and mine.

Ernie transformed his pattern of idolatry through repentance. Once again, he was healed through God's forgiveness for him. The peace that passes all understanding comforted his contrite heart.

Some time later, one of those friends contacted me. He wanted to visit Ernie in prison to grant him forgiveness, but he was fearful of going alone. He knew that I had been visiting Ernie, and he asked if I would accompany him.

I was privileged to witness the miracle of reconciliation as this injured friend forgave the man who had betrayed and hurt him so deeply. Although God blessed Ernie with this friend's forgiveness, that friend was blessed by God to do what we can never do on our own—forgive as the Lord has forgiven us.

I will never forget the tears shed that day as a broken relationship was healed through Christ's love and forgiveness. These brothers in Christ experienced God's love and grace in ways neither will ever forget. Nor will I.

Scripture counsels those whose desires turn into demands:

Delight yourself in the LORD, and He will give you the desires of your heart. Commit your way to the LORD; trust in Him, and He will act. He will bring forth your righteousness as the light, and your justice as the noonday. Be still before the LORD and wait patiently for Him; fret not yourself over the one who prospers in his way, over the man who carries out evil devices! Refrain from anger, and forsake wrath! Fret not yourself; it tends only to evil. (Psalm 37:4–8)

As far as I know, the third friend did not forgive Ernie. Ernie was released from prison and moved away, and I have lost contact with him.

But Ernie's peace was not dependent on forgiveness from this last friend. His peace, his comfort, his joy, his delight were all realized as he fixed his eyes on Jesus, the author and perfecter of his faith (Hebrews 12:1–3).

HOW DOES THIS APPLY TO ME?

1. What offense did you commit that caused someone to not forgive you?

2. How do you know that God has forgiven you for that offense? Answer that question after reviewing 2 Corinthians 5:21; 1 John 1:9; 1 Peter 2:24; and Romans 8:1.

3. Why was your offense so hurtful to the other person? What earthly consequences are you bearing for your sin?

4. How have you demanded in your heart to be forgiven by the person you sinned against?

5. How have you expressed your expectation that this person needs to forgive you?

6. Review the diagram "The Development of an Idol" from this chapter. Identify your thoughts, words, or actions that correlate to the different parts of the development. What will happen if you do not stop the development of this idol? What is the way to stop your idolatry and fix your eyes on Jesus?

7. Write a prayer. First, confess before God that you are demanding forgiveness from the one you have offended. Next, pray that God protects that person from their own bitterness and that they be healed from the harm you caused. Third, ask God to give you patience as you place your hope in Him. Commend yourself, the other person, and everyone else affected to God's care. Finally, thank Jesus for the forgiveness you have in Him.

PRAYER TEMPLATE

(See chapter 3, "How Should I Pray?")

INTRODUCTION

REFERENCE TO GOD'S WORK

PETITION

RESULT

CONCLUSION

CHAPTER 14

WHY NOT JUST FORGIVE AND FORGET?

The deed is done, words have been said
That linger in the heart and head,
And all attempts meet with regret
To just forgive and then forget.

The hardest part is to forget
Those haunting memories, and yet
Our Lord Himself provides a way
To keep our troubled thoughts at bay.

God's memory is unlike ours;
He conquered sin with all its powers
Through Jesus' blood, which sets us free.
Forgiven, we at peace may be.

You have probably heard the adage "forgive and forget." It's a catchy saying that is often given as a piece of wisdom to those who are struggling to forgive. Yet, the psychological and theological fields both agree that this is poor advice.

This phrase implies that we should move on and no longer think about how we were wronged. But does forgiving require that you forget? Is it possible that I could forgive and still remember how the person sinned against me? It is difficult to forget about transgressions that have pierced our core.

Joyce was a fun-loving person and enjoyed being outside on the farm. She was dependable, hardworking, and compassionate. But every time she drove past the land that her husband and children spent many years farming, she remembered with meticulous clarity the sinful actions of her brother-in-law. While her father-in-law was still living, her brother-in-law Charles convinced his father to change his will. There always had been an understanding that Joyce and her family would inherit the family farm owned by her father-in-law. But in the new will, the farm went to Charles.

This land was not merely dirt—it was their legacy. Farming this land was more than a job. It was a way of life. They prayed over this land when there was no rain. They rejoiced when the crop was plentiful. Their family wedding pictures were taken down by the creek. Charles had other ideas. Not only did he take away the hope for Joyce's family to inherit the farm, but he sold the farm without giving Joyce's family the opportunity to purchase the land.

Eventually, Joyce felt she could forgive Charles, but she could never forget.

FORGETTING IS IMPOSSIBLE

"Forgive and forget" implies that a sin can only be forgiven if we can forget. That would mean Joyce would have to forget the fact that her brother-in-law sinned against her and deeply hurt her family in order to genuinely forgive him.

The hurt that Joyce felt slashed her heart open and left a gaping hole. Her family's lifetime dream had been taken from them. This is not the kind of wound that is forgotten. Pretending that her brother-in-law never sold the land out from under her family does not make the pain of loss go away.

If someone took a chain saw and cut your arm off because she was angry with you, you would not walk around ignoring the fact that you only have one arm. When people asked you about how you lost your arm, you wouldn't respond, "Oh, I kind of forgot I was missing an arm. I don't really remember how I lost it."

Trying to forget what happened will impede your ability to forgive. Ignoring sin and acting as if nothing ever occurred will cause bitterness to fester within you.

The more you try to forget about it, the more you think about it. And the more you think about it, the more you blame yourself for not being able to forgive because you can't forget what took place. Ruminating in this way only encourages the cognitive cycle to loop around and around and around.

Attempting to forget so that you can forgive is an ungodly approach to forgiving that keeps us in the prison of unforgiveness. We do not forgive to forget. Neither do we wait to forgive until we forget. We forgive others because God in Christ forgives us. Connecting forgiveness with forgetting takes our focus off Jesus and what He has done and promises for us.

Telling someone to forgive and forget is telling them that forgiveness depends on their ability to forget what took place. The responsibility is on the person who was wronged rather than on what Jesus has done for us. This burdens a person whose heart has been ripped apart and is not capable of ignoring the damage.

We tell ourselves that the day will come when we are able to forgive and forget. But it doesn't. We keep recalling the sin, stuck in the downward spiral of unforgiveness that separates us from God and our neighbor. We spend time and resources working to forget, only to be reminded every day of the wound caused by another person's sinful behavior. We can't forget, and so we convince ourselves we have not forgiven.

DOES GOD FORGET?

Some believe that God forgets our sins when He forgives us. The confusion comes from the passage in Jeremiah where God declares, "I will forgive their iniquity, and I will remember their sin no more" (31:34).

This passage might sound as if God forgets sin, as if He has amnesia about the evil things we said or did once He forgives us. It is understandable that this could bring comfort to people. Such a god would always see you as a perfect person who has never fallen short of his commandments.

But God knows all about our sinful history. He knows that we have sinned against Him and our neighbor. God does not suffer from amnesia or dementia. He has not forgotten our sin. God has forgiven our sin. He chooses not to remember, meaning that He does not bring up our past sins and use them against us.

The Scriptures clearly articulate the sins of the people in the Old and New Testaments. In the book of Genesis, we are told that Adam and Eve sinned by eating from the forbidden tree. This sin was not forgotten by God, but it was forgiven. He no longer held their sin against them. If God had forgotten what Adam and Eve did, He would never have spoken of it again. He never would have told us about it in His Word.

The Bible also recounts the sins of Moses, the Israelites, King David, and many others.

God does not forget. He forgives and chooses not to hold our sins against us. Paul says,

Therefore, just as sin came into the world through one man, and death through sin, and so death spread to all men because all sinned—for sin indeed was in the world before the law was given, but sin is not counted where there is no law. Yet death reigned from Adam to Moses, even over those whose sinning was not like the transgression of Adam, who was a type of the one who was to come. (Romans 5:12–14)

God has not forgotten.

The writers of the New Testament knew about Adam and Eve because God's Word tells of their sin. Paul knew that sin came into the world through Adam, and by this sin all human creation now struggles with sin and faces eternal death. God has not forgotten, but He chooses not to remember those sins.

Paul also writes, "For as by a man came death, by a man has come also the resurrection of the dead. For as in Adam all die, so also in Christ shall all be made alive" (1 Corinthians 15:21–22). God did not forget or try to hide what Adam did and how this affects us as fallen people in a fallen world. Instead, He gave us His Son for the forgiveness of our sins, making us heirs of eternal life.

Paul warns Christians, "But I am afraid that as the serpent deceived Eve by his cunning, your thoughts will be led astray from a sincere and pure devotion to Christ" (2 Corinthians 11:3). Paul knew that his readers would be aware of the sin of Adam and Eve and how the devil deceived them. The devil still threatens us today. Paul exhorts us to be careful lest the devil lead us away from Christ in the same way that he led Adam and Eve away from God's Word in the garden.

God never forgot about the sin of Adam and Eve, which caused the whole creation to fall into sin. God never forgot about the sin of Moses, who killed a man (see Exodus 2:11–22) and struck the rock (see Numbers 20:11–12). God never forgot about the sins of King David when he misused his authority, committed adultery with Bathsheba, and had her husband killed in battle (see 2 Samuel 11–12). God never forgot about the sin of Jonah, who refused to go to Nineveh (see Jonah 1). God never forgot about the sins of Peter, who sliced off the ear of a servant (see John 18:10) and denied he knew Jesus (see Luke 22:54–62). And God has not forgotten your sin. God knows you are a sinner and that you deserve the punishment of hell (see Matthew 13:42; Romans 3:23; 6:23).

God has not forgotten your sin. He has *forgiven* your sin. He remembers your sin no more and does not hold your sin against you. You are a child of your heavenly Father.

Remembering sin no more means that God does not act upon that sin and remembers it differently. When God says, "I will remember their sin no more," He is saying that He will not give us what we deserve. "For by grace you have been saved through faith. And this is not your own doing; it is the gift of God, not a result of works, so that no one may boast" (Ephesians 2:8–9).

When God recalls the transgression of Adam and Eve, He could remember it as the sin that destroyed His creation and condemned all people to hell. But that is not how God remembers. Adam and Eve sinned, but God provided a way of forgiveness. God remembers their transgression as forgiven through the promise fulfilled in His Son, Jesus Christ.

God does not recall our sins for our condemnation. Rather, He remembers according to His mercy and grace. The goal of forgiveness is not to forget. The goal of forgiveness is to remember that God forgives sin by the blood of Jesus (see Hebrews 9:15–22).

MARK

My research participants all remembered how someone sinned against them and could vividly describe it. They could not forget their suffering. But how they told their stories depended on if they were unforgiving or forgiving of the transgression. Unforgiving people tell their stories with anger, bitterness, or a desire for revenge. When forgiving people tell their stories, they confess their anger, bitterness, and desire for revenge as sinful reactions that need forgiveness so they can forgive the transgressor. Forgiving people of God tell the story differently than unforgiving people do.

Logan stated, "The way I kind of see forgiveness is if you forgive somebody, you remember it but you don't hold it against them anymore. You're no longer obsessing over what somebody else has done to you." Logan was able to forgive his wife and live out his faith in Christ. He remembers the incidents with his wife, but he remembers them differently because of forgiveness. Without forgiveness, he would remember with all the anger and bitterness he felt in those moments. But with forgiveness, he remembers them as sins forgiven by Christ, which freed him from the prison of unforgiveness that was destroying his marriage.

CAN WE RELY ON OUR MEMORIES?

By nature, we place great value on our memories. We assume that our memory is like a recording device that accurately accounts for every detail. You can observe how this has been reflected in the value placed on eyewitness accounts of crimes. For some time, eyewitness testimonies were considered reliable evidence to convict someone of a crime.

Psychologist Elizabeth Loftus is a leading expert on the reliability of memories.[11] Her interest in our ability to remember was stirred by a court case where a man named Steve Titus was falsely accused of rape. Loftus described the Titus case and her involvement in a TED Talk.[12] The victim picked Steve out of a lineup, claiming he looked most similar to the person who attacked her. During the trial she confidently identified Steve as her attacker. However, after further investigation, Steve was found innocent. The crime was horrendous, but the wrong person was charged and imprisoned because of a faulty memory.

Loftus's research reveals that our memories should not be trusted. We remember situations according to our own interpretation of what took place. As we recall an incident repeatedly in our mind, we tend to reframe the details to fit our interpretation instead of remembering the reality. Our memories can be distorted and contaminated.

People commonly remain in unforgiveness because they fixate on how they remember the event. Take the example of Logan and his wife arguing about the hole in their bathroom during a blizzard. From Logan's perspective, he was trying to protect his wife when he would not let her have the car keys. Yet, from his wife's perspective, he was controlling her. They experienced the same event

---

11 Elizabeth F. Loftus, *Eyewitness Testimony* (Cambridge: Harvard University Press, 1996).

12 See Elizabeth Loftus, "How Reliable Is Your Memory?" TEDGlobal 2013, https://www.ted.com/talks/elizabeth_loftus_how_reliable_is_your_memory. See also her book *Eyewitness Testimony* (Cambridge: Harvard University Press, 1996).

but interpreted what happened differently. Their memories of what took place were distorted based on their interpretations.

Memories can't be trusted because we are not perfect recording devices. Yet, often people will refuse to forgive based on their memory—or more precisely, their interpretation—of a situation. We trust in what we think took place, how we recall it. But it is possible that we do not remember it accurately because our perspective was skewed. Sometimes unforgiveness is based on an inaccurate interpretation of what took place.

TED

In mediation, I am often amazed at how a misunderstanding between two parties can lead to a significant offense. The offense severely damages their relationship, and the misunderstandings snowball from there. Each party's memory of what happened reflects his or her interpretation. Because of the perceived offenses, they stop listening to each other. In their separation, their accounts of the offensive events change to justify their hatred of each other. With the guidance of a mediator, they are able to tell their stories without interruption and with less tension. When that happens, they begin to listen to each other and understand the other person's perspective, which challenges their own memories or interpretations. Compassion, love, and forgiveness replace disgust, hatred, and unforgiveness.

Do they forget what happened as they reconcile? No. But they remember the events differently.

I experienced this myself as a party in a business conflict that resulted in litigation. The court failed to resolve the conflict in three hearings. I had become angry and bitter over the year this dispute continued. But in just two days of Christian mediation, we not only resolved our business dispute but we also reconciled as brothers in Christ through confession and forgiveness. Two years later, a man called me who was involved with my former adversary to ask about my experience with him. I remembered what took place, but how I shared my story with this man was dramatically different from my description before I had forgiven my opponent. I left out details that I relived in my mind for months during the conflict. Instead, I told him how we forgave each other in Christ.

WHY NOT JUST FORGIVE AND FORGET?

Forgiving and forgetting is not possible. Trying to do so takes our focus off our Savior, the source of forgiveness. The goal of forgiveness is not forgetting. God did not forget. He chose to remember our sin no more. He chose not to use our sin against us. He chose to forgive our sin.

By the power of the Holy Spirit, we do not forget the transgression, but we remember that it is forgiven by the blood of our Savior, Jesus Christ. We trust in the fulfilled promises of our God. God does not remember our sins according to what we deserve. He remembers our sins according to what His Son has done for us. "For our sake He made Him to be sin who knew no sin, so that in Him we might become the righteousness of God" (2 Corinthians 5:21).

Don't burden yourself by trying to forgive and forget. Instead, change how you remember. You can choose to remember the sin as unforgivable. Or you can choose to remember the sin as forgiven by God through Christ.

God has chosen to remember your sin as forgiven. Because of His love for you, He can help you do the same with those who have sinned against you.

HOW DOES THIS APPLY TO ME?

IF YOU ARE STRUGGLING WITH "FORGIVE AND FORGET"

1. Write down what you remember about the offense. Be sure to include the parts that caused the most offense for you.

2. Review what you have written. Identify the parts of what happened that you have rehearsed over and over in your mind.

3. Mark those areas that you believe have been impacted by your emotions (such as hurt, embarrassment, anger, betrayal, or feelings of injustice). How might your interpretation of these events have become skewed because of your emotions?

4. Read Psalm 103:1–13. How does God respond to your sin, according to these verses?

   ▶ Verse 8

   ▶ Verse 9

   ▶ Verse 10

   ▶ Verses 11–13

5. In Psalm 103:3–5, what is the first benefit God gives to you? How does this benefit lead to the other benefits listed?

6. Read Jeremiah 31:34 out loud, inserting your name in the verse as follows: "I will forgive [name's] iniquity, and I will remember [name's] sin no more." Why does God make this promise to you? (See 1 Peter 2:24; 2 Corinthians 5:21; Romans 8:1.)

7. Did Jesus die for the sins committed against you? What is the eternal impact to you? to the offender?

8. Write a prayer thanking God for your forgiveness in Jesus. Ask the Holy Spirit to help you remember differently what is burdening you for the sake of Jesus. Pray for the person who has hurt you so deeply. Confess any sinful thoughts you had as you recalled this offense over and over.

PRAYER TEMPLATE

(See chapter 3, "How Should I Pray?")

INTRODUCTION

REFERENCE TO GOD'S WORK

PETITION

RESULT

CONCLUSION

CHAPTER 15

WHAT ABOUT JUSTICE?

When wrongs are done before our eyes,
And calls for justice will not cease,
What penalty can we devise
That brings the victim's heart true peace?

Are we like gods? May we impose
A sentence like "Eye for an eye"?
For when we sin, *we* may suppose
Sin's wages justly must apply.

But Christ in mercy and in love
Brings to believing souls release,
Our punishment and guilt removes,
And wraps us in His robe of peace.

TED

While talking with a pastor in India, I spoke about forgiveness and the peace it brings. He told me, "Without justice, there is no peace."

I asked what he meant. He explained that if a victim is not satisfied with the justice levied against the offender, then the victim can never experience peace. As we talked, I realized he was talking about earthly justice.

I reminded him that Jesus paid the full punishment for the sins of the whole world (John 3:16), satisfying God's requirement for justice. Jesus' suffering and death on the cross provides peace for those who believe in Christ: "Therefore, since we have been justified by faith, we have peace with God through our Lord Jesus Christ" (Romans 5:1).

Still, this man insisted that if he was not satisfied with the punishment for the one who sinned against him, he could have no peace.

I learned during my work in India that many people there are obsessed with justice. I wondered whether living in a Hindu culture based on a caste system contributed to this obsession. Everywhere I went, people were striving to be recognized as someone with worth, especially those from low castes or the outcastes. They felt oppressed by societal norms that determined their value according to what caste they were born in. Based on their standing in society, they are often treated unjustly compared with those of higher castes. I concluded that living in oppression increases one's longing for justice.

But the ideology that peace depends on justice served is not unique to India. Protests for fair treatment in the United States and other countries also reflect this theme. Demonstration signs include messages such as "No Justice, No Peace." Activists promote the idea that justice requires eliminating prejudice and only then can there be peace.

In television shows featuring murder and other injurious crimes, law enforcement officials often state that capturing and convicting a perpetrator will finally bring peace to the survivors and their families. But when a survivor of the crime speaks near the end of the program, they rarely indicate that they are at peace. Frequently, survivors complain that justice was not served. Or if they agree that the punishment was adequate, they indicate that the sentence still did not provide peace.

That's also what I have experienced in reconciliation work. Although someone may be required to provide restitution or suffer other consequences for his offense, the person he hurt does not experience peace just because the offender was punished. In many cases, victims declare that the consequences fall short of justice, that the offenders got away without truly paying for their crimes. In other words, there was no justice. Therefore, the offended lacks peace.

The yearning for justice has been a part of the human experience since man's fall into sin. People in the Bible lamented when justice fell short of their expectations. Many psalms express the need for justice.

Job exclaimed, "Behold, I cry out, 'Violence!' but I am not answered; I call for help, but there is no justice" (19:7).

Habakkuk complained, "So the law is paralyzed, and justice never goes forth. For the wicked surround the righteous; so justice goes forth perverted" (1:4).

In Luke 18:1–8, Jesus taught about prayer using the parable of the persistent widow. She continued to appeal to the judge for justice. He refused her requests for a while, but he finally succumbed to her pleas because of her persistence. But then Jesus sums up His teaching on this parable: "And will not God give justice to His elect, who cry to Him day and night? Will He delay long over them? I tell you, He will give justice to them speedily. Nevertheless, when the Son of Man comes, will He find faith on earth?" (vv. 7–8).

Jesus declares that God will bring about justice for His people. But Jesus seems to place more emphasis on faith than justice.

We should expect justice and do what we can to achieve it. God calls us to "do justice, and to love kindness" (Micah 6:8). However, we often do not have the ability to make justice happen, especially in a way that meets our expectations. In a sin-filled world, justice often falls short, and justice on our terms rarely brings the peace we seek.

WHAT DOES JUSTICE LOOK LIKE?

God is just, and He created us to desire justice.

However, our idea of justice does not always match our Creator's. Our understanding is tainted by sin and limited to our own perspective. Only God can judge rightly. He alone judges the hearts of people. We are unable to see others' hearts as God does. Our omniscient God understands everything from an eternal perspective. We live in a material world and view life primarily from our earthly understanding. God knows the details of every situation. Our knowledge of others and events around us is limited, and we often fill the gaps with speculation.

Thus, what we view as just often differs from God's view. Not surprisingly, our view also differs from the views of those around us.

One aspect of our Maker's justice requires that all are treated equally and fairly. God views each person He created as worthy of fair treatment, regardless of social status. We see this theme repeated in Scripture as God calls us to treat everyone justly, especially caring for those who are vulnerable in our communities—for example, the widows, the orphans, and the poor. "He has told you, O man, what is good; and what does the LORD require of you but to do justice, and to love kindness, and to walk humbly with your God?" (Micah 6:8).

Another aspect of justice is judging the guilt of an accused wrongdoer. Those judged not guilty are acquitted. Justice for those falsely accused requires treating them as if they never offended. Those found guilty are punished based on the merits of the case. The offender suffers the consequences of her crime. (See chapter 10, "Does Forgiveness Release Consequences?" for the purpose of consequences.)

So what does God's justice look like?

To put it bluntly, anyone born in sin or who acts sinfully is justly condemned to spend eternity separated from God in hell.

According to God's Word, that means all people.

All we like sheep have gone astray; we have turned—every one—to his own way. (Isaiah 53:6)

As it is written: "None is righteous, no, not one; no one understands; no one seeks for God. All have turned aside; together they have become worthless; no one does good, not even one." (Romans 3:10–12)

For all have sinned and fall short of the glory of God. (Romans 3:23)

Do you really want God's justice?

The answer is yes! But why?

Because God in His infinite wisdom chose to execute the justice we deserved on His Son, Jesus.

He knew that we were powerless to do anything about our condition. Without His intervention, all people would be condemned to hell. Jesus willingly took on our sin and its condemnation. The Father turned His face away from His Son as Jesus hung on the cross. Jesus' words reflect His Father's rejection: "My God, My God, why have You forsaken Me?" (Matthew 27:46). Because Jesus took on our sin, He suffered the rejection we deserved and died a cruel and painful death.

Because Jesus paid the full price for our punishment, the Father gave us His Son's righteousness. Thus, God sees us as sanctified. In other words, we have been made holy in God's eyes because the price for our sin was paid in full by Christ. "For our sake He made Him to be sin who knew no sin, so that in Him we might become the righteousness of God" (2 Corinthians 5:21).

This kind of justice evades our human understanding. Who among us would sacrifice our only, innocent child to pay for the horrendous crimes of evil people? What person would do such a crazy thing? But our God did just that.

Because of His love for us, God bestowed on us His mercy and grace. Mercy is not receiving what we deserve—in this case, hell. Grace is receiving what we do not deserve—heaven. In Jesus, we are beneficiaries of God's mercy and grace. We are not condemned because of our sin. We are made heirs of His heavenly promises and will spend eternity with Him. While His mercy and grace were made available for all, only those who believe benefit from this unfathomable gift.

> For God so loved the world, that He gave His only Son, that whoever believes in Him should not perish but have eternal life. For God did not send His Son into the world to condemn the world, but in order that the world might be saved through Him. Whoever believes in Him is not condemned, but whoever does not believe is condemned already, because He has not believed in the name of the only Son of God. (John 3:16–18)

Jesus died for all sinners. But in God's justice, only those who believe in the gift benefit from it. In God's justice, the most horrid of sinners benefit if she believes. In His justice, the most saintlike person who does not believe retains his own condemnation and is not saved.

Hard to understand. We can only receive this truth by faith. Only those who believe in God's gift of Jesus can grasp this form of justice. "Evil men do not understand justice, but those who seek the LORD understand it completely" (Proverbs 28:5).

WHAT ABOUT EARTHLY JUSTICE?

Ah, that's the rub, isn't it?

As Christians, we trust in God's justice for eternity, even if it surpasses our limited understanding. We accept the eternal blessings for believers and condemnation for nonbelievers based on faith.

But as God's creatures, we expect—and sometimes we demand—justice on earth. We were created with a sense of justice: first, that all should be treated equally and fairly; and second, that those who hurt others must suffer the consequences of their crime.

God knew that society would fall into chaos if everyone could execute justice as they desired. We would be unable to survive if everyone meted out their own justice. Remember the first murder? Cain slew his brother Abel because of jealousy. Cain executed "justice" on Abel because his brother found more favor with God. We have seen how vigilante justice often is unjust and dangerous.

Out of love for us, God appointed people in our communities to be rulers and judges of justice. Accordingly, He commands that we submit to the authorities He put in place for our protection.

> Let every person be subject to the governing authorities. For there is no authority except from God, and those that exist have been instituted by God. Therefore whoever resists the authorities resists what God has appointed, and those who resist will incur judgment. (Romans 13:1-2)

Sometimes we serve in a position of authority—parent, teacher, pastor, or manager. We may even serve as civil authority in law enforcement, as a district attorney, or as a court judge. In our positions of authority, we determine what is just and decide appropriate penalties for offensive behavior.

But more often, we have limited authority to determine a just punishment for those who harm us. We may have little or no influence on the decision for the penalty. We must depend on those who have the authority and responsibility to fulfill the laws of justice.

When our pain is great, we may not feel satisfied with the punishment our offender receives. We may feel that the punishment does not deliver sufficient hurt to the offender compared to the pain we endure. We may believe that we have not received adequate restitution for the loss we incurred as a result of the offense.

Must we forgive? We are called to forgive as God through Christ has forgiven us. But as discussed in chapter 10, "Does Forgiveness Release Consequences?" there are still earthly consequences that may apply. We require appropriate consequences for our injuries.

IT'S NOT FAIR!

TED

A pastor friend of mine was counseling a woman in his office when he heard his next appointment arrive in the reception area. A husband and wife had requested marriage counseling, and they entered the church office arguing loudly. The pastor ended the session with the woman and went out to greet the couple, who didn't cease fighting. He motioned for them to enter his office and take a seat, where they continued quarreling for ten minutes.

Finally, the pastor rose from his seat and stood right in front of the couple. They both stopped bickering, looking up at him. Making the sign of the cross, he said, "In the name of the Father and of the Son and of the Holy Spirit. Amen. You may now continue."

The couple sat stunned for a moment, and then the husband blurted out, "That's not fair!"

The husband was right. It's not fair that while we were still sinners, Christ died for us. It's not fair that God made Him who knew no sin to be sin for us, so that we might become the righteousness of God. It's not fair that the Father has shown such love to us that we should be called the children of God, and that is who we are. Thank God it's not fair!

When the punishment for an offense fails to meet our expectations, we are tempted to cry, "It's not fair!" We criticize the decision. Our response may be godly, for we were created to desire justice. Our response may be affected by our sinful nature, desiring retribution for the pain we are suffering. It may even be a combination of both!

Whether justice is realized or not, what or whom we worship is revealed in our response. If we trust God for our peace, despite the injustices of the world around us, we will respond in a way that reflects our faith. If we trust our own demands for justice, and our personal peace depends on the outcome we expect, our trust will have turned away from God. We trust our own judgment, our own demands, and our own ability to make others suffer for this unfair situation. In other words, we make ourselves god. And peace eludes us.

While my father's estate was in probate, a state department of revenue rejected a major deduction on our estate return, resulting in a large tax increase. As my tax attorneys reviewed the rejection, they showed me the tax law that clearly allowed the deduction. The agent was obviously in error. After conversations with the revenue agent failed to get results, our only recourse was to request a hearing. Months went by before we were granted a hearing date. A few weeks before our hearing, that revenue agent left the department. Our hearing was delayed for another six months while we waited for his replacement. The new agent was reluctant to agree with my attorneys, so a new hearing date was set months later. (My attorney explained that it was likely agents newly assigned to our case didn't want to be responsible for reducing taxes on returns they did not originally review. Our best recourse was a hearing before a judge outside of the department.) Before the second hearing date, that agent also left the department. Once again we were delayed. Agents leaving the department and the delayed hearing dates went on for six years.

Needless to say, I was furious. This was so unfair! I firmly believed with my attorneys that the tax assessed was illegitimate, and it amounted to tens of thousands of dollars. After each delay, I would lie awake at night, fuming over the unfairness of this whole process. At those times, whom was I trusting for justice? And what was I depending on for peace? My fear, love, and trust were not most of all in God.

Finally, I calculated what it was costing the estate to continue fighting this battle. Every time the hearing was postponed, I received invoices from the attorneys for their work. I projected what the actual hearing would cost. The repeated delays and resubmitting documents for each new agent, plus the fees for our estate to be represented at the hearing, would cost more than the total tax increase. And there was no guarantee that we would prevail.

My responsibility to the estate was to pay all debts and provide the largest settlement for the beneficiaries. Thus, I stopped my pursuit of the matter and paid the tax. Did I believe that paying the tax was fair? Absolutely not! But in the end, I felt compelled to do what was most beneficial for the beneficiaries.

But what about peace? I prayed that God would give me peace of mind that I did what I could. I submitted to the tax authorities whom I believed were wrong. But I trusted that God would bless the outcome of my work. I had finally learned to trust God regardless of what I wanted. I was at peace. As I later reflected on the situation, I realized that God had given the estate big breaks in other matters that more than made up for the unfair tax we paid. During my attempts to get justice, I had forgotten just how blessed I was. In my most angry moments, I let my pursuit of earthly justice overshadow God's justice, which made me His forgiven child, an heir of heaven.

When we obsess over a lack of justice, it can develop into an idol. Our peace becomes dependent on our personal idea of justice rather than what God has done for us in Christ. We may compare our personal righteousness to the sinfulness of the offender, a form of self-righteousness. We may grumble and complain against authorities, including God, for the unjust results. We gossip about and slander anyone who fails to meet our expectations. We unconsciously make ourselves into a god who alone can determine the appropriate fate of the condemned and judge authorities who add insult with unjust decisions.

Paul warns us:

> Do all things without grumbling or disputing, that you may be blameless and innocent, children of God without blemish in the midst of a crooked and twisted generation, among whom you shine as lights in the world, holding fast to the word of life, so that in the day of Christ I may be proud that I did not run in vain or labor in vain. (Philippians 2:14–16)

When justice fails to meet our expectation, how can we be at peace?

HOW DOES JUSTICE BRING PEACE?

Sin separates us from God because our holy God does not tolerate sinful beings in His presence. "Your iniquities have made a separation between you and your God, and your sins have hidden His face from you so that He does not hear" (Isaiah 59:2).

Sin breaks the relationship between us and our Creator. Without the hope of the Gospel, we face eternal death.

Because Christ took on the punishment of our sins and gave us His righteousness, our relationship with our heavenly Father is restored. "But now in Christ Jesus you who once were far off have been brought near by the blood of Christ" (Ephesians 2:13).

Our restored relationship as children of God makes us heirs of His heavenly promises.

> But when the fullness of time had come, God sent forth His Son, born of woman, born under the law, to redeem those who were under the law, so that we might receive adoption as sons. And because you are sons, God has sent the Spirit of His Son into our hearts, crying, "Abba! Father!" So you are no longer a slave, but a son, and if a son, then an heir through God. (Galatians 4:4–7)

This restored relationship with God brings peace that passes all understanding.

> Therefore, since we have been justified by faith, we have peace with God through our Lord Jesus Christ. (Romans 5:1)

> And the peace of God, which surpasses all understanding, will guard your hearts and your minds in Christ Jesus. (Philippians 4:7)

We find peace in the justification we have through Jesus' death and resurrection because His sacrifice for us restores our relationship with God. Heavenly justice through the Gospel brings peace. Earthly justice, whether we approve of it or not, does not bring peace that passes understanding.

We have peace, not based on whether the offender has suffered sufficient consequences but because Christ bore the full consequences of our sin. We experience peace whether we have received appropriate restitution or not. We receive peace because we are forgiven by God, not because an offender is justly punished or because we have received what we believe we deserve. "But He was pierced for our transgressions; He was crushed for our iniquities; upon Him was the chastisement that brought us peace, and with His wounds we are healed" (Isaiah 53:5).

The peace we seek—the peace we truly need—is not found in earthly matters. It is found only in Jesus Christ and the forgiveness of our sins. "For in Him all the fullness of God was pleased to dwell, and through Him to reconcile to Himself all things, whether on earth or in heaven, making peace by the blood of His cross" (Colossians 1:19–20).

HOW CAN I RESPOND TO INJUSTICE?

Some injustices require people to respond to bring about godly change. When we find ourselves with opportunity to bring about justice, God calls us to do so: "He has told you, O man, what is good; and what does the LORD require of you but to do justice, and to love kindness, and to walk humbly with your God?" (Micah 6:8).

But all our efforts for godly change require thoughts, words, and actions that reflect our faith in Christ. Holy ends do not justify sinful means. Our fighting for justice impacts our own hearts as well as others around us.

> But in your hearts honor Christ the Lord as holy, always being prepared to make a defense to anyone who asks you for a reason

for the hope that is in you; yet do it with gentleness and respect, having a good conscience, so that, when you are slandered, those who revile your good behavior in Christ may be put to shame. (1 Peter 3:15–16)

We are tempted to respond to our assessments of injustice by our sinful nature. Long-term anger can evolve into hatred and bitterness. We may attempt personal retribution, taking justice into our own hands like vigilantes. We can fall into a pit of hopelessness and eventually depression because we are looking for peace in the wrong places. For these temptations, you may want to refer to chapter 6, "How Does Anger Give Opportunity to the Devil?"

Peter teaches us how to respond to unjust suffering by pointing to our Savior:

Servants, be subject to your masters with all respect, not only to the good and gentle but also to the unjust. For this is a gracious thing, when, mindful of God, one endures sorrows while suffering unjustly. For what credit is it if, when you sin and are beaten for it, you endure? But if when you do good and suffer for it you endure, this is a gracious thing in the sight of God. For to this you have been called, because Christ also suffered for you, leaving you an example, so that you might follow in His steps. (1 Peter 2:18–21)

Notice how Jesus responded to the great injustices He faced: "He committed no sin, neither was deceit found in His mouth. When He was reviled, He did not revile in return; when He suffered, He did not threaten, but *continued entrusting Himself to Him who judges justly*" (vv. 22–23, emphasis added).

As Jesus was unjustly accused, convicted, beaten, publicly shamed, and executed, He "continued entrusting Himself to Him who judges justly." He took no sinful action to stop His unjust treatment or suffering, even to death. And what was the result? Healing, salvation, and peace for you and me. "He Himself bore our sins in His body on the tree, that we might die to sin and live to righteousness. By His wounds you have been healed" (v. 24).

Jesus empowers us to entrust ourselves to Him who judges justly. At the cross of Jesus, we find healing from the pain of the original offense and the hurt caused by the lack of justice. Long-term anger, personal retribution, and hopelessness lead us away from Christ. Jesus invites us: "Come to Me, all who labor and are heavy laden, and I will give you rest" (Matthew 11:28).

Seek comfort and encouragement through God's Word:

Let the word of Christ dwell in you richly, teaching and admonishing one another in all wisdom, singing psalms and hymns and spiritual songs, with thankfulness in your hearts to God. And whatever you do, in word or deed, do everything in the name of the Lord Jesus, giving thanks to God the Father through Him. (Colossians 3:16–17)

Cry out to God with your pain. Ask for healing, patience, understanding, and forgiveness—and peace in the midst of your suffering. "Do not be anxious about anything, but in everything by prayer and supplication with thanksgiving let your requests be made known to God. And the peace of God, which surpasses all understanding, will guard your hearts and your minds in Christ Jesus" (Philippians 4:6–7).

Remember that we live in a temporary world tainted by sin. Justice in a world of sinners often is not what we think it should be. Trust God that He provides His justice from an eternal perspective.

Pray for God's direction, comfort, help, and healing. Thank Him for the many blessings He has given you, even as you suffer in this world. Instead of focusing on the lack of justice, fix your eyes on Jesus and the blessings you have in Him.

Finally, brothers, whatever is true, whatever is honorable, whatever is just, whatever is pure, whatever is lovely, whatever is commendable, if there is any excellence, if there is anything worthy of praise, think about these things. What you have learned and received and heard and seen in me—practice these things, and the God of peace will be with you. (Philippians 4:8–9)

Should we fight for justice in our world, especially when vulnerable people are being oppressed or unfairly treated? Yes. But we need to be careful not to sin as we strive to bring about godly justice. When we sin to achieve our goals, no matter how godly we think they are, we have crossed a line and made ourselves god. May God grant us the wisdom to seek justice while still honoring His precepts.

HOW DOES THIS APPLY TO ME?

1. Describe the situation where you believe justice has not been served. Describe what you think would be the fulfillment of justice.

2. Identify the emotions you are experiencing because of this lack of justice. How are your emotions affecting your faith?

3. God hates sin, including yours. How did God execute justice for your sinful nature and actual sins?

4. Fill in this blank: If only _____, then I would have peace and satisfaction that justice has been served.

   ▶ In whom are you trusting for justice?

   ▶ What does your answer suggest to you about your belief in your source of peace?

   ▶ How can Jesus help you find peace in your search for justice?

5. Consider whether you have an opportunity to help bring about godly justice. How can you improve justice while displaying a Christlike attitude and behavior?

6. Seek out your pastor or a spiritually mature friend who will listen to your hurts and guide you through God's Word for comfort, healing, and peace. Invite him or her to specifically help you identify your own sinful attitudes that you may confess them before God. Ask your pastor or friend to assure you of your forgiveness in Christ.

7. Write a prayer for God's help and healing with the following elements:

    ▶ Praying that you find comfort and encouragement in God's Word

    ▶ Praying for all those hurt by the offender

    ▶ Praying for those in authority who determine earthly justice in this situation

    ▶ Praying for the offender

    ▶ Commending all for whom you pray to the justice, mercy, and grace of your loving God

    ▶ Thanking Jesus for taking the full punishment for your sin and giving you His righteousness

PRAYER TEMPLATE

(See chapter 3, "How Should I Pray?")

INTRODUCTION

REFERENCE TO GOD'S WORK

PETITION

RESULT

CONCLUSION

CHAPTER 16

HOW DO I PROCLAIM FORGIVENESS?

When we would speak a word of grace,
Help us stand in the other's place
To understand their point of view;
With gentleness our words imbue.

Show us the log in our own eyes
Before the speck that in theirs lies;
Curb our emotions, guard our voice,
That we, forgiven, both rejoice.

Jim was in middle school when his alcoholic father drenched their family home in gasoline and burned it to the ground. Over the years Jim only saw his father once or twice but never intended for his father to be a part of his life. But Jim's faith began to grow through regular church attendance with his wife.

Jim said, "There was like this growing desire that I felt I wanted him to know that I forgave him. Because all along I think in my mind I could tell myself, 'Oh yeah, I've forgiven him, and I'll just go on.' But then I think as I got older, and even the thought of him getting older, I started to have more of a desire to talk to him about forgiveness, to tell him that I'd forgiven him and I wanted him to know."

Twenty-seven years after his father burned down the house, Jim saw his father at a family reunion. Jim had prepared himself to speak words of forgiveness to his father by talking to his pastor and attending a workshop on biblical reconciliation.

Jim described his father this way: "Okay, now you've got to remember, my dad at this point was in his late sixties, a big guy, like six foot three about three hundred pounds. Hard life, farmer, and manual labor his whole life. He came from a family born in [the] '30s, '40s, you know. And his parents had ten kids in the family. So not the kind of person who talked about their feelings. If I would say to him, even now, 'How did that make you feel, Dad?' he'd probably look at me like I was crazy."

At the family reunion, Jim and his father had good conversations about what was going on in their lives. When it was time for Jim to leave, he went over and sat next to his father.

"Well, we're taking off," Jim said. "You know, I don't know if you need to hear it or not, but I just want you to know that I forgive you and that I love you. You are forgiven in Christ's name."

His father nodded and reached out for Jim's hand and said, "I wish things could have been different."

PREPARATION

Think of all the things that you prepare for—an athletic event, a business pitch, a trip, an emergency, a pregnancy, an interview.

The outcome of the event is heavily dependent on how one prepares. The athlete who trains every day, eats properly, and receives coaching has significantly better odds of winning than the athlete who does not train, eats junk food, and refuses to be coached. The homeowner who has flashlights, batteries, food supplies, and a weather radio will ride out the storm much better than the homeowner who has none of these things in place.

When we are not prepared, we react to a situation without thinking, without curbing our emotions, and without considering the impact of our behavior. For example, consider the mother with three small children standing in the checkout line at the grocery store. She already had to deal with her kids trying to place things in the cart and fights about who was going to sit in the cart and who was going to help push the cart. She waited with a cart full of food and three children begging for candy bars that are strategically placed at a child's eye level.

Her ten-year-old son whined, "I want a candy bar."

"Not today," Mom patiently responded.

With more intensity, he pleaded, "But I want one! Can I have one?"

Showing her frustration, Mom responded more firmly: "I said no!"

Then, with as much strength and passion as a ten-year-old can muster: "Buy me a candy bar right now!!"

Without thinking, without checking her emotions, without considering the impact of her behavior, Mom reacted. She grabbed her son by the arm and swung him around. She bent down and looked him in the face and shouted with as much strength and passion as a worn-out mother could muster: "I said no! And don't ask again, or else!"

The mother reacted out of frustration instead of responding to her son with reasonable discipline. Reactions are centered in the moment and are not thought through. They are filled with emotion and ungodly behavior. However, when we take time to prepare for such a moment, it is easier to respond instead of react. Preparation helps us to assess our cognitive, emotional, and behavioral responses.

Before you proclaim forgiveness to someone, you need to prepare both yourself and the other person to encourage a godly response rather than an ungodly reaction.

PREPARING YOURSELF
TO SPEAK FORGIVENESS

In the Sermon on the Mount, Jesus taught His disciples:

Why do you see the speck that is in your brother's eye, but do not notice the log that is in your own eye? Or how can you say to your brother, "Let me take the speck out of your eye," when there is the log in your own eye? (Matthew 7:3–4)

We are proficient at confessing the sins of other people and ignoring our own sins. When people discuss a particular conflict, we tend to describe how the other person sinned. Very few people begin by saying, "So let me tell you what I did wrong." It often sounds like this: "So let me tell you what Kyle did wrong."

Yet, Jesus reminds us that we are no better than Kyle. We are only seeing part of what is really going on because our own sin gets in the way. Like a scientist looking at a specimen, we place Kyle's sin under a microscope and magnify his failures for all to see. From our assumed position of power over Kyle, we are like a god who desires to control him. But zooming in on Kyle's sin impedes my ability to clearly see Kyle. Moreover, I am unable to clearly see myself.

Therefore, Jesus says, "You hypocrite, first take the log out of your own eye, and then you will see clearly to take the speck out of your brother's eye" (v. 5).

Place yourself on the specimen slide and ask someone to help you identify how you sinned in the situation. Any Christian who practices self-examination, confession, repentance, and forgiveness can assist you in identifying the log in your eye. Pastors and spiritual leaders are specially trained to help.

MARK

All my research participants were able to forgive after they received care from a fellow Christian. In many cases, their pastor gently identified how they were contributing to the conflict. The pastor helped his member focus on her own sin so that it could be confessed and forgiven rather than magnify the sin of the other. The member was then able to approach her offender as a forgiven child of God.

How you approach your offender makes a difference. If you approach with a large log in your eye, you will not see clearly what is really going on with your offender and yourself. And you are likely to do more harm to your offender and your relationship.

Dorothy initially approached Kyle without addressing the log in her eye. Kyle had sinned against Dorothy. But Dorothy was quick to gossip and slander Kyle at her place of work and through social media. Rather than seeking to restore, she attacked Kyle with words. Her sinful reaction did not bring Kyle to repentance. Instead, her log of sin pounded his heart like a battering ram, causing Kyle to raise his defenses. Kyle walled himself off from Dorothy and protected himself from her assault.

Jesus says, "Do not give dogs what is holy, and do not throw your pearls before pigs, lest they trample them underfoot and turn to attack you" (v. 6). One way to interpret this verse, especially in light of Jesus' teachings on sin and judging others in the previous verses, is that the holy things and pearls are Christians—your brothers and sisters in the faith. When you ram your log of sin into a fellow Christian, you knock them down to be trampled. And by doing so, you will likely be trampled as well.[13]

Dorothy ignored her own sins, focusing solely on the speck in Kyle's eye. She approached a fellow Christian, who is a holy pearl, with the intent of crushing him. She would forgive him only if he groveled at her feet.

Jesus is clear that we should not hypocritically condemn others by making ourselves like a god, magnifying the sins of others through a microscope.

Preparing to forgive someone involves taking the log out of your own eye before you try to take the speck out of your offender's eye. Then you can approach your offender as a forgiven child of God.

PREPARING THE OFFENDER TO RECEIVE FORGIVENESS

Preparing yourself to speak forgiveness begins with admitting your own sin. It is not easy to acknowledge that you did wrong. Most people expend significant energy blaming others and minimizing their sins. Think about how difficult it has been for you to acknowledge your own sins. How long did it take you to confess that log of sin in your eye? Was it difficult to hear someone else tell you about the sin? Did you repent right away or did it take some time before you were able to repent? Did you accept the efforts of others to restore you or did you push them away?

---

13   This is not the predominant interpretation of this verse. Most commentators will interpret the holy things and pearls as the Gospel that should not be thrown before dogs and pigs. However, Jeffrey Gibbs provides a contextual interpretation of Matthew 7:6 that reflects this perspective. See Jeffrey A. Gibbs, *Matthew 1:1–11:1*, Concordia Commentary (St. Louis: Concordia Publishing House, 2006).

Understanding your own experience with sin will help you to be more empathetic toward the person who has sinned against you. Your approach to the situation will help prepare the offender to receive forgiveness.

Approach your offender with grace and gentleness. "Do nothing from selfish ambition or conceit, but in humility count others more significant than yourselves" (Philippians 2:3).

Address your offender as a fellow sinner whom God has gifted with the forgiveness of Jesus. You are not more important than he is. You are both specimens that can easily have your sins magnified. Paul continues, "Let each of you look not only to his own interests, but also to the interests of others" (v. 4). Considering the interests of others helps us to pause and think about how to approach the offender so that they will receive what we offer.

In conflict, there can be confusion about what took place and what is considered a sin. After some time has passed, write down from your perspective what took place, your sin, and your perception of the other person's sin. In other words, how did the offender's behavior affect you? Then, discuss it with a fellow Christian to help you process your thoughts and feelings about the situation. This will help you prepare to engage in conversation with your offender.

Dorothy prepared herself for a conversation with Kyle. She rehearsed what she was going to say and how she was going to say it. When the time came, she approached Kyle with grace:

> Kyle, thanks for meeting with me today. I want to assure you that it is not my intent to harm you. My hope is that we can have a reconciled relationship. There are a few things we need to talk about that I think will move us in that direction. First, I want to confess that I have gossiped and slandered you at work and through social media. I felt hurt by what you did to me and I did not respond in a godly way. It is my prayer that you could forgive me.

This approach demonstrates how a Christian should address situations of sin. Dorothy showed Kyle compassion by thanking him and telling him that she was not there to attack him. She let him know what she hoped to achieve by meeting together. And she admitted her own sinfulness. Dorothy did not approach Kyle from the position of looking down through a microscope at his sin. She approached Kyle as a fellow sinner needing forgiveness.

The offender may need some help seeing his sin. One approach would be very direct. Dorothy could say, "You fired me in front of everybody. You said that I was lazy and incompetent for the whole team to hear." By taking this approach, Kyle would mostly likely take a defensive position and start walling himself off from Dorothy.

The godly approach allows the other person to share their perspective of what took place. Consider alternative phrases that Dorothy could use to help Kyle explore the situation with greater depth:

> Firing me in front of everyone hurt me deeply. If you could go back in time, would you do anything differently?

> Terminating me was hard for both of us. What was the most difficult part of the situation for you?

This provides space for Kyle to share his perspective of the situation. Kyle will sense that Dorothy cares about him and is listening to him.

As Kyle speaks, Dorothy should respond with active listening skills rather than react with emotion.

An emotional reaction might look like Dorothy is trying to defend herself or make accusations against Kyle. Suppose Dorothy replied like this: "But Kyle, if you would not have started this whole thing, I would not have gossiped about you." Such a reaction would hinder good communication. Dorothy should also consider her nonverbal reactions. Rolling her eyes, grimacing, looking at her feet rather than at Kyle—these might give the impression she is dismissing what he is saying.

Reactions are rarely thought through and often make it harder to discuss difficult topics. But with practice, we can learn good responses that create a favorable environment.

Active listening skills encourage productive conversation. Here are some active listening techniques and a few example responses to put in your toolbox.

PARAPHRASE WHAT YOU HEAR THEM SAYING:

"I get the impression that . . ."

"The way you see it . . ."

"You must really care about . . ."

CLARIFY WHAT YOU HEAR THEM SAYING:

"Tell me more about . . ."

"Can you give me an example . . ."

"I don't think I heard you correctly. Could you say that in different words?"

SUMMARIZE WHAT YOU HEAR THEM SAYING:
"Let me summarize what I have heard you say . . ."

Active listening encourages Kyle to tell his story in a more productive manner. With active listening, Dorothy will likely learn things about the situation by giving Kyle the space to talk about it from his perspective. Dorothy may not agree with everything he says. Active listening is not a debate. Rather, active listening helps create a conversation where both parties can express their experience and opinions in a beneficial way.

After Dorothy has taken time to listen to Kyle, she will have earned more respect to offer her perspective. It will sound something like this: "Kyle, thanks for sharing your perspective of what took place. You have helped to clear up some misunderstandings I had. Would it be okay with you if I shared from my perspective what took place?"

GUIDELINES FOR PROCLAIMING FORGIVENESS

Forgiveness is a gift of God that was purchased by the blood of Jesus Christ (see 1 Corinthians 6:19–20; 7:23; 1 Peter 1:18–19). God clearly speaks this forgiveness in His Word, and all who believe have this gift of salvation. God also speaks this forgiveness through us. We can speak forgiveness to one another and receive the peace and joy of our sins being washed away.

As you prepare to proclaim forgiveness, the following guidelines will help you respond to a transgression in a God-pleasing way.

PROCLAIM FORGIVENESS AS A CHILD OF GOD

Remembering your identity as a child of God is part of your preparation for proclaiming forgiveness. You are part of God's kingdom. You already have the gifts of life, salvation, and forgiveness of sins in the name of Jesus Christ (see Galatians 3:26; 4:7; John 1:12). As a child of God, you are aware of your own sinfulness, and you have already confessed the log of sin in your own eye and received the gift of forgiveness (see Matthew 7:5).

A child of God approaches the offender as a sinner who has been forgiven in the name of Jesus Christ. A child of God approaches as someone who has also been forgiven and washed by the blood of Jesus Christ. "But if we walk in the light, as He is in the light, we have fellowship with one another, and the blood of Jesus His Son cleanses us from all sin" (1 John 1:7).

A child of God does not proclaim forgiveness as one who is holy on her own account. We have done nothing to earn any part of our own salvation. There is nothing good in us.

> They have all turned aside; together they have become corrupt; there is none who does good, not even one. (Psalm 14:3)

> For I know that nothing good dwells in me, that is, in my flesh. (Romans 7:18)

God's children proclaim the forgiveness that was gifted to them by the Holy Spirit.

As people forgiven by Christ, we approach our transgressor with the gift we have received—Christ's forgiveness. The forgiveness of Christ is not conditional. God does not say, "You must do this or I will not forgive you." He simply declares, "You are forgiven." Forgiveness is a gift that was purchased by the blood of Jesus Christ for all people (see John 3:16).

Therefore, we do not offer conditional forgiveness either.

We might be tempted to say, "I forgive you, but if you do it again there is no more forgiveness." We might want to say, "I will forgive you only if you promise . . ." Avoid using words such as *if*, *but*, *unless*, *as long as*, or *provided*. These statements make forgiveness conditional, and it is no longer a gift.

Go as a forgiven child of God who believes and trusts in the gift of forgiveness.

PROCLAIM FORGIVENESS WITH GENTLENESS

It might be difficult to speak forgiveness with gentleness. Sometimes, in our hurt, we want to be vengeful. But when we have time to prepare, we can temper our emotions and respond with gentleness. Paul encourages us, "Brothers, if anyone is caught in any transgression, you who are spiritual should restore him in a spirit of gentleness. Keep watch on yourself, less you too be tempted" (Galatians 6:1).

Without preparation we might react impatiently and come across as argumentative. But Paul encourages us to remember who we are in Christ:

> And the Lord's servant must not be quarrelsome but kind to everyone, able to teach, patiently enduring evil, correcting his opponents with gentleness. God may perhaps grant them repentance

leading to a knowledge of the truth, and they may come to their senses and escape from the snare of the devil, after being captured by him to do his will. (2 Timothy 2:24–26)

Children of God prepare themselves to approach with gentleness and patience. We anticipate that the person may not have repented of the sin or even want to repent. The goal is to speak with gentleness the Gospel of Jesus Christ and let God grant the repentance.

The granting of forgiveness is not dependent on repentance. God's forgiveness is for all people. But receiving the gift of forgiveness is dependent on repentance and faith. As far as Jim knew, his father had not repented of his sins at the time he proclaimed forgiveness. But Jim was prepared to forgive his father with the hope that God would grant him repentance that would lead to the knowledge of the truth that he is forgiven in Christ.

How Jim approached his father was important. If Jim had approached his father in anger with a confrontational attitude, it would not have made it easy for his father to hear the proclamation of forgiveness. If Jim had acted as if he were God, his father would not have respected Jim's words. Jim was prepared to approach his father with gentleness. He knew his father was not an emotional man. There was no need for Jim to make his father uncomfortable with a flowery speech. The proclamation of forgiveness was simple and to the point, the way his father could best receive it. Jim looked to the interests of his father and considered how best to serve him.

When you prepare to speak forgiveness to someone, consider their character and personality. Paul encourages us, "Let each of you look not only to his own interests, but also to the interests of others" (Philippians 2:4). The way Jim proclaimed forgiveness to his father might be different from the way he proclaims forgiveness to his wife, his coworker, or his neighbor. He might be more physical with his wife, giving her a hug and a kiss. He might be more professional with a coworker, talking with her after work. He might be more casual with his neighbor, talking outside in the yard. Our gentle approach may look different depending on the person we are speaking to, but what we say should always be rooted in the gift of forgiveness in Jesus Christ.

A child of God must also be ready for the gift of forgiveness to be rejected. Not everyone will respond to our forgiveness with gentleness. We might fantasize that they will say something like "That is the best thing I have heard all day!

Thank you so much for forgiving me." Some people might be angry, defensive, or resentful. But that does not change how we speak forgiveness.

Peter urges us to prepare and says,

> In your hearts honor Christ the Lord as holy, always being prepared to make a defense to anyone who asks you for a reason for the hope that is in you; yet do it with gentleness and respect, having a good conscience, so that, when you are slandered, those who revile your good behavior in Christ may be put to shame. (1 Peter 3:15–16)

Approach with gentleness, taking into consideration the other person's interests, trusting God to move him to repent and receive your gift in faith.

PROCLAIM FORGIVENESS WITH SPECIFICITY

Context makes a difference!

Kathy had been fretting over something her husband said to her a couple of weeks earlier. She was doing housework and asked for his help. He said, "I don't do dishes, I don't take out the trash, and I don't do laundry. That is your duty. And to be honest, you don't do a very good job at it."

For two weeks Kathy replayed that incident in her head so many times. She created a loop that fed her anger. Her rumination on his words drove her to despair.

But then Kathy decided to forgive her husband. One day after dinner, Kathy said to him, "I forgive you for what you said that made me so mad at you." Her husband sat there perplexed, wondering what he had said.

We often assume that others know what they have done. In some cases, they may know, but not always. Jim's father knew. Burning down the family house was a significant event. But whether the offender knows or not, we need to identify the sin we are forgiving. This prepares the offender for forgiveness.

Kathy's husband was confused by her proclamation of forgiveness because he was unaware of his sin and how much turmoil it had caused his wife. When Kathy walked out of the room, he was confused and simply dismissed the whole thing, thankful that she was not going to use whatever he had said against him. But he was not able to appreciate the gift of forgiveness, and it did not give him the opportunity to repent. Neither would it help him to avoid repeating the offense.

Proclaiming sin depends on context. Sometimes, it is obvious what is meant. But some occasions require that we specify what is being forgiven. Remember to consider the other person's interests.

People may say things like "I forgive you from the depths of my heart" or "I want you to know we are cool." They might say, "What you did last week, it is forgotten," or, "I was hurt by what you did but don't worry about it, it's okay." Maybe you have heard people say things like this when they offer forgiveness. However, they do not specifically forgive in the name of Jesus. The phrases focus on self and the ability to dismiss what took place. They lack context and specificity meant to bring healing and relief to the offender.

Forgiveness does not excuse sin. Forgiveness takes sin away. This can only be done in the name of Jesus Christ. When you proclaim forgiveness, you do so in the name of Jesus Christ. Paul says, "There is salvation in no one else, for there is no other name under heaven given among men by which we must be saved" (Acts 4:12).

Specifically identify the sin you are forgiving, and intentionally forgive in the name of Jesus Christ.

PROCLAIM FORGIVENESS AND WAIT ON THE LORD

Jim's proclamation of forgiveness was simple yet significant. Jim addressed his father from within a larger context than that moment at the reunion. Jim understood his father's personality. Jim spoke forgiveness as a child of God. He wanted his father to know that he was able to forgive him because of his faith in Jesus Christ. Jim took all these things into consideration when he prepared himself to forgive his father.

Jim was also prepared to wait on the Lord. Jim said, "I didn't expect anything because he is the way he is. He's seventy years old. I didn't go with any kind of strings attached like, 'Okay, I'm going to forgive you, but we're going to have a relationship now, and you're going to call me.' That wasn't the reason that I did it."

But Jim did not need to wait very long. The two of them emailed, and his father stayed at Jim's home various times.

It was a joyous reunion and reconciliation between a father and son. However, it does not always turn out that way. After we speak forgiveness, we wait on the Lord, and sometimes we do not see anything positive. This can be difficult to understand and accept.

Even Jesus experienced such reactions. He offered the gift of salvation to a rich young man who walked away from the gift (see Mark 10:17–31). Jesus and Stephen each prayed, "Lord, forgive them, for they don't know what they are doing" (Luke 23:34; Acts 7:60). Their forgiveness did not stop their executions. Nevertheless, some who participated later received the gift through faith. Saul witnessed Stephen's execution with approval but later became a zealous follower of Jesus named Paul.

We cannot force people to receive the gift of forgiveness. We offer it and wait on the Lord.

Waiting on the Lord is an act of faith. The psalmist says, "I believe that I shall look upon the goodness of the LORD in the land of the living! Wait for the LORD; be strong, and let your heart take courage; wait for the LORD" (27:13–14). It may seem as if the Lord is not acting, but His timing may not be ours (see Isaiah 55:8–9; 2 Peter 3:9).

As we wait on the Lord, we pray. Pray that the Holy Spirit will have many opportunities to speak God's Word into their lives. Pray that the good news of salvation will work on their hearts so that they will receive the free gift of forgiveness. Pray that they receive the gift that has been purchased for them by the blood of Jesus. Ask God to give you patience and increase your trust in Him.

Give the gift of forgiveness and wait on the Lord to work in their hearts.

FINDING THE RIGHT WORDS

The Bible does not prescribe a step-by-step process for speaking forgiveness. Depending on the situation there can be many ways to approach someone. But the guidelines above provide a biblical understanding of how to prepare yourself and the other person to give and receive the gift of forgiveness.

Jim was prepared by his pastor and the reconciliation workshop to remember the gift of forgiveness that was already his in Christ Jesus. Jim recognized his own sinful attitudes and thoughts about his father. He repented and was refreshed by being forgiven. Now Jim needed to prepare his father to receive the gift of forgiveness that was already his. Jim, a child of God, did this by gently approaching his father, specifically forgiving in the name of Jesus, and waiting on the Lord to work in his father's life.

After applying the above guidelines, prepare your proclamation. You may use phrases such as:

> I have good news for you. You are forgiven in the name of
> Jesus Christ.

> As God in Christ has forgiven both you and me, I also forgive you.

> As a sinner also in need of forgiveness, I forgive you in the name of the Father and of the Son and of the Holy Spirit.

A powerful way to proclaim God's forgiveness is to use Scripture, inserting the person's name into the verse. This personalizes the verse, comforting the person with the assurance of God's love from His Word, like so:

> [Roger,] He Himself bore our sins in His body on the tree, that we might die to sin and live to righteousness. By His wounds[, Roger,] you have been healed. (1 Peter 2:24)

Then add your personal forgiveness: "As God through Christ has forgiven both you and me, I also forgive you your sins against me."

Many Scripture verses work well for proclaiming God's forgiveness. Here are a few you might use:

> Blessed is [Name] whose transgression is forgiven, whose sin is covered. Blessed is [Name,] against whom the LORD counts no iniquity, and in whose spirit there is no deceit. (Psalm 32:1-2)

> For as high as the heavens are above the earth, so great is His stead-fast love toward [Name] who fear[s] Him; as far as the east is from the west, so far does He remove [your] transgressions from [you]. (Psalm 103:11-12)

> [Jesus] was delivered up for our trespasses and raised for our justification. Therefore, [Name,] since we have been justified by faith, we have peace with God through our Lord Jesus Christ. Through Him we have also obtained access by faith into this grace in which we stand, and we rejoice in hope of the glory of God. (Romans 4:25-5:2)

> There is therefore now no condemnation for [Name] who [is] in Christ Jesus. (Romans 8:1)

> [Name,] for our sake [God] made Him to be sin who knew no sin, so that in Him [you] might become the righteousness of God. (2 Corinthians 5:21)

> [Name,] the blood of Jesus His Son cleanses [you] from all sin. (1 John 1:7)

WHEN YOU SHOULD NOT PROCLAIM FORGIVENESS

The gift of forgiveness was accomplished by Jesus Christ, and He offers that gift to everyone. However, not everyone is willing to repent of their sins and believe in Jesus. In some cases, people are openly unrepentant and claim a right to their sin. Suppose you asked the offender, "If you could go back in time, would you do anything differently?" Someone clinging to their sin might respond, "I would not change a thing. And if given the opportunity, I would do it again."

Matthew 18 provides direction for restoring those who have strayed. Jesus encourages His disciples to engage the sinner over and over with the hope of restoration. Specifically in verses 15–20, He teaches us how to approach those who have sinned against us.

> If your brother sins against you, go and tell him his fault, between you and him alone. If he listens to you, you have gained your brother. But if he does not listen, take one or two others along with you, that every charge may be established by the evidence of two or three witnesses. If he refuses to listen to them, tell it to the church. And if he refuses to listen even to the church, let him be to you as a Gentile and a tax collector. Truly, I say to you, whatever you bind on earth shall be bound in heaven, and whatever you loose on earth shall be loosed in heaven. Again I say to you, if two of you agree on earth about anything they ask, it will be done for them by My Father in heaven. For where two or three are gathered in My name, there am I among them.

Jesus uses the refrain "if he . . . , then you are to . . ." five times in this text.[14] We should not abandon the person who has not repented, but consistently engage them with the hope that they will not reject the gift of forgiveness.

There is no guarantee that the sinner will repent. But as far as it depends on us, we faithfully speak God's Word into their lives with the hope that they will let go of their sin.

---

14 Jeffrey Gibbs provides an excellent commentary of this text that highlights God's desire to give the sinner the gift of forgiveness. Gibbs points out that Jesus could have stopped with verse 15 and ended the matter. But it is a deadly thing for a person to remain in sin. Therefore, every attempt should be made to restore the sinner so that they can enjoy the gift of forgiveness. See Jeffrey A. Gibbs, *Matthew 11:2–20:34*, Concordia Commentary (St. Louis: Concordia Publishing House, 2010).

We do not give the gift of forgiveness to openly impenitent people who claim a right to their sins. "If he refuses to listen to them, tell it to the church. And if he refuses to listen even to the church, let him be to you as a Gentile and a tax collector" (v. 17).

The person's congregation has the responsibility for their spiritual well-being. When someone refuses to repent, they act as if they do not need or even believe in Christ's forgiveness. Their eternal welfare is at stake. Thus, such a person who claims a right to their sin could be put outside of the church through the process of excommunication in the hope that they will repent and believe in the forgiveness of sins. (For more on this, see chapter 8, "What If They Don't Repent?" and chapter 17, "Is There Any Unforgivable Sin?")

But such a decision does not end our responsibility to the offender.

In Jesus' parable of the weeds (see Matthew 13:24–30), the weeds and the wheat continue to live together until the harvest. At Jesus' second coming on the Last Day, He will separate the believers from the nonbelievers. Jesus says we should still attempt to speak God's Word into their lives with the hope that they might repent until that last harvest day. For our God "desires all people to be saved and to come to the knowledge of the truth" (1 Timothy 2:4).

In some cases, it may be difficult to know if a person is claiming a right to a sin or if they are struggling with repentance. We should not speak words of forgiveness to a person who has overtly claimed a right to a sin. That person needs to hear God's Law. However, it is appropriate to speak forgiveness to someone who is wrestling with repentance.

Paul says, "Or do you presume on the riches of His kindness and forbearance and patience, not knowing that God's kindness is meant to lead you to repentance?" (Romans 2:4). When we show God's kindness to a person who is struggling with sin, it shows them the gift of forgiveness. God's kindness can lead them to repentance.

God is patient with people because He does not want them to die eternally. "The Lord is not slow to fulfill His promise as some count slowness, but is patient toward you, not wishing that any should perish, but that all should reach repentance" (2 Peter 3:9).

Thank God for His mercy, His grace, His love, and His patience with all His people! Praise Him for the forgiveness we have in Christ Jesus!

HOW DOES THIS APPLY TO ME?

1. Describe a situation where someone has sinned against you and you want to proclaim forgiveness.

2. Before you meet with anyone, identify how you sinned in the situation. Maybe your sin was in reaction to her initial sin. Did you have sinful thoughts? Did you gossip? Did you plan ways to retaliate?

3. Set up an appointment with your pastor or a spiritually mature friend. First, ask for his commitment to confidentiality. Let him know that you are looking for guidance as you prepare to reconcile with someone through confession and forgiveness. Then, reflecting on your own sins in the relationship, ask him to hear your confession to God so that he can proclaim God's forgiveness to you. Refer to the section "Finding the Right Words" above and encourage your pastor or friend to use Scripture as he absolves you. Hearing God's forgiveness proclaimed to you verbally helps prepare you to do the same for the other person.

4. Next, discuss how best to approach the other person.

   ▶ You might write out your confession of sin that you could speak to the other person.

   ▶ If the other person seems unaware of how she has sinned against you, write out possible ways you could help her see her sin. Work toward being empathetic and showing Christian love.

   ▶ Write out how you will proclaim God's forgiveness. Consider using Scripture, inserting the person's name, as described in this chapter.

   ▶ Rehearse all of what you plan to say with your pastor or friend.

5. Anticipate how you will respond if the offender is not receptive

   ▶ to your confession.

   ▶ to you identifying his sin.

   ▶ to you proclaiming forgiveness.

6. Discuss your response with your pastor or friend.

7. Write a prayer for God's guidance, including petitions for

   ▶ a pastor or friend who will give you godly counsel;

   ▶ the ability to get the log out of your own eye;

   ▶ the courage to meet with the other person;

   ▶ the opportunity to approach the other person with gentleness and empathy; and

   ▶ the other person, that God would lead her to repentance and forgiveness in Christ.

PRAYER TEMPLATE

(See chapter 3, "How Should I Pray?")

INTRODUCTION

REFERENCE TO GOD'S WORK

PETITION

RESULT

CONCLUSION

CHAPTER 17

IS THERE ANY UNFORGIVABLE SIN?

Holy Spirit, by Your grace
We may see our Savior's face.
Guard our faith that it may be
Constant to eternity.

Ask ten people to name an unforgivable sin, and you are likely to get as many different answers.

We tend to judge certain heinous sins as unforgivable—murder, rape, sexually assaulting children, torture, and more. Some believe that evil leaders who have directed mass tortures and killings are guilty of unforgivable sin.

But to identify any sin as unforgivable, except as specified in God's Word, is to minimize the atoning work of Christ. Such judgment of that sin, or of a person committing that sin, suggests that Jesus' suffering and death were insufficient or that His redemption was not for all people.

Jesus' sacrifice on Calvary paid the full penalty for all sin. In His words from the cross, Jesus declared, "It is finished" (John 19:30), meaning the debt for all of humanity's sin has been paid in full.

Christ died for the sins of the whole world, as He asserted: "For God so loved the world, that He gave His only Son, that whoever believes in Him should not perish but have eternal life" (John 3:16). "The world" includes all people.

> But He was pierced for our transgressions; He was crushed for our iniquities; upon Him was the chastisement that brought us peace, and with His wounds we are healed. All we like sheep have gone astray; we have turned—every one—to his own way; and the LORD has laid on Him the iniquity of us all. (Isaiah 53:5–6)

> In Christ God was reconciling the world to Himself, not counting their trespasses against them. (2 Corinthians 5:19)

Nevertheless, the Bible does identify one sin that is "unforgivable."

SIN AGAINST THE HOLY SPIRIT

During Jesus' ministry, the Pharisees accused Him of casting out demons by the power of the devil. Jesus initially discredits the false notion that Satan would cast out Satan. But then Matthew records Jesus' stern warning about their unbelieving testimonies:

> Therefore I tell you, every sin and blasphemy will be forgiven people, but the blasphemy against the Spirit will not be forgiven. And whoever speaks a word against the Son of Man will be forgiven, but whoever speaks against the Holy Spirit will not be forgiven, either in this age or in the age to come. (Matthew 12:31–32)

Mark also records Jesus' express admonition:

Truly, I say to you, all sins will be forgiven the children of man, and whatever blasphemies they utter, but whoever blasphemes against the Holy Spirit never has forgiveness, but is guilty of an eternal sin. (Mark 3:28–29)

Jesus mentions this same sin when He contrasts the outcomes for those who confess faith in Him with those who deny Him:

And I tell you, everyone who acknowledges Me before men, the Son of Man also will acknowledge before the angels of God, but the one who denies Me before men will be denied before the angels of God. And everyone who speaks a word against the Son of Man will be forgiven, but the one who blasphemes against the Holy Spirit will not be forgiven. (Luke 12:8–10)

WHAT IS BLASPHEMING AGAINST THE HOLY SPIRIT?

Simply put, blaspheming against the Holy Spirit is rejecting faith in Jesus and His atoning work on the cross.

How is rejecting faith in Christ blaspheming against the Holy Spirit?

The Bible teaches that the Holy Spirit brings us to faith in Christ. By nature, we are spiritually blind, dead, and enemies of God.

The natural person does not accept the things of the Spirit of God, for they are folly to him, and he is not able to understand them because they are spiritually discerned. (1 Corinthians 2:14)

And you were dead in the trespasses and sins in which you once walked, following the course of this world, following the prince of the power of the air, the spirit that is now at work in the sons of disobedience. (Ephesians 2:1–2)

For the mind that is set on the flesh is hostile to God, for it does not submit to God's law; indeed, it cannot. (Romans 8:7)

Although we cannot come to faith on our own, the Holy Spirit enables us to believe.

Therefore I want you to understand that no one speaking in the Spirit of God ever says "Jesus is accursed!" and no one can say

"Jesus is Lord" except in the Holy Spirit. (1 Corinthians 12:3)

Jesus answered, "Truly, truly, I say to you, unless one is born of water and the Spirit, he cannot enter the kingdom of God. That which is born of the flesh is flesh, and that which is born of the Spirit is spirit." (John 3:5–6)

To reject faith in Christ, a gift of the Holy Spirit, is to sin against the giver of that gift. Those who refuse to believe in Jesus' forgiveness for them blaspheme the Holy Spirit of God.

Because Jesus bore the full consequences for our sin, we are forgiven. The consequences of eternal death (hell) are taken away for those who believe. "There is therefore now no condemnation for those who are in Christ Jesus" (Romans 8:1).

But those who refuse the gift retain their own sins and the consequences of eternal separation from God.

[Jesus said,] "For God so loved the world, that He gave His only Son, that whoever believes in Him should not perish but have eternal life. For God did not send His Son into the world to condemn the world, but in order that the world might be saved through Him. Whoever believes in Him is not condemned, but whoever does not believe is condemned already, because He has not believed in the name of the only Son of God." (John 3:16–18)

Thus, it is not any particular sin judged by people as heinous that condemns, but rather it is the sin against the Holy Spirit—not believing in Jesus as Savior—that condemns. Those who reject the Gospel resist the Holy Spirit and remain condemned by their own account. "Whoever believes and is baptized will be saved, but whoever does not believe will be condemned" (Mark 16:16).

Sin against the Holy Spirit may be called the unforgivable sin because rejection of faith in Christ results in eternal judgment. Rejecting Christ means retaining one's own sin and declaring His forgiveness unnecessary—in other words, self-justification. Those who refuse the Holy Spirit demonstrate a hardened heart. They refuse to repent and thus reject forgiveness through Christ. The Holy Spirit does not force anyone to receive His gift of faith. But those who reject His gift retain their own sins to their eternal damnation. "Whoever believes in the Son has eternal life; whoever does not obey the Son shall not see life, but the wrath of God remains on him" (John 3:36).

HOW CAN I AVOID
THE UNFORGIVABLE SIN?

First of all, if you are concerned about sinning against the Holy Spirit, take comfort. You likely have not committed this sin, or you are on a journey to repent of this sin. Those who blaspheme the Holy Spirit are not worrying about it. Your concern demonstrates your fear of God and faith in Him. Pray that the Holy Spirit strengthens your faith and reassures you of God's promise for you. Let God comfort you with His promises in Scripture:

Believe in the Lord Jesus, and you will be saved. (Acts 16:31)

The LORD is merciful and gracious, slow to anger and abounding in steadfast love. He will not always chide, nor will He keep His anger forever. He does not deal with us according to our sins, nor repay us according to our iniquities. For as high as the heavens are above the earth, so great is His steadfast love toward those who fear Him; as far as the east is from the west, so far does He remove our transgressions from us. As a father shows compassion to his children, so the LORD shows compassion to those who fear Him. (Psalm 103:8–13)

In Him we have redemption through His blood, the forgiveness of our trespasses, according to the riches of His grace, which He lavished upon us, in all wisdom and insight making known to us the mystery of His will, according to His purpose, which He set forth in Christ as a plan for the fullness of time, to unite all things in Him, things in heaven and things on earth. (Ephesians 1:7–10)

Your salvation is based not on your own works but on faith in Christ. "For by grace you have been saved through faith. And this is not your own doing; it is the gift of God, not a result of works, so that no one may boast" (Ephesians 2:8–9).

God's forgiveness is yours as you repent and believe in Jesus. "If we confess our sins, He is faithful and just to forgive us our sins and to cleanse us from all unrighteousness" (1 John 1:9).

The unforgivable sin, blaspheming against the Holy Spirit, is denying what Jesus has done for you, rejecting the forgiveness of sins, and justifying yourself before God.

As to whether others have committed this sin, this is not our individual judgment to make. Only God knows the heart (Psalm 44:21). Jesus authorized the church to withhold forgiveness from the openly unrepentant because they act as if they do not believe in the forgiveness of sins (see Matthew 16:17–19; John 20:23). The church takes this action to help bring back a straying soul from the brink of eternal death. The wandering sinner is restored when he repents and confesses faith in Christ. We commend the eternal welfare of ourselves and others to our God.

Nevertheless, those who initially reject faith in Jesus but later believe before they die are forgiven and enter heaven. The thief on the cross next to Jesus confessed faith shortly before his death, and Jesus assured him, "Today you will be with Me in paradise" (Luke 23:43).

Thanks be to God that He is merciful and gracious, even granting eternal life to those with last-minute conversions!

Jesus said, "I am the resurrection and the life. Whoever believes in Me, though he die, yet shall he live, and everyone who lives and believes in Me shall never die" (John 11:25–26).

HOW DOES THIS APPLY TO ME?

1. Based on Scripture, for what sins has Jesus not died?

2. According to the Bible, what is the only sin that God declares unforgivable if not repented of before death?

3. How has this chapter challenged your thinking on what sin is unforgivable?

4. Why does the unforgivable sin not apply to you?

5. If you continue to struggle with what kinds of sins are unforgivable, seek out your pastor or a spiritually mature friend to discuss this chapter (and the rest of the book).

6. Write a prayer that God comforts you in your faith and takes away your temptation to judge others' hearts. Thank Him for the grace and mercy He has shown you and others.

PRAYER TEMPLATE

(See chapter 3, "How Should I Pray?")

INTRODUCTION

REFERENCE TO GOD'S WORK

PETITION

RESULT

CONCLUSION

CHAPTER 18

CAN THERE BE FORGIVENESS WITHOUT RECONCILIATION?

Our sins may cause a separation
From those we wrong—and from the Lord.
Desiring reconciliation
We seek relationships restored.
The only way that this can be
Is through forgiveness full and free.

But what if they do not receive us
Through will or inability?
We must rely on God's forgiveness,
Since God in Christ has set us free.
Then trust in His consoling Word
And leave the outcome to the Lord.

FORGIVEN AND RECONCILED WITH GOD

Jesus told a parable about a son who demanded his share of the inheritance from his father. This was an unusual request because the father would need to give up that which he used to support himself. Stranger yet, the father agreed and gave his son the full share of his inheritance.

The son was now free to leave the family and live a lifestyle very different from his father's. The son traveled to a faraway place and freely spent the inheritance without any concern for the future.

The son rejected his father and squandered his inheritance on reckless living. But his extravagant lifestyle came to a sudden end when the money ran out. The son was destitute and would soon perish.

Therefore, the son hired himself out to do the most reprehensible thing for a Jewish man—feed pigs. The Old Testament prohibited God's people from eating pigs; they were unclean animals to God's people (Leviticus 11:7-8). The son was so desperate, so impoverished, so close to death that he lived among unclean animals. Yet, it was not enough to fill his stomach and save him from perishing.

We sometimes think we can sustain a life of disgraceful living. We are so eager to turn our backs on a gracious Father to pursue freedom and autonomy. But when our resources are depleted, we sit in the corner of a dark room filled with regret and shame for what we have done.

Kevin had a girlfriend for two years. They enjoyed going to movies, hiking in the mountains, and cooking. But Kevin's desire for a more physically intimate relationship was shut down by his girlfriend. Kevin decided he wanted the freedom to pursue other people and broke off the relationship. With the availability of the internet and various apps that specialize in hooking up, it did not take long for his physical desires to be met. Additionally, he was not shy when posting on social media about his new autonomous lifestyle. He also posted gossip and slander concerning his ex-girlfriend.

Everything came crashing down when one of his hook-ups stole his bank cards and wiped him out financially. Two weeks later, he became ill and learned that he had contracted a deadly sexually transmitted disease. He was destitute and would soon perish. He had rejected a faithful woman to pursue his own sinful desires. And there he sat in the corner of his dark room, filled with regret and shame for what he had done. He was terrified of dying and convinced that he would go to hell.

In Jesus' parable, the son who squandered his father's inheritance decided to return to his father and beg for forgiveness. "Father, I have sinned against heaven and before you. I am no longer worthy to be called your son. Treat me as one of your hired servants," he planned to say (Luke 15:18–19).

What would you have done if your wayward child returned home after being such a disgrace to the family? You might choose to shun the child, reject the child, or refuse to speak to the child. You might lecture the child about what he did and let him return home only as a servant or hired hand but not as one of your children.

The father does a very unexpected thing. He runs to his son while is he still a long way off, embraces him, and puts decent clothes on him. A family ring is placed on his son's finger, indicating that the father recognizes the man as his son. He then throws a celebratory dinner for him and says to everyone, "For this my son was dead, and is alive again; he was lost, and is found" (v. 24). The forgiving father reconciles with his prodigal son.

This is what our heavenly Father does for us. God forgives us and reconciles us to Himself.

All this is from God, who through Christ reconciled us to Himself and gave us the ministry of reconciliation; that is, in Christ God was reconciling the world to Himself, not counting their trespasses against them, and entrusting to us the message of reconciliation. (2 Corinthians 5:18–19)

God could have chosen to shun us, reject us, and refuse to speak to us. He could have sentenced us to hell. He could have chosen to forgive us but force us to live as His servants on earth with no hope of eternal life in heaven. But our loving Father chose to forgive us and reconcile with us. He made us His children and heirs of His heavenly promises.

See what kind of love the Father has given to us, that we should be called children of God; and so we are. (1 John 3:1)

For in Christ Jesus you are all sons of God, through faith. (Galatians 3:26)

So you are no longer a slave, but a son, and if a son, then an heir through God. (Galatians 4:7)

Kevin was a prodigal son who turned away from that which was good to pursue the desires of his sinful flesh. Such a road often leads to despair and destruction. But when there is repentance and faith, God is quick to forgive and reconcile us back into His kingdom.

Kevin was blessed with a Christian friend who listened to him, prayed with him, and reminded him of the forgiveness of Jesus Christ. God would not abandon Kevin, and He would not treat him as a second-class citizen of heaven. Kevin was fully forgiven, reconciled to his Father by the blood of Jesus Christ.

> In Him we have redemption through His blood, the forgiveness of our trespasses, according to the riches of His grace, which He lavished upon us, in all wisdom and insight making known to us the mystery of His will, according to His purpose, which He set forth in Christ as a plan for the fullness of time, to unite all things in Him, things in heaven and things on earth. (Ephesians 1:7–10)

You, dear reader, are a forgiven and reconciled child of God. When God forgives sins, He also restores us—reconciles us—to Himself. With God there is forgiveness *and* reconciliation.

WHAT IS RECONCILIATION?

The Bible clearly teaches that we should forgive one another. Jesus says, "And whenever you stand praying, forgive, if you have anything against anyone, so that your Father also who is in heaven may forgive you your trespasses" (Mark 11:25).

While Jesus hung on the cross, He prayed, "Father, forgive them, for they know not what they do" (Luke 23:34). When Peter asked Jesus how many times he should forgive, Jesus answered, "I do not say to you seven times, but seventy-seven times" (Matthew 18:21–22). Jesus did not mean that forgiveness is limited to seventy-seven times but rather that we are to forgive as often as needed. He taught His disciples to pray, "and forgive us our sins, for we ourselves forgive everyone who is indebted to us" (Luke 11:4). Paul reminded the church in Ephesus, "Be kind to one another, tenderhearted, forgiving one another, as God in Christ forgave you" (Ephesians 4:32).

Forgiveness is washing the sin away through the blood of Jesus Christ. When God forgives us, He promises not to use our sin against us. That sin will not prevent us from being His children or being part of His kingdom. When I forgive another person, I do so as a person who has also been forgiven by the work of Christ. Forgiving one another is important because it reflects the forgiveness we have in Jesus. Unforgiveness results in bitterness and contradicts our faith in our Savior's forgiveness.

> Strive for peace with everyone, and for the holiness without which no one will see the Lord. See to it that no one fails to obtain the grace of God; that no "root of bitterness" springs up and causes trouble, and by it many become defiled. (Hebrews 12:14–15)

Reconciliation between us and God occurs when no sin separates us. Our relationship is restored as if no break in the relationship ever occurred. Reconciliation between sinners takes place when no sin separates them from one another. Usually, this requires both parties to confess their sins and forgive one another.

Eric and Steve grew up together in the same town. They played sports together, went to the same school, attended the same church, spent time at each other's homes, and shared the same friend group. Eric became an electrician, married the pastor's daughter, and had three children. Steve worked at the local lumberyard and remained a bachelor. The conflict between them started when both men began courting the pastor's daughter. Steve was consumed with disappointment when she dumped him for Eric.

Eric visited the lumberyard on a regular basis to purchase supplies for his electrical business. Steve always felt a knot in his stomach when Eric walked in. Over the years Eric accused Steve of cheating him out of supplies. Steve gossiped about Eric with other customers. The tension between the two of them was well known in their town of twelve thousand.

To make matters worse, Eric was the church treasurer, and Steve was the church president. And their congregation was struggling to survive financially.

The congregation held its annual meeting after the Sunday worship service. Steve called the meeting to order and asked for the treasurer's report. Eric reported that finances were poor and he was concerned that, if the trend continued, they would not be able to pay their bills in the next three months.

Steve looked straight at Eric and said, "I hope you and Pastor have not been skimming from the offering plate."

Eric jumped out of his chair and lunged at Steve, yelling, "You're a loser! You couldn't get the girl! You didn't do any advance schooling beyond high school! You're a loser!"

The meeting ended as other congregants stepped between the two men to prevent a physical altercation.

Eric and Steve had sinned against each other and failed to provide a good Christian witness.

The congregation contacted a Christian mediator to meet with Eric and Steve, hoping they could be reconciled. The mediator began by meeting with each of them individually to identify sins that needed to be confessed to the other person.

With the help of the Christian mediator, Eric and Steve met together over a period of several days. But it was this moment that changed everything:

Eric took a breath and said, "Steve, I have not always been fair to you. I have gloated about my accomplishments. I have ridiculed you in public and threatened to do you physical harm. I have sinned against God and against you. I hope that you can forgive me."

Steve responded, "I do forgive you. I have not been perfect either. I have struggled with being jealous of you my whole life. It was not right of me to accuse you of stealing from the offering plate. I wanted to find something I could use against you to make myself feel better. That was not right to do."

Eric and Steve confessed their sins to each other and forgave each other in the name of Jesus Christ. They reconciled and their relationship was restored.

FORGIVEN BUT NOT RECONCILED

Kevin repented of his sins and received the gift of God's forgiveness. He was reconciled to God. However, his ex-girlfriend was deeply hurt by his behavior and could not bring herself to forgive or reconcile with Kevin. She wanted nothing to do with him.

Kevin was forgiven but not reconciled with his ex-girlfriend. Forgiveness and reconciliation happen simultaneously with God. Your sins are washed away, you are forgiven, and you are restored as a child of God in His kingdom. But a forgiven child of God may not always experience reconciliation with the other people involved. A potential consequence of betrayal is loss of trust, which results in breaking a relationship.

In Kevin's situation, his ex-girlfriend did not want to forgive him or reconcile with him. Kevin experienced God's forgiveness, but reconciliation with his former girlfriend was not realized. There may be other factors that prevent reconciliation with another person.

Debra had a long-standing conflict with her father. It all started when her father disapproved of the man she was dating. Debra got pregnant and had an abortion. She later got pregnant again and married. Three children later, she divorced and was struggling to find employment. Her father refused to help her. In return, she refused to let him see his grandchildren.

Time does not heal all wounds. But it will either provide you with the opportunity to bury your pain more deeply or the opportunity to address the pain in a godly way. Debra buried her pain for many years, thinking that it would go away. It never did. Long-term bitterness set in.

Years later she decided to visit her father, who was living in a nursing home. Her second husband, Jack, was the kind of man her father would have been proud of. Jack had no issues with drugs or alcohol, and he provided for Debra in ways that her first husband did not. Over time, Debra learned to live a godly life and desired to be reconciled with her father.

Debra and Jack packed up the car and drove eight hours to her father's small town. Debra was nervous about seeing her father after all these years. But she was also excited to introduce him to Jack and hoped this would be a new chapter in their relationship.

One of the staff members led them down a hall and into a room. There was a man sitting in a reclining chair, sleeping.

"Dad. Dad, it's me, Debra."

Her father slowly opened his eyes. "Debra. Good to see you."

Debra gestured to her husband and said, "I want to introduce you to my husband, Jack."

"Nice to meet you, Jack. Will you be my new roommate?"

Unsure how to respond, Jack gave Debra a nervous look.

"No, Jack's not your roommate. He's my husband, and I wanted you to meet him," Debra said.

"Oh. Well, have a good day," replied her father.

"Dad, I want you to know that I am sorry for everything. I was not always a good daughter, but I hope that we can reconnect."

The old man reclining in the chair sat up with a confused look. "Should I know you? Are you going to be my new roommates?"

Debra was forgiven and reconciled with her heavenly Father. And she had forgiven her earthly father. But dementia prevented Debra from being reconciled with him.

It can be difficult to live in this type of situation—forgiven by God but not reconciled with those around us. Perhaps it's an ex-girlfriend who does not want to be reconciled. It may be a father who has dementia. It might be a loved one who died or a friend who moved away. It may be that you have forgiven someone and want reconciliation, but the other person refuses. There are many reasons why you won't always be able to reconcile with someone.

In those moments, we take comfort in the forgiveness and reconciliation we have with God through Jesus Christ.

SEEKING RECONCILIATION

A forgiven and reconciled child of God will desire to be reconciled with others. Paul tells us, "If possible, so far as it depends on you, live peaceably with all" (Romans 12:18). Jesus Himself said, "You have heard that it was said, 'You shall love your neighbor and hate your enemy.' But I say to you, Love your enemies and pray for those who persecute you, so that you may be sons of your Father who is in heaven" (Matthew 5:43–45).

A broken relationship with your neighbor will affect your relationship with God. Therefore, Jesus illustrates the need for reconciliation when He said,

> So if you are offering your gift at the altar and there remember that your brother has something against you, leave your gift there before the altar and go. First be reconciled to your brother, and then come and offer your gift. Come to terms quickly with your accuser while you are going with him to court, lest your accuser hand you over to the judge, and the judge to the guard, and you be put in prison. (Matthew 5:23–25)

If you have a shattered relationship, it is your responsibility to try to reconcile with that person. It is not wise to abandon your neighbor so that you or they can remain in anger, bitterness, or sin. Children of God who desire to partake of the Sacrament of the Altar need to first seek reconciliation with their brothers and sisters. Anyone who refuses to be reconciled with their neighbor risks harming their relationship to God. Therefore, such a person should not partake in the Lord's Supper, because they no longer give witness as someone forgiven in Christ.

However, it is not our responsibility to make others reconcile with us. Paul instructed Timothy in this way: "And the Lord's servant must not be quarrelsome but kind to everyone, able to teach, patiently enduring evil, correcting his opponents with gentleness" (2 Timothy 2:24–25a). If someone has something against you, go with gentleness to correct the wrong and be reconciled.

But we are not responsible for the work of changing a person's heart. Paul says that we go to those who are in error with the hope that God will grant them repentance: "God may perhaps grant them repentance leading to a knowledge of the truth, and they may come to their senses and escape from the snare of the devil, after being captured by him to do his will" (vv. 25b–26).

We make every effort to live in peace with others. "If possible, so far as it depends on you, live peaceably with all" (Romans 12:18). You are responsible for your actions to initiate reconciliation—"if possible, so far as it depends on you." But you are not responsible for the other person's response. You cannot force others to love you, to confess, to forgive, or to reconcile.

So what does the child of God do when the other person refuses to reconcile? Exhaust your opportunities to reconcile (see chapter 8, "What If They Don't Repent?"). Then pray, commending yourself and the other person to God's care.

HOW DOES THIS APPLY TO ME?

1. Identify a situation where you have forgiven someone but reconciliation has not taken place.

2. Describe the specific reasons why reconciliation did not take place.

3. If the other person is alive and well enough to meet, identify ways that you might encourage reconciliation with the other person.

4. Describe what it would look like if you were reconciled with the other person.

5. If the other person is not alive or is not well enough to meet, or if other conditions prevent you from meeting, describe what you can do at this time.

6. Write a prayer thanking God for the gift of forgiveness through His Son, Jesus Christ. If you have not yet forgiven, pray for God's strength to forgive even if you are not able to reconcile. Ask God for patience as you wait for the day you can be reconciled with the other person. Ask God for continued opportunities that might lead to reconciliation. Pray for the other person. Then commend both yourself and the other person to God's grace and mercy.

PRAYER TEMPLATE

(See chapter 3, "How Should I Pray?")

INTRODUCTION

REFERENCE TO GOD'S WORK

PETITION

RESULT

CONCLUSION

CONCLUSION

In the introduction, we posed these questions:

> Who is the unforgivable in your life? Is it someone who hurt you or someone you love? Do you consider yourself unforgivable?
>
> What is the unforgivable sin? What was the offense that is so painful for you?
>
> What seems beyond any hope for forgiveness?

As you revisit these questions, we hope that you have found answers like those summarized below:

Who is the unforgivable? Christ died for all people. That includes the one who has hurt you or someone you love. And it includes you. You both are forgiven!

What is the unforgivable sin? Christ died for all sins. The only unforgivable sin is rejecting God's gift of forgiveness by not believing in what His Son has done for sinners.

What seems beyond any hope for forgiveness? With God, all things are possible. Even the miracle of forgiving as God has forgiven you.

Our prayer for you is that with God's help you can forgive the unforgivable, just as God in Christ has done for you.

Still struggling? Don't worry. Forgiveness from God is instantaneous and constant. But with people, forgiveness often takes time. It's a journey of faith. But as a child of God, you don't walk this journey on your own. Your Savior, the one who died and rose again for you, promises to be with you always.

I will not leave you or forsake you. (Joshua 1:5)

And behold, I am with you always, to the end of the age. (Matthew 28:20)

In your struggle to forgive, He is there with you to forgive you again and again, to strengthen your faith, to enable you to do what you can never do on your own—forgive as God forgave you. In your journey, keep your eyes fixed on Jesus:

Therefore, since we are surrounded by so great a cloud of witnesses, let us also lay aside every weight, and sin which clings so closely, and let us run with endurance the race that is set before us, looking to Jesus, the founder and perfecter of our faith, who for the joy that was set before Him endured the cross, despising the shame, and is seated at the right hand of the throne of God. Consider Him who endured from sinners such hostility against Himself, so that you may not grow weary or fainthearted. (Hebrews 12:1–3)

Review the chapters of this book on your journey. Choose the one that describes what challenges you most. Use the questions to apply the principles of that chapter to your situation. But as you read, focus on the Scriptures that are referenced. The Holy Spirit will work through God's Word to change your heart and enable you to do God's will. Ask your pastor or another spiritually mature friend to accompany you on this journey. For further reading, see the resource list at the back of this book.

Now may our Lord Jesus Christ Himself, and God our Father, who loved us and gave us eternal comfort and good hope through grace, comfort your hearts and establish them in every good work and word. (2 Thessalonians 2:16–17)

Your brothers in Christ,
Ted Kober and Mark Rockenbach

RESOURCES

Ambassadors of Reconciliation. *Forgiven to Forgive: Six Weeks of Daily Devotions.* Billings, MT: Ambassadors of Reconciliation, 2010.

———. *A Reason for Hope: Six Weeks of Daily Devotions.* Billings, MT: Ambassadors of Reconciliation, 2019.

Bonhoeffer, Dietrich. *Life Together.* Translated by John W. Doberstein. New York: Harper and Row Publishers, Inc., 1954.

Cloud, Henry, and John Townsend. *Boundaries: When to Say Yes, How to Say No to Take Control of Your Life.* Grand Rapids: Zondervan, 2017.

Gibbs, Jeffrey A. *Matthew 1:1–11:1,* Concordia Commentary. St. Louis: Concordia Publishing House, 2006.

———. *Matthew 11:2–20:34,* Concordia Commentary. St. Louis: Concordia Publishing House, 2010.

Kober, Ted. *Built on the Rock: The Healthy Congregation.* St. Louis: Concordia Publishing House, 2017.

———. *Confession and Forgiveness: Professing Faith as Ambassadors of Reconciliation.* St. Louis: Concordia Publishing House, 2002.

———. *Conflict Resolution vs. Reconciliation.* Billings, MT: Ambassadors of Reconciliation, 2017.

———. *Go and Be Reconciled: What Does This Mean?* Billings, MT: Ambassadors of Reconciliation, 2016.

———. *Reconciling under the Cross: Resolving Conflict and Restoring Relationships Using the Bible.* Billings, MT: Ambassadors of Reconciliation, 2023.

Koehler, Walter J. *Counseling and Confession: The Role of Confession and Absolution in Pastoral Counseling.* St. Louis: Concordia Seminary Press, 2011.

Lockwood, Michael A. *The Unholy Trinity: Martin Luther against the Idol of Me, Myself, and I*. St. Louis: Concordia Publishing House, 2016.

Marrs, Rick W. *Making Christian Counseling More Christ Centered*. Bloomington, IN: WestBow Press, 2019.

Mangalwadi, Vishal, Vijay Martis, M. B. Desai, Babu K. Verhese, and Radha Samuel. *Burnt Alive: The Staines and the God They Loved—Missionaries Murdered in Manoharpur*. Mumbai, India: GLS Publishing, 1999.

Seinkbeil, Harold L. *Dying to Live: The Power of Forgiveness*. St. Louis: Concordia Publishing House, 1994.

Tripp, Paul David. *Instruments in the Redeemer's Hands: People in Need of Change Helping People in Need of Change*. Phillipsburg, NJ: Presbyterian and Reformed Publishing, 2002.

Veith, Gene Edward, Jr. *The Spirituality of the Cross*, third ed. St. Louis: Concordia Publishing House, 2021.

Welch, Edward T. *Addictions—A Banquet in the Grave: Finding Hope in the Power of the Gospel*. Phillipsburg, NJ: Presbyterian and Reformed Publishing, 2001.

SUGGESTED HYMN TUNES

CHAPTER 1

ERHALT UNS, HERR (*LSB* 655)

CHAPTER 2

MEINEN JESUM LASS' ICH NICHT (DARMSTADT) (*LSB* 609)

CHAPTER 3

SURSUM CORDA (*LSB* 788)

CHAPTER 4

KINGSFOLD (*LSB* 444)

CHAPTER 5

MERIBAH (*LSB* 698)

CHAPTER 6

DER AM KREUZ (*LSB* 421)

CHAPTER 7

SOUTHWELL (*LSB* 424)

CHAPTER 8

DER MANGE SKAL KOMME (*LSB* 510)

CHAPTER 9

FOUNDATION (*LSB* 728)

CHAPTER 10

IN GOTTES NAMEN FAHREN WIR (*LSB* 581)